NOT QUITE TO PLAN

MY EXPERIENCE OF THE GLOBAL PANDEMIC AND A MILITARY COUP WITH A NEWBORN BABY.

MILLA CHAPLIN RAE

Not Quite
To Plan
*My experience of the global pandemic and
a military coup with a newborn baby*

By
Milla Chaplin Rae

Copyright © 2023 Milla Chaplin Rae

ISBN 978-1-3999-4750-3

Cover Design: Simon Thompson

Author Photographs: Payal Kumar of Sunshine Stories

Published by Blue Masala Press

All rights reserved. No part of this publication may be reproduced, stored in a retrieval system, or transmitted, in any form or by any means, without the prior written permission of the publisher.

For contact information or to find out more about the author, please visit www.millachaplinrae.com

*For Jasper and Dylan -
without you, none of this would have been possible.*

PROLOGUE

THERE'S an unofficial playbook for people responding to a coup in Myanmar and for the first twenty-four hours it reads something like this: act fast, raid the ATMs to withdraw all money from banks, hoard peanut oil and rice, and bury your stash of loose gemstones underground for safekeeping. I do none of these things. I do send my husband, Dylan, down to the supermarket to buy nappies though. Even in an apocalypse I wouldn't want to be cleaning up that mess.

On the morning of 1 February 2021, I wake early. As I drag my still-half-asleep body towards my fussing two-month-old son Jasper's cot, I switch on my phone. Almost instantly, it is engulfed by a wildfire of messages, news and social media alerts telling me that the Myanmar military, also known as the Tatmadaw (which translates as Great or Grand Army), has deposed the leaders of the elected government before they can be sworn into parliament today. We are in the early stages of a Coup d'etat and I am suddenly very much awake.

Muscle-memory and habit lead me to the living room, but not before I have woken Dylan with an understated but urgent "oh shit". They say everyone has a fight or flight reflex. What they don't say is that there is a third option of staying very, very still and very, very quiet until you become one with your sofa. I am mainly still because Jasper needs to feed - something which hasn't come naturally to either of us. But I am quiet because I don't quite know what to say or how to react. I don't want to overreact and spread undue panic among friends and family, but equally, I don't want to underreact in case the situation takes a sharp turn for the worse and we are unprepared.

Dylan joins me on the sofa as he takes in the bombardment of messages and alerts on his own phone, showing popular images and posts to me and asking, 'did you see this?' with increasing disbelief. It's not yet 7 am. He turns on the TV to look for news coverage and is greeted by a technical error message on the channels that would usually give us the BBC News or CNN. That figures. Our Wi-Fi is still working so he switches to an internet TV provider and we see that news of the coup has already spread internationally.

'Our families will be worried,' I say, calculating that Dylan's Australian relatives will soon see this on their lunch time news. For mine in the UK, it will be a few more hours before they know.

Dylan nods. 'But it could settle down again,' he says, putting into words what we are both thinking.

Rumours of a possible coup have been swirling for days, but with our relatively limited knowledge of the complex politics behind these rumours, we weren't actually expecting it to happen. Whether because we don't want to accept that it *has* now happened, or because we are naive, we are both holding out half a hope that things might resolve themselves peacefully.

'You should probably go to the shop as soon as it opens,'

I tell Dylan. 'We don't want to be caught without enough nappies if we end up in a lockdown.'

I settle Jasper down in his day bed now that he has finished feeding. I don't know what to do next. Time takes on a strange, shapeless form. At some point Dylan leaves for the supermarket. I try to decide if I'm hungry. Maybe I am just thirsty. I should probably stop re-reading the same, increasingly alarming news. I go to the balcony and look out over the residential estate in which we live. It is always quiet, because we are far from the centre of the city, but I think today it is probably even quieter. We live in a newly built, twenty-eight storey apartment tower in which very few apartments have yet sold. We are the sole occupants. I usually find this funny and talk in jest to friends about 'our tower'. Today, however, I feel isolated. I should probably get dressed.

I look around the apartment. It is our home; filled with custom furniture, bespoke artwork, ornaments, photographs, utensils, gadgets, books and souvenirs collected over the six years Dylan and I have been living and working in Myanmar. And then there are the more recent acquisitions of the baby monitor, the Moses basket, the pile of muslin cloths and the stroller: the telltale trappings of a new addition to the family. Our home has been our safe haven throughout my pregnancy, which coincided with the pandemic. It is cosy and private and personal and when I am here, I can forget that there's a world outside our new, little family. But not today. Today things feel different. Despite the quiet, the world outside feels as though it's clamouring to break in.

After a while, Dylan returns from his shopping trip, laden with nappies and some fresh milk. I feel better now that he is back and it occurs to me that this is the first time I have ever felt vulnerable in all the years I have lived in

Yangon and all the time I have been with Dylan. I am back on the sofa, dressed, and with Jasper now sleeping on me.

'Did you see anyone we know? What are people saying?' I ask him in a low, urgent voice, covering Jasper's available ear with my hand.

'It's eerily quiet out there apart from the line at the supermarket. I don't know what I expected, but there's a strange atmosphere. I saw a few people I recognised but none of our friends. One of my old colleagues was there, and he confirmed there's been a coup,' he says as he places the shopping bags down beside the sofa and comes back to sit with Jasper and me.

'Well, we knew there had been a coup from Facebook. Did he seem worried?' I ask, eager to find a benchmark for my own reaction.

'Kind of. He told us to stock up on cash, and food, and to wait and see what happens over the next few days. He said the ATMs will run out,' Dylan responds.

'He didn't tell us to hide all our gems? I have definitely seen that advice circulating on social media. So did you get cash?'

'No, there was a line so I thought I'd go down later or tomorrow, once the initial panic is over.'

Dylan's casual complacency in the face of our first military coup is admirable and concerning in equal measure. It has never been his place in our relationship to worry - that's my job. I want to find his attitude reassuring, but the idea of having no money ignites a fear in me and I mentally scan all the usual places we scatter cash around the house and wonder if this might just be the emergency that all these small deposits have been set aside for.

'Oh, my colleague did say that Aung San Suu Kyi has been detained,' adds Dylan, interrupting my calculations.

'Oh wow. They went straight to the top.'

'How's the little guy?' Dylan asks, stroking Jasper's head and giving me a familiar look which tells me that my thoughts are leaking out onto my face. I exhale.

'Oh, he's fine. Oblivious, which must be nice. So, what do we do now?' While I do the worrying, Dylan usually does the planning, and I search his face for a sense of urgency or concern. I don't find it.

'I think we just wait. Wait and see what the military does next. Oh, Tony's calling.'

Dylan's father Tony, a lifelong expat himself, lives in the next-door tower to us. He, like us, has been in Myanmar for several years, and unlike us, elsewhere in Southeast Asia for many years before that.

'You're on speakerphone, Tony, Milla's here too. Did you hear there's been a coup?' Dylan says as he answers the call.

'Yeah, so? I've seen three of them,' comes Tony's gruff brush-off of the topic.

'What? Tony, I said there's been a coup,' repeats Dylan.

'Yeah. And I said I've seen three of them. In Thailand. It's old news. Nothing will happen.'

'Tony, this doesn't feel like a Thai coup. This feels more serious than that,' I venture, rolling my eyes at Dylan. Tony's dismissive optimism comes as no surprise. 'They've detained Aung San Suu Kyi, and all the other senior politicians. The news we're hearing from friends doesn't sound good.'

'Where did you see that? The news they've detained Aung San Suu Kyi,' Tony asks, suddenly a little more interested.

'Dylan's colleague told him, but I'm sure it'll be all over Facebook by now,' I say, while Dylan is out of earshot, stashing the nappies in Jasper's room. 'I sent him out early on an emergency nappy run. You might want to get down to the shop if you are running low on supplies.'

'Oh right, I'll take a look. And I'll see you later - still on for lunch?' says Tony.

'Of course!'

I hang up the call and go back to doom scrolling social media to see if any new information has surfaced. They say panic breeds panic, and in the first couple of hours after the news of the coup breaks, so it does; the more the images circulate of panic withdrawals at ATMs, the more people panic and try to withdraw at ATMs. The more people share images of empty shelves and crowded supermarket aisles, the more people rush out to buy emergency rations. The more photos and videos that emerge showing lines miles long outside petrol stations, the more people want to buy petrol. I wonder if there is something more that we should be doing, beyond waiting, but the thought of leaving our cocoon and taking Jasper out into the world makes me feel afraid. The anger starts to swell online as people react to the threatened return of a military regime. And then suddenly, it all stops.

The military have switched off the internet. Bizarrely, we still have our fibre internet connection, but the blackout of the telecoms networks nationwide plunges us into a void. We can talk to people and watch news broadcasts from thousands of miles away, but we know very little about what's happening around us in the city we live in. I feel unsettled, as though I know that the rug is about to be ripped out from under me. My mind starts to race. We are already in the middle of a global pandemic, which is why Jasper was born in Myanmar in the first place.

'What do you think this will mean for travel?' I wonder out loud to Dylan. 'Do you think we will have to leave? Will we even be able to leave? And if we leave, where would we go? And what about all our belongings? There's already a backlog at the port from the pandemic and that Suez Canal issue. Do you think we'd be able to ship anything, or will we have to sell it all? And what about Jasper's passport? I put the application in a couple of weeks ago and I haven't heard anything back. Do you think they can expedite it? I hope it reaches us before there's any more disruption to deliveries or anything. Maybe you should go back and line up at the ATM. Do we need to buy tinned food? Do you think the shelves will be restocked? What else do you think we are going to need while we wait for this to play out? Do we have petrol in our car? Maybe we need more nappies ...'

The worries tumble out of me in an erratic stream of consciousness, despite Dylan's best attempts to offer reassurance. I wish I could be as composed as he is, but such is our dynamic that my response is always as emotional as his is rational.

'And what if we get COVID? What if Jasper gets COVID?'

'You're starting to overthink things, and I can understand why, but I think we have to try and stay calm,' says Dylan. 'There isn't really anything we can do but wait to see what happens next.'

He's right. There really *isn't* anything we can do besides waiting. I grip Dylan's hand and I hug Jasper in close as he starts to squirm, releasing some gas as he does. I can't help but smile at his tiny toots. I want to shield myself from my imagination by focusing on my two favourite people. I think back to Jasper's entry into the world just a couple of months earlier, which was traumatic. And then to being pregnant through the pandemic: admittedly a mixed blessing. I think back to the meticulous preparation I tried to do for motherhood: the books I read cover to cover, the apps I downloaded and the fitness programs I mostly followed. And then I think back further to the whirlwind of the early days of Myanmar's reopening and the thriving social scene which brought Dylan and I together all those years before. The tidal wave of memories might have knocked me off my feet were I not already part of the sofa.

Yangon isn't just where Dylan and I met, it is where we have chosen to build a life together; a life that just twenty-four hours earlier was tantalisingly close to perfect.

PART I

1

A YANGON LOVE STORY

'Change of plan! I'm moving to Myanmar,' I said to my mother the moment she answered the phone, as I walked through Green Park at pace.

It was 2015 when three-and-a-bit years in London confirmed to me that I was better suited to a more unpredictable life. Before London I had been living in Beijing in my third and final year of a marketing and communications graduate program that offered me 'three years, three companies, three countries'. I had completed my trio of placements in London, New York and Beijing and had left China after a wobble in my commitment to an expat life led me back to the UK to think some more.

'What? Myanmar? Is that what used to be Burma?' my mother asked.

'Yeah, it's what was Burma. Or for some countries it still is Burma, I think. Including the UK. I had to look it up. I think Burma was what the Brits called it when they were there, but the name has been changed in recent years. I am sure I'll know more once I am there!' I gabbled excitedly.

'Why the change? I thought you were going to Vietnam?

I had only just got my head around that, to be honest,' my mother responded with a hint of exasperation.

In her defence, there were only a few weeks before I was due to leave my job and my life in London to move across the world in search of what I had defined as 'the organised chaos of a developing market', so it was understandable that she wasn't expecting a change of destination this late in the day.

'Yes, I know I *was* going to Vietnam. But I just spoke with my new boss and she's based in Yangon or Rangoon. The agency is based in Saigon, but the client is in Yangon, so it makes more sense for me to go to Myanmar. She thinks I'll like Yangon.'

My short stint in the UK had been more than enough to make me realise that I not only enjoyed living abroad, but I thrived on the energy of it, and so I was setting off in search of fulfilment and adventure. I expected to like Myanmar, but I had no idea how completely and utterly it would change my life.

I arrived in Yangon on 26 July 2015, in the middle of the monsoon, which made house-hunting infinitely more difficult than it might have been had I arrived during the dry season. I had given myself two weeks before my official start date at my new agency, during which I needed to find somewhere to live and to get a feel for the place. Yangon was awash with an intensity unlike anything I had experienced before. The rain came down in juicy, plump dollops which exploded on impact and, in the brief respite between downpours, the immediate heat drove the moisture back off the roads like steam off a pudding.

I had long enjoyed a love-hate relationship with house-hunting. I had done plenty of it - initially looking for accommodation while studying abroad as a language student during my university days and later finding places to live while on my professional secondments. I saw it as a kind of initiation ritual - the fastest way for me to immerse myself in my new life, to understand a new city's infrastructure, to visit neighbourhoods that perhaps my daily routine wouldn't ordinarily lead me to, and to begin to see how I might adapt to and adopt the culture, habits and customs of my new home. I looked out for the shops and services I might need, for the transport I might use, and for the community I might like to be a part of.

Despite this not being my first international move, I found it hard to get my head around Yangon, which surprised me. For starters, there was no Central Business District, no obvious area where expats tended to congregate or live, and there was terrible, standing traffic. It was also the city that Google Maps forgot; landmarks and businesses which did appear in the app were almost always pegged in the wrong place, and directions often assumed roads which were long gone. As I tried to keep the apartment viewing appointments I made, I was reliant on taxis to get about and, on more than one occasion, I tried to direct my ride through someone's private driveway (without success). But I was as eager as I was inexperienced and collected my wrong turns like trophies. My solo adventure made me feel intrepid and more alive than I ever had in London.

There was no Uber or Grab yet and the taxis were unregulated and unmetered. Not long before I arrived, thousands of taxis had been reportedly taken out of circulation for being unroadworthy. Given the state of those still operating, I didn't put much faith in the baseline for roadworthiness. There appeared to be very few do's and don'ts as far as driving in Yangon went. I saw more arms flailing out of windows than I saw use of indicators. Once I was even asked by a taxi driver to flail *my* arm because he wanted to signal to the vehicles on my side of the car. I politely declined. Horns and headlights were honked and flashed to let other drivers know of our existence and of the driver's intention to do something questionable (not to warn of danger or to give way).

Not much English was spoken in Yangon, which made my taxi fare negotiations brief and predictable, and it was always a pleasant surprise to arrive at the destination I had in mind. I did encounter the odd taxi driver who was surprisingly fluent in English. Once, a brief conversation with one of these drivers explained he had been a university student in the eighties, studying law, when a nationwide popular uprising had led to deadly crackdowns from the ruling military powers. It was during this political crisis that Aung San Suu Kyi had emerged as a national icon for democracy, but also during this period that an entire generation's dreams were stolen. Universities were closed because they were seen as the origin of the so-called dissent. An already crippled economy (under infamous military dictator General Ne Win) was destroyed. People's futures were irrevocably damaged by violent oppression, jail sentences and the further closing off of the country from international influence - people like my driver, who was now driving a taxi instead of practising law.

I despaired when taxis were nowhere to be found once a heavy rainstorm turned Yangon's struggling streets into rivers; rivers of warm, brown water littered with food wrappers, lettuce leaves and the odd lonely, floating flip flop. I had been told that walking even short distances was not advisable during the monsoon. This was not because of the certainty of getting caught in a downpour or because of the treacherous mould slicks on the pavements, but because of the risk of electrocution when some of the haphazard electrical cabling fell into a puddle. I lost count of the long, soggy hours I wasted trying to flag down taxis in inclement weather. On one particularly memorable occasion I was relieved to see the headlights of a vacant taxi, elongated by the streaming rain which caught the glare and carried it down onto the coursing river of a road, swerving dangerously across several lanes to reach me. It was only as the car drew closer to where I stood that I noticed a Buddhist monk waiting patiently a little further upstream than me. Illuminated in the taxi's lights, his maroon robes gave him the look of a flame flickering in the stormy darkness. The taxi was coming for him, not for me. That I, a foreigner who would undoubtedly have paid double what any local rider would have been charged, was dismissed in favour of a monk told me everything I needed to know about the status of Buddhism in society.

Public buses I quickly decided weren't for me. The bus system was a lawless, cowboy country. Crumbling, spluttering minibuses raced one another from stop to stop, competing for fares. The drivers did not care if they set off with people hanging half in or out. As a pedestrian, it was wise to give these rickety rust buckets a very wide berth, to avoid being spat on by an occupant. The projectile saliva jets expelled from the open windows of these minibuses were blood red, stained with betel juice. Chewing betel nuts was prolific in Yangon in my early days there, although it reduced considerably over the years. Comprising an areca nut wrapped in a betel leaf and flavoured with dangerously corrosive lime paste, betel nuts were available on every street corner. They were a pungent and highly addictive stimulant. A betel chewer was easily identifiable with red-stained teeth, twitchy, over-alert behaviour and an almost constant need to spit out excess saliva. I was hit several times, fortunately never in the face (unlike a friend of mine) and I quickly learned the distance to give these vehicles at traffic lights.

Adding to the danger of the death-defying speed at which the minibuses were travelling was the problem that they were right-hand drives, driving on the right-hand side of the road. Overtaking was a game of chicken and alighting passengers were frequently deposited in the middle of fast-moving traffic. I learned this was a legacy issue from the seventies; the result of former military dictator, General Ne Win, responding to advice (rumoured to be from an astrologer) that he should move the country politically to the right. The symbolic action he took was to switch the side of the road that his subjects drove on. Overnight, he decreed that vehicles should abandon the British-introduced road rules and swap sides. Some of the minibuses had fashioned themselves new doorways by punching out a panel from the right-hand side, (without much effort given the decaying state of the metal). Chaos this most definitely was. Whether it was organised or not was another matter. Even after a brand new, air-conditioned, left-hand-drive bus fleet was commissioned by the government a few years into my stay in Yangon, I never dared to experiment by riding in one.

I found my first apartment at the very end of my two-week hunt, by which time I had seen some very weird and not very wonderful places. I quickly learned that an agent, in the house-hunting sense, is merely an intermediary who wants to take a fee for connecting an apartment with a tenant. They do not care how long this process takes or how many times they fail at it. My request for a clean, light, two-bedroom apartment with living room, kitchen and one and a half bathrooms was met with a five-bedroom house, a single-room studio and (my personal favourite) a two-bedroom-two-bathroom place whose living room appeared to have been tiled up like an abattoir, complete with sink and hose to wash down the nasties. I saw places where the walls didn't reach the ceiling, or were actually curtains. I saw places that only had the traditional squat toilets, despite having requested otherwise. I saw several places with a toilet too close to the food storage in the kitchen for my comfort (although I learned this was the norm for many of the older properties). I saw a place with a kitchen counter which barely came up to my thighs. I saw places with no windows in any of the bedrooms. I saw a place with a living room window into the main stairwell of the building, instead of outside into natural light. 'You said you wanted windows!' came the feeble justification.

I began to refuse to see places that the agent had clearly never set foot in and was dragging me along to so that they could take some photos for other prospective tenants. Despite all the false starts, the agents were unavoidable. And, as I kept reminding myself, the scavenger hunt was certainly showing me Yangon from all sides. Finally, only days before I gave up and extended my stay in the hotel (where my employer had put me up) I found somewhere. I almost abandoned the viewing, but something told me that it was worth waiting the half hour that the agent was late by and risking dengue fever (offering up my bare legs as a mosquito banquet in the middle of a spectacular thunderstorm). I had a good feeling about the neighbourhood which was cosy, quiet and had a small supermarket which I had identified as a rare treat.

What swung this place for me was that it was empty and its walls were white. Too many of the apartments I had viewed had been painted a garish mint green and loaded with oversized teak furniture which had the effect of shrinking an otherwise spacious home. I had to pay a year's worth of rent, up front and in cash, which gave me momentary cause to question whether I had made the right decision in moving to Yangon. I initially assumed that the requirement to pay up front and in cash was a 'foreigner tax', but I soon learned that it was normal in Myanmar's cash-based economy where the people didn't trust the banking system enough to keep their money there, and didn't trust the legal system enough to believe in contracts. I was exhausted from traipsing all over the city, I was itchy from the monsoon mosquitoes and I felt very alone. But, in the time it took me to wire the money from the UK, withdraw it from local bank and lug it over to my new home in a holdall, I had talked myself back into looking forward to becoming acquainted with the city while I bought furniture. I knew no one in Yangon, so I had plenty of free time on my hands for exploration.

I was surprised to learn from my new boss that there was a hockey club in Yangon. Despite having been a member of a club in London, I hadn't brought any of my kit with me after I failed to find any information on anything sport-related during my pre-departure research. I soon discovered that this was more indicative of the nascent internet connectivity in Myanmar and the weak presence of Google rather than of a lack of sports facilities.

One August Saturday at 9am, a month into my Yangon adventure, I took myself off to the hockey pitch which, to my surprise, enjoyed a prime location right in the middle of the city. I joined the weekly training session. It was about 35°C already, and a break in the monsoon meant powerful sunshine and thick, heavy air to breathe. As my betel-chewing taxi driver unceremoniously deposited me, and a glob of phlegm, at what I had to hope was the entrance to the compound containing the hockey pitch, I took in the vinyl banner on the gates advertising a traditional Myanmar Lethwei fight in the boxing stadium I saw to my left. To my right, as I walked tentatively through the gates, I could see a row of food hawkers with their metal tables and tiny plastic chairs under a tarpaulin and corrugated iron roof. A pack of stray dogs basked in the early morning heat. Dogs were an unwelcome but common sight in Yangon; the city's human population was divided on whether the dogs should be culled, and despite some attempts at control, (both humane and otherwise) dog attacks and rabies were rampant. I walked quietly and as far from them as I could.

In front of me, deeper into the compound and on the other side of a car park (full of secondhand minivans) was the pitch. There appeared to be one other person there, already warming up. I was as awkward as a teenager; nervous to approach a stranger, to join a new club and to put myself out there to make new friends. I considered chickening out and coming the following week, but realised how silly I was being. The player on the field looked up, saw me and waved a hello, before starting towards me. I called out a hello back and put on what I hoped was a look of confidence. The stranger turned out to be Dylan, an Australian who had accompanied his father to Myanmar to set up a construction company, and, although I could not yet know it, my future husband.

The pitch itself was Astro turf, which surprised me, but it was covered in thick black mould, which did not. A neglected, concrete spectator stand gave several sleeping or maybe dying dogs (it was always hard to tell) some much-needed shade on wide steps painted in the fading red, yellow and green of the Myanmar flag. Hockey not only became part of my weekend routine but also the centre of my social circle for the six years I would end up living in Yangon. From that very first session (when one of the other girls invited me to join her at a house party that evening), to when Dylan and I became an item a little over half a year later, to the string of sad farewells we said amid COVID and then the coup d'état, the Yangon Pythons Hockey Club was the epicentre of my Yangon experience. It was the most inclusive and welcoming club I have ever been a part of, which made it worth the early start and the significant risk of dehydration posed by two hours of hot hockey every week. Sadly, even if COVID hadn't wiped out most of the club's members through repatriations and relocations, the coup would have put an end to it because the pitch was on military-owned land. Not to mention that our most regular opponents were a fun-loving, ragtag team made up of Myanmar navy personnel.

My first job at the advertising agency ended after just six months when the agency withdrew from the market. I didn't move to Vietnam, as I had initially imagined I might had the Yangon role not worked out. I was too caught up in the country's momentum and too engaged in setting up my life there. If there was one word to describe Myanmar back in 2015 it was optimistic; the cities buzzed with an irrepressible energy, the countryside mesmerised visitors with its raw, untouched beauty. The country had opened up to foreign investment in 2011, after fifty years of isolation at the hands of a brutal military regime. This gave the feel of a country and a population which had woken up from a very long nap, bursting with enthusiasm for everything to which they now had access. Three telecommunications giants, one of which was my client at the agency, were racing to roll out towers and mobile phones across the country. State by state, township by township, village by village, family by family, fifty-one million people were being introduced to the power of connectivity. Up until this moment, most people in Myanmar hadn't even heard of the internet, let alone dreamed of having access to it through a mobile device.

Myanmar skipped the journey through dial-up connections, desktops and laptops and jumped straight into smartphone connection, which earned it the moniker Leapfrog Nation. Dylan had arrived a few months before me and had paid two hundred US dollars for his SIM card before the internet roll out had properly begun. I paid just a couple of dollars for mine.

The longer we stayed, the more transformation we witnessed. Yangon, although not the official capital of Myanmar, was the cultural and commercial hub, and was where progress was at its most accelerated. The downtown streets, a grid system distinctly colonial in architecture, groaned under people and traffic. Billboards shouted about newly available international brands and products, the city's first shiny, new, Thai-style shopping malls sprung up out of the ground and new overpasses eased the flow of commuters as everyone hurried to take their place in a new future. That Yangon was where I fell in love with Dylan undoubtedly rose-tints my memories of the city and of my time there. Expat life is often a balancing act of risk against reward; the highs can be very high and the lows very low. For me, the risk in moving there was that I might not enjoy it, or that I would find the culture shock too great, or that the political landscape wasn't stable enough in the long term, but the reward was that I met my soulmate in Dylan and we rode the high of building a life there together for as long as we could.

To this day, if you ask Dylan what made the biggest difference to his life in Yangon, he will answer the arrival of bottled, fresh milk on supermarket shelves. I, apparently, come a close second. Dylan and I moved in together after only a couple of months of dating, taking an apartment in the beating heart of downtown Yangon, a stone's throw from landmarks such as Bogyoke Aung San Market (formerly Scott Market), famous for its wholesale fabrics, gems and artisanal crafts, Yangon Railway Station, the iconic Secretariat Building and the majestic Strand Hotel. House guests would comment on the noise; without double glazing, it was as though the honking and chugging of cars and buses came right through the floor-to-ceiling windows into the living room, together with the noise of street hawkers and migrating crows at dawn and dusk. Our township was a melting pot of cultures not hugely typical of Myanmar's majority Buddhist culture and, at various times of day and night, we would hear church-bell chimes, Hindu bells, Buddhist chanting and the call to prayer from the mosque next door. Some cities have a hum to them, but Yangon sang at the top of its voice and all I wanted to do was join in.

Apart from when we were working, Dylan and I did everything together. We were an inseparable team, known in the expat community as more than a little sport mad. Besides hockey and the hockey club (which we ended up running for a while), we played tennis, squash and golf. For almost two years, we took 6am boxing classes on our balcony, much to the bemusement of our neighbours and the sleepy security guards at the rundown hotel across the street. Our teacher, Ko Ye, had model good looks, bones of lead and abs of steel. He regularly showed us two versions of a move, saying, 'This is how you do it in the ring. And this is how we do it on the street.' Thankfully, neither Dylan nor I have needed to use any of our moves except for staying fit, but I have no doubt that Ko Ye could have floored a man twice his size with one nudge.

The Yangon expat scene was relatively new and very close-knit. It predominantly attracted young, ambitious, hard-working professionals who saw an opportunity in

Myanmar to do both good and interesting work. We all fell in love with the potential, the drive and the local people. Burmese colleagues and friends I shared my years with in Myanmar were warm, kind and generous. I don't imagine many people arrive in London and describe the first people they meet in those terms, but the Myanmar people were these things and more. Besides their caring, family-focused natures, my Myanmar counterparts were a force to be reckoned with. Against the odds, and with an outdated learn-by-rote education system behind them, there was a rapidly expanding community of go-getters and entrepreneurs who were ambitious, smart, hungry for change and excited to learn. The internet gave them access to international institutions and qualifications which they took full advantage of.

In Yangon, professional networking and personal socialising were one and the same. People I encountered through work would appear at social events and vice versa, and I think the blurred lines between professional and personal relationships formed a huge part of the appeal of Yangon long term. I never felt as though I had to choose between my work or my personal life. They were closely intertwined with one another and that worked for me. The flagship events we attended each year were the Burns' Night, a ceilidh which saw over a hundred Yangon residents reeling and drinking whisky in the garden of the British Ambassador's house, and the Oktoberfest which ensured the annual destruction of a hotel ballroom in a triumph of oompah and weissbier. And every year, I came away from these events having met someone new and interesting, with an innovative idea about how to support Myanmar's developing economy and infrastructure. We joked among friends that the slightly strange visa rules, and the relative obscurity of Myanmar as a tourist destination, acted as a highly effective filter which only let a certain calibre of person through.

We joked about it, but in my experience, it was true. Expats in Myanmar gave so much of themselves to the country's future that perhaps it was inevitable that being forced out by something like a military coup would leave us all feeling as though we had lost a part of ourselves.

By the time we married in 2019, Dylan and I planned to stay in Yangon long term.

'How much longer do you think you'll stay in Myanmar?' friends and relatives asked at our wedding in Jersey.

'At least another ten years,' one of us would answer. 'We have always said that we will stay there until our child, (if we have one and if he or she is anything like us) is old enough to need competitive sports. And then we'll move to Australia. There aren't a lot of sports for children in Yangon sadly and anyway, it would be easier for a child to move before high school.'

'Or,' the other of us would say, tongue firmly in cheek, 'if the military decides they want their power back. Tanks rolling down the streets of Yangon would send a pretty clear message that we should leave.'

2

THE MAGIC OF MYANMAR

OUTSIDE YANGON, Myanmar presents a very different side of its personality. If Yangon captivated my mind and fired me up, then it was this softer side of Myanmar which stole my heart and gave me space to breathe.

Myanmar is the largest of the mainland Southeast Asian countries by area, with a population estimated at around fifty-one million people. It shares borders with five other countries: India, China, Bangladesh, Thailand and Laos. In the early twentieth century Burma, as it was then known, was seen as the 'rice bowl of Asia' on account of its lush, fertile Irrawaddy Delta from which much of the world's rice originated. Myanmar is rich in natural resources, most eye-catching of which are the rubies and sapphires from the heavily restricted area of Mogok, also known as 'Ruby Land'.

The telecoms company I initially worked for was rapidly expanding its network into the four corners of the country. This required me to quickly get my head around the complex geography. Administratively, Myanmar is broken into seven states, seven divisions and one union territory which houses the capital city of Naypyitaw. The seven states are mainly in the uplands and roughly mirror the areas inhabited by the seven official main ethnic minority groups. The seven divisions are in the plains and are home to a population of predominantly Bamar ethnic origin (the largest ethnic group). Myanmar is diverse in about as many ways as it's possible to be diverse. It has snow-capped mountains, sun-soaked beaches, flood plains, jungles and islands. It is officially home to hundreds of ethnic groups, although the exact number is unknown. A wide chasm divides the rich from the poor. And sadly, for the past seventy years, the home of outwardly peace-loving people of Myanmar has been the stage for long-running civil wars between several ethnic armed groups and the Myanmar military, over disputed autonomy, authority, oppression and equality.

Myanmar is predominantly rural, with less than thirty percent of the country's population living in urban environments (according to the 2014 Population and Housing Census which was conducted by the Department of Population, Ministry of Labour, Immigration and Population with technical assistance from UNFPA). And when I say rural, in many cases I mean in homes built from wood or bamboo with no electricity and often limited running water. The same report estimated that only a third of the population have access to electricity, and only thirty percent were assessed at that time to be using safe drinking water. While visiting a regional market on a work trip to Kayah State, I watched a mother feeding her very young child beer. When I asked my guide about this, he told me 'drinking beer is safer than drinking water sometimes.' This was not uncommon in the rural areas according to accounts I heard from Burmese friends and colleagues, in the same way that many babies were raised on sweetened condensed milk, straight from the tin, on the understanding that it might contain more nutrients than could be provided by the mother.

The different ethnic groups in Myanmar with their own languages, customs, stories, traditions and dress, make for very colourful, captivating tourism experiences for both international and domestic visitors. Some customs were beginning to take a back seat to developmental progress, such as the brass neck rings worn by women of the Kayan tribe, or the face tattoos seen on the women of the Chin Tribe, while others such as the water play at the Thingyan Water Festival which marks the Myanmar New Year, embraced a more commercial (less religious) side, growing bigger, wetter, louder and drunker each year, especially in the big cities.

Much of the advertising we produced was printed on durable, waterproof vinyl, which would be found interwoven into the thatching on peoples' roofs and walls once the campaign was over. It was always jarring to see a home with no electrical power, no sanitation and no running water flying the flag for 4G internet. The simple way that most Myanmar people lived, and still live, did nothing to dampen their generous spirits and welcoming natures. Myanmar has repeatedly topped the Charities Aid Foundation's World Giving Index: a list of the world's most benevolent nations and a list on which Myanmar has never fallen outside the top ten since its inception in 2013. And this from a country which not only has had a tumultuous political history, but which also falls victim to regular natural disasters with deadly weather systems such as cyclones causing flooding and landslides each year.

The Myanmar people are the warmest and most painfully honest I have met anywhere in the world - their generosity evident everywhere. In my first year there, a friend came to visit from the UK and while touring Myanmar's beautiful Inle Lake in Shan State, she left an envelope of money in her hotel room. The envelope was unmarked and it was almost a week before she realised the money was missing. I helped her to phone the hotel.

'Oh thank you for calling,' the receptionist gushed when I relayed my friend's story and asked whether they had found any money. 'We were waiting for Miss Jessica to call us. Our cleaning staff found the money in her room but we had no phone number for her. It is waiting at reception for collection.'

Five hundred dollars could have been life changing for a member of the cleaning staff, and I admit we were not holding out much hope of the money still being there. But then, this was Myanmar. And as this and so many stories like it would constantly remind me, there was something very special about Myanmar and its people. I was once chased down the street by someone, for a good few blocks, I should add, because I was doing my best to ignore and outpace the 'hello, hello, HELLO!' behind me, for a young man to return my 500 Kyats (then around thirty-five cents) which had fallen from my bag as I stepped out of a taxi. Actions that we, as westerners, might see as random acts of kindness were baked into the Burmese way of life.

The honesty of the Myanmar people also manifested itself in unsolicited, unfiltered observations. I lost count of the number of times I was told that I had either gained or lost weight, or that my face looked 'some kind of strange' when I forgot to put any make-up on, or that I looked tired or sick when I felt fine. However unwarranted they might have seemed to me, these observations came from a good place. Or more accurately, from a place of concern. The observer wanted to help, and the observation would be quickly followed by the offer of a solution. I had the distinct impression that if there was something that a Myanmar person could do to improve my day, they would go out of their way to do it. It might not have happened immediately, but at some point, something would materialise. And if it wasn't exactly what was wanted or needed, it would be a pretty close approximation of it.

The Burmese have a wonderful word *'kanalay'*. It translates as 'moment' or 'in a moment' and is as versatile as it is vague. It stands in for 'please wait', 'I'm thinking', 'I'll be right back', 'just a little while longer', and 'I have no idea what the delay is but I am sure if we hang around, something will turn up'. I have waited anywhere between a few minutes to a few days for something which was due to happen 'kanalay'. Deliveries for example, a response to an email, confirmation on a travel booking, the arrival of a boat driver or a drink being served at a bar. I will never forget ordering the cheeseboard from the menu at the Red Mountain winery in Inle Lake, first being told no, and then quickly *'kanalay'*, and then waiting almost an hour for a plate of four slices of white bread topped with cheese slices (with the plastic still on) to materialise at my table. I think perhaps we were the first people to order the cheeseboard and the waiter had done his best to provide it, by sending out for cheese and then arranging what had returned as best he possibly could. Given the elasticity of moments in Myanmar, it wasn't surprising that nobody outside of Yangon ever seemed to be in any hurry.

I travelled as much as I could when I first arrived. I fell in love with the kindness, the calm and gentle pace outside Yangon and the predictable unpredictability of life there. I am glad that I made the most of having few fixed engagements and fewer responsibilities in the early days and took as many weekend trips as I could. Not only because after several months in Myanmar, my social and professional lives started to get in the way of short-hop flights, long-distance bus rides and whimsical boat trips, but also because had I only known Yangon, I wouldn't really have known Myanmar. If I caught wind of someone organising a trip, I was the first to sign up which helped widen my social circle as well as broaden my understanding of Myanmar. I would be hard-pushed to choose a favourite mode of transport from my travels because each one had its own endearing quirks.

To fly was to put my life in the hands of what felt like an ageing, airborne, hop-on, hop-off bus tour. There were a handful of domestic airlines and, for the most part, they all flew to the same handful of tourist-safe destinations: the urban centres of Yangon and Mandalay, the temples of Bagan, the beach at Ngapali, Heho for access to the enchanting Inle Lake and the pine forests of Kalaw and, of course, the official capital city of Naypyidaw. There were parts of Myanmar which were still closed off to foreign visitors - some because of on-going fighting, others because they were along illicit trade routes. The airlines themselves were mostly new, but the planes they were flying and the ways in which they were operating were not. Many of the airlines flew a circular route through most or all these places, dropping off and picking up passengers while others waited on the plane. Flying was exciting in Myanmar in 2015; the departure time, airline *and* destination were all likely to change with barely a few hours warning. More than once, I found myself racing to the airport to catch a flight a good two hours earlier than I had originally booked, with a different airline and stopping in at least one wrong airport before the one I was trying to reach. On arrival at Yangon's Domestic Terminal, it could take as little as a few minutes to get from the check-in desk where they issued me a boarding pass and a coloured sticker, tagging me to indicate to the airport staff which aircraft I should be loaded into, to the gate. The gates were all in the same room. I suppose they weren't as much gates as doors to and from the runway. The waiting hall was vast and wanted to be grand, with ornate, carved teak pillars holding up the roof, but was instead filled with lines and lines of decaying plastic chairs. There was no air conditioning and nothing to dampen the sound of the ticket-holding hordes. I would take a seat somewhere amidst the throng of unhurried air travellers, keeping an eye out for other perplexed foreigners straining to understand the Tannoy announcements and looking around in vain for an information screen. If I enquired about the status of my flight, I was told 'kanalay' – of course!

At some point, someone holding a clipboard would invade my personal space to peer at the sticker on my chest. I felt as though I'd won the lottery when I was plucked from the crowd as the lucky passenger who had been selected for a seat on the as-yet unspecified plane heading to my destination at some point in however convoluted a manner. Sometimes I felt sure that they were simply waiting to fill the seats in a plane before they finalised the route it would take. As I say, it was exciting.

The planes themselves, although old, were functional and perfectly acceptable for an hour's flight. Everywhere took an hour, give or take. Just enough time to tuck into a small cardboard snack box containing a bottle of water, a rock-solid pastry, a chocolate truffle and a square of cake. Dylan and I used to play a game of 'Guess what colour cake?' whenever we flew together. I usually guessed pink, and he usually guessed yellow. One of us was usually right, except when it was green. Landing anywhere other than Yangon meant a no-frills welcome; a casual stroll across the runway to an unassuming terminal building, hand-delivered baggage only released after production of the matching baggage receipt and some heavily armed security personnel checking passports and visas.

Long-distance bus rides were best enjoyed overnight, in my opinion. That way I wasn't quite as aware of how near the misses were with other vehicles, cows and potholes the size of craters in unfinished roads. That the road between Yangon and Myanmar's capital Naypyidaw was nick-named The Death Highway was enough to put me off ever making that journey. The incessant honking didn't make for a perfect night's sleep on an overnight bus ride, however, and nor did the customary middle-of-the-night pitstop in the middle of nowhere. When the bus pulled into the bumpy, gravelly forecourt of a roof on legs, passengers were all evicted to stumble bleary-eyed towards a fruit stall, deep fryer or a squat toilet. Besides the lights on and in the building itself, there was nothing to see for miles around. Somewhere out in the black there might have been tiny, stilted huts for farmers and grazing livestock and sweeping farmland, perhaps even a mountain or a stream, but it was all shrouded in darkness and silence. Bus tickets were cheap, about one tenth of the cost of a flight, and in some ways the surprisingly comfortable coaches ran on a tighter schedule, but they were not for the weak of mind or of bowel.

Burma Belly came for all of us at one time or another. I endured a nerve-wracking three hours on a bus between Hsipaw and Pyin Oo Lwin with a rogue bacteria performing gymnastics in my small intestine. I didn't lose my dignity, but I don't think I've ever clenched so many parts of my body at the same time or for so long. There is nothing quite like discussing the ins and outs, and the exact consistency of the outs, of your digestive system to help you make fast, firm friends in a new place. One fellow Brit, who would later be

Dylan's best man at our wedding, confessed to me after a few months of burgeoning friendship that he had been 'afraid to fart' since arriving in Myanmar over a year earlier, for fear of less easily dissipated follow-through. A truer consecration of comradeship there never was. Restaurant reviews and recommendations I gave to friends would often include a commentary as to whether the food had ever 'got me'. Sometimes, the food was delicious enough to make it worth the risk, but other places would be struck off the roster as soon as I was able to leave the safety of the toilet.

This brings me to boat rides. I took an especially memorable trip to the Myanmar Andaman Islands in 2016 with a rag-tag bunch of expats cobbled together by someone who was looking to fill a twelve-person-live-aboard boat for a few days of island hopping. On arrival in Myeik, the port from which we would be departing, we were sad to discover that, in the words of our dishevelled boat driver, 'the boat shit itself.' To this day, we don't know much more than this, but the result was that we bundled onto a speed boat instead of a slow-chugging dive boat, and slept two magical nights in tents on the white sands of entirely deserted beaches. With the environment around us silent and still but for the lapping of the crystal-clear waters on the sun-warmed sand, and the distant chattering of cicadas in the thick jungle behind the beach, all attention was on the stars. Miles from any light pollution and months away from the monsoon, the night sky glistened and sparkled. The moon shone a shimmering, silver path between the beach and the horizon, a path across which ripples danced in the evening's gentle breeze. We bathed in a bucket in the middle of the empty beach and sidled behind rocks or trees to do our private business. Everyone had their very own loo with a view. We ate nothing but barbecued squid on this trip, which, fortunately, had the opposite effect of Burma Belly. Our boat driver traded some beer and whisky with a passing fishing boat for our 'dinner' each evening, which turned out to be freshly caught but unaccompanied squid. We did venture into a fishing village for breakfast one morning out of three and enjoyed an odd combination of fresh fruit, peanut butter sandwiches and fried noodles. We also had time for a short hike up a hillside to reach a scenic spot from which we could watch the fishing boats setting off across an aquamarine sea, half-hidden behind a curtain of hot pink bougainvillea. That trip around the rarely visited Myanmar Andaman Islands took us well beyond the reach of the newly rolled out internet connectivity, making it feel even more other-worldly than ever.

Besides Ngapali Beach, the tropical paradise where I insisted on spending my late-October birthday every year, my favourite place in Myanmar was Southern Shan State. An hour's flight from Yangon, the small but officious airport of Heho was the gateway to cooler climes, sweeping agricultural landscapes, the birthplace of delicious Shan Noodles (Myanmar's racier answer to spaghetti bolognese) and several deserving tourism hotspots. Shan State is vast and many areas are still heavily restricted due to the ongoing civil wars which continue, particularly in the north. During my time in Myanmar I never saw any danger personally, but I was aware of more than one occasion on which tourists were injured or killed by landmines while trekking in Shan State.

On arrival at Heho Airport, after passing through immigration, tourists had the choice of turning left to drive towards the state capital of Taunggyi, passing the vast and serene Inle Lake on the way, or turning right towards the former British hill station of Kalaw. The road in either direction took a similarly undulating route through villages and farms, twisting around hillsides with breakneck bends and very little by way of road markings. At different times of year, the entire landscape would be painted in the faded orange of summer or the deep green of monsoon.

The first few times I visited Shan State, there was no car rental service, but even once a local conglomerate launched a fleet of hire cars, Dylan and I still opted to leave the driving to the professionals. At least, to those people who were more accustomed to dodging stray cattle, avoiding surprise ditches and anticipating sharp turns while executing a blind overtaking manoeuvre on a road that was itself barely clinging to the side of a mountain. I loved the drive, whether to Kalaw or Inle Lake, because as the car wound through the countryside I wound down from the pace of Yangon life. Despite having lived in some of the world's densest and most impatient cities, I am far more at home in the country. The gentle cadence and expansive skies of Shan State replenished the energy I lost in the city. I am sure it also helped that it was like travelling back in time and holidaying in a bygone era, but one where both my money and my mobile worked seamlessly. Myanmar could be simultaneously hypnotically calm and wildly disorganised. As my father commented once, on a visit to Inle Lake, as he sat watching the wooden boat traffic in a bottleneck at the market town of Nyaung Shwe, 'It looks like absolute chaos, but somehow it works perfectly.'

I must have travelled to Shan State a dozen times over the years. Sometimes with visiting friends or family members, and other times only with Dylan, as a breather from Yangon. In Kalaw I stayed in friendly, family-run chalets which wouldn't have looked out of place in Switzerland, went on day hikes through the pines with local guides, ran the odd half-marathon as part of the annual Kalaw Run and patronised the cluster of picturesque, sustainable coffee shops which sprang up in the town over the years. In Inle I barely took my eyes off the lake, staying at hotels best accessed by the traditional narrow, wooden boat with an ear-splitting outboard motor and spending my days cycling around the lake to marvel at it from various vantage points in various lights. These trips helped to remind me of how lucky I was to live within a short flight's distance of such soul-reviving beauty and of how fortunate I was to have both the time and the means to enjoy it.

Once a year, however, the graceful tranquillity of Inle Lake and its surrounds was disturbed by the unbridled mayhem of what was arguably Shan State's most unique attraction: The Taunggyi Balloon Festival. It never appealed to me, having heard stories of how dangerous it was and having seen the stunned faces of friends who had spent a few hours at the festival before returning to Inle Lake to recover, their ears ringing and their eyes wide with adrenalin. The Taunggyi Balloon Festival was a three-day-long fire balloon and firework extravaganza in a mountainside field arena. It was a competition to see who could build the most beautiful hot air balloon and put on the most spectacular pyrotechnic display as it ascended. Local artisans spent months designing and building hand-painted balloons which were so beautiful it was a shame they were only admired for a matter of minutes before being released into the night sky, never to be seen again. There were no people in these balloon baskets, only fireworks at the end of a long, carefully timed fuse.

I finally attended the festival in 2019, not so much by choice as by duty, in my role at a large, local financial institution where I worked for my last three years in Myanmar. I had heard accounts of how, every year, there was some disaster, or worse, a tragedy as the result of a hot air balloon with its basket laden with hundreds of fireworks, failing to reach a safe altitude before the fuse met the gunpowder. I hoped that safety measures had improved over the years, but when I found myself running for cover under plastic tarpaulin already punctured with the scars of unsuccessful protection from previous flaming downpours, I saw how well placed my reluctance to attend had been. The festival was nothing short of insanity; wild, colourful, awe-inspiring insanity. The balloons lifted off every half hour or so from dusk until midnight with the drunkest festival goers tightly wrapped around the ignition pit for the best views, and the other fifty-odd thousand partying at bars, food stalls and a dilapidated funfair, directly below the flight path. Working there, as a sponsor, meant three long nights of breathless exhilaration and genuine fear for my life. I am not sorry I didn't go sooner.

Whenever someone came to visit Myanmar, I would advise them to get out of Yangon as quickly as possible. I had spreadsheets of tried and tested itineraries, designed to show off the very best of what Myanmar had to offer by way of history, culture, food, scenery and accidental adventure. It wasn't that I didn't want to see them, but I preferred to let Myanmar charm them with its quiet, unassuming beauty and then listen to them fumbling around for the appropriate superlatives over a beer back in Yangon at the end of their trip. And then I would help them fill their bags with artisanal gifts from Yangon's Bogyoke Aung San Market, a popular tourist destination and a mecca for souvenirs, before sending them trudging towards their homeward flight.

Market shopping was an absolute joy in Myanmar, and I don't say that lightly. I am a seasoned haggler and thoroughly enjoy a feisty game of negotiation with an opportunist stall-holder who sees nothing but dollars behind my grey-blue eyes. I honed my craft in China where, thanks to my degree-level fluency in Mandarin, I was able to bring prices down from their lofty ten-fold tourist hikes to a more reasonable market rate. I bartered with a smile. I enjoyed the theatre of the pretend outrage and the walk-away, as long as the shopkeepers were amused by it too. It was fun, but it was also exhausting. Bartering my way through my Christmas shopping list in Beijing was about as efficient as trying to run through water.

But in Myanmar, I never once had a chance to quibble over a price tag because they were always fair. Even at Bogyoke Aung San Market, the store owners gently quoted a fair price and left the choice up to the shopper. I had my favourite stalls there and, the more I visited, the more they dropped their prices, at no request from me. When I picked up sixty mini, hand-painted Pathein umbrellas and sixty scented wooden fans as favours for our wedding guests, the House of Rattan threw in some placemats as a gift. Part of me wished that, for their sakes they had taken a little more advantage, but the other part of me kept coming back - because they didn't. It is the first place in the world where I have shopped until I've dropped and come away feeling as though I would have paid more for less. In the six years I was in Myanmar I never felt taken advantage of.

Despite its natural beauty, its unique range of ethnic cultures and its friendly people, Myanmar remained off the beaten tourist track, even before COVID or the coup came along to all but wipe out its fledgling tourist industry. Selfishly, that's also something I loved about the country. I felt as though I was in on a wonderful secret. It was more expensive, less well documented by guidebooks and not as well served by international airlines as its Southeast Asian neighbours, which kept out the slouchy, elephant-panted backpackers chasing cheap thrills. The people who did make it to Myanmar were there because they really wanted to be there, rather than because they *did not* want to be somewhere else. And this was true for both tourists and expats.

Myanmar was a leapfrog nation, a frontier market and a bewitching travel destination. To Dylan and I, it was simply the place we called home.

3

THE NEW NORMAL

THE WONDERFUL LIFE we enjoyed for so long in Yangon changed beyond all recognition in 2020, with the onset of the pandemic which ravaged the entire world. Myanmar somehow avoided a major wave of the virus in 2020, but the government brought in preventative measures modelled on other government responses.

For most of the year we lived under 'COVID restrictions' until it had a rebrand towards the end of the year and became 'The New Normal'. The New Normal enforced mask wearing in public places, restricted domestic travel, banned international travel (except for the odd relief flight) and required restaurants to pass a rigorous COVID safety inspection before they were OK-ed to open. Temperature checks were the norm, as were contact tracing forms. Anyone who could work from home did so and large gatherings were a thing of the past. Vast quarantine centres like field hospitals popped up in fields and convention centres across the major cities, sponsored by big, local corporations, including the financial institution I was working for then. These were ready to welcome any positive cases once they had been located and rounded up by a parade of hazmat suits. When a positive case was identified, the gate to the offending residential compound or apartment block would be cordoned off with black and yellow police tape, and terrified neighbouring communities would do their utmost to hinder any through traffic from the infected area. People feared COVID, with many having seen what it had done in other countries around the world, and others simply scared of its stigma. The authorities set up a COVID hotline but most people I spoke to were too scared to call it in case their simple request for advice cast suspicion on them or their families.

We too lived in fear of catching COVID but it wasn't the illness we were afraid of, it was the public quarantine conditions. Stories emerged of poor sanitation, no privacy, no charging points for phones and laptops and little or no access to feminine hygiene products. Among our friends, people spoke about rumoured COVID cases in a secret code of nods and winks. If anyone we knew did catch the virus that year, they kept very, very quiet about it.

For Dylan and myself the early days of the pandemic were very stressful professionally; while the rest of the world seemed to be making sourdough and singing to one another, we were buried under crisis management protocols - Dylan for the residential estate we had moved in to a few months before the pandemic and me for the financial institution. Despite a conspicuous lack of positive COVID cases, Dylan spent much of 2020 preparing apocalyptic orders of baked beans, eggs, rice and frozen chickens to feed the three thousand inhabitants of our community in case of a full lockdown. And I commissioned upbeat jingles to encourage queueing bank customers to wash their hands and keep their distance. My team, working from home and dotted all over Yangon in their apartments, were hindered by the relentless hot season power cuts. Power cuts were normal for March and April time but, with everyone trying to work from home instead of in the office, with its backup generator, the daily outages did nothing to boost morale. It was hard for us to meet our deadlines on the communications frontline, now that everyone was stashed away in corners of crowded homes, trying to focus on their tasks, while other members of their multi-generational families worked on their own business in the same space. For several hours a day, different townships had no power, as per the outage roster that the government posted on Facebook each week. It was like working on a merry-go-round; team members jumped in and out of files and documents, picking up from wherever their predecessor had left off, as and when they could.

Dylan and I were on call night and day and, in a country like Myanmar, where education levels are generally low and where the government lacked the sophistication and reach in its own communications to have any real impact, the pressure on private businesses to save lives through educational materials was enormous. As the language of COVID started to develop around the world, my team was busy trying to create appropriate translations of the new terms, such as 'social distancing', into Burmese.

'Where are we on the social distancing video to play in the branches and offices?' my boss would ask from where he was based in the UK.

'Let me check which designer has power today,' I would answer. 'I know we were almost done with subtitles yesterday, but most of the team have been without power overnight and this morning, so we have been slow to get going today.'

These busy months coincided with my first trimester of pregnancy, and I couldn't be sure if my breathlessness and sudden need to take my afternoon calls lying down was due to the information overload and pressures to deliver under tight deadlines, or to hormonal changes. I was lucky that our apartment building had a back-up generator which kicked in almost instantly, so we were not affected by the grid outages. The mandate, that all staff who could work from home should do so, suited me just fine with my unrelenting, but fortunately mild, nausea. We did return to the office for a brief period when I was four months along and my fifty-minute car journey each way, coupled with a need to find respectable clothes which still fitted me, confirmed that pandemic pregnancy was an absolute gift. And not only because being pregnant in the confines of my own home was far easier than being pregnant out in public, but also because pregnancy was the perfect distraction from what was going on in the world around me.

Besides the work my team and I were doing to keep people safe, there was also a huge amount of work to be done to help proliferate digital payment systems to avoid physical contact. I had started my role back in 2018, at what was an undeniably exciting time for the country's finance industry: the dawn of mobile payments. My first three months were a baptism by fire into the world of fintech and it was thrilling. Having just built a mobile wallet, the company was on the brink of rolling it out across the entire country, deploying thousands of staff nationwide as brand ambassadors, salespeople and customer support representatives. Given the rapid adoption of mobile devices and internet connections, there was no reason not to reach for the stars as far as mobile wallets were concerned. Between 2018 and 2019 we brought millions of customers on board. The sign-up numbers were staggering, even if usage was a little slower on the uptake. But the fact remained that Myanmar was still very reliant on cash. The issue with anything other than cash was always trust. If people couldn't see and touch the money, they didn't fully trust that it was there.

For those of us in the mobile payment industry, therefore, COVID was something of a godsend. Suddenly, everyone wanted and needed a secure, contactless payment system and mobile wallets jumped at the opportunity to fill the gap. I proudly promoted our mobile wallet, extolling its virtues to friends and acquaintances, teaching them how it worked, helping them to top up and showing them all the places where they could use it. I would cheer, sometimes out loud, every time I paid with my mobile and revelled in the ability to use such a sophisticated payment system in a country that had only embraced mobile technology a few years before.

It was something of a mystery how Myanmar avoided a serious wave of COVID-19 for as long as it did. I remember reading an article in the *New York Times* in March 2020, which talked about how some of Myanmar's Buddhist leaders had been '*promoting nonmedical remedies. One famous monk said that eating a lime and three palm seeds would keep the virus away. Another monk recommended seven ground peppercorns.*' Maybe that was it? I prefer to think that it had more to do with the tireless work of teams like mine, preparing posters, banners and social media cartoons to teach people the importance of good hygiene and avoiding crowded places, or the fact that Myanmar was never an international transit hub. It wasn't merely a case of low testing levels or underreporting at this stage, either; both mine and Dylan's employers were monitoring staff health conditions daily and, with a combined workforce of over twenty thousand people, none with even anecdotal reports of the virus among friends or families, the data, suggesting Myanmar skipped the global first and second waves, was fairly compelling.

Despite this, there was no complacency and the Myanmar public rallied together to minimise the threat of the pandemic. For the most part, people followed the guidelines and rules set out by the government and by local businesses. The prevailing mood was one of nervous pessimism; everyone expected the virus to arrive at some point, and when it did, they expected the results to be devastating. This was due, in large part, to the state of the medical system in Myanmar: people knew it to be understaffed, and reliant on old equipment and outdated practices. And that was in the major cities where the standards were far higher than in the more remote towns and villages. Many of my colleagues lived with old and infirm grandparents whom they did not want to put at risk. I found it eye-opening to read about people flouting and resisting the restrictions in the west. In Myanmar, a country in which salary cuts and job losses had the potential to plunge millions of people back below the poverty line, and where a severe respiratory illness would be deadly to thousands of people with underlying health conditions and without access to medicines (let alone ventilators), people understood the importance of pulling together and playing their part. That said, for many of these people, crowded accommodation and grocery shopping at poorly ventilated markets was unavoidable, so there was a limit to how effectively the preventative measures could be followed. Despite being fit and healthy and despite having the means to pay for private medical care, my pregnancy put me automatically in the vulnerable category as far as my employer and the medical professionals were concerned, so every time the case numbers rose even the tiniest amount, I was advised to stay home.

It was during one of these periods of heightened alert and reinforced stay home advice, in late July 2020, that I started to think seriously about where I was going to give birth. In an ideal world, I would have chosen to go to Bangkok for the birth. Bangkok had been Dylan's and my go-to escape from Yangon over the years. It was only a ninety-minute flight away and once there, we used to be able to do everything we couldn't do in Myanmar: go bowling, see a movie at the IMAX cinema, enjoy metered taxis, use public transport, gorge ourselves in Michelin-starred restaurants, splurge in H&M and bask in the luxury of anonymity. Plus, Tony's wife Jen was there. Before COVID, Tony had split his time between Yangon and Bangkok; working in Yangon but living in Bangkok. Jen was still in Bangkok, as yet undecided on whether the pandemic was going to be disruptive enough to travel for her to move back to Australia to wait it out while Tony doubled down on Yangon. Bangkok also had world-class medical facilities, although I had never needed them before. Most expats and financially able Burmese lived by a kind of unwritten rule that for anything more serious than a scratch, you were best to head to Bangkok. There was a story about someone who knew someone who knew someone that had broken their arm and had it set in Myanmar. As the story went, the arm had never been the same again because somewhere between the doctor, the X-ray and the cast, something had been misunderstood and the setting had gone wrong. We once played golf with a heart surgeon who told us that, even with his expertise, he would advise patients to get on the first plane out as soon as they were stable. How true the arm story was, I never knew, but I took its message to heart: for something important, go to Bangkok.

I reviewed all the birth packages at the big Bangkok hospitals and took advice from other Yangon-based friends who had given birth in Thailand before, albeit under pre-pandemic circumstances.

'Ooh look - this is the one Juliette mentioned, where you

can push the two gurneys together to make a double bed for us! It looks amazing,' I exclaimed to Dylan over lunch one day. 'And this one offers a maternal mani-pedi and a newborn photoshoot as part of the package. I mean, it's totally unnecessary but why not, right? Marie said that her hospital was more like a 5* hotel than a hospital, with an entire floor dedicated to passport and visa admin so you don't even have to leave the hospital to get all the forms to fill in.'

'Bangkok does have amazing hospitals,' responded Dylan thoughtfully. 'When I caught typhoid from eating at that dodgy restaurant in Mandalay that Tony sent me to, I was treated at Bumrungrad Hospital in Bangkok. I pretty much stumbled in and died on their lobby floor, but I still remember it being amazing.'

Usually when Dylan told this story it ended with the punchline that typhoid made him superhuman and enabled him to bowl his best ever bowling score while delirious. But now wasn't the time for chest-puffing.

'That said, I think maybe we need to think about the practicalities of it all. Like when would you need to leave here, and when would I join you, and where would we stay in Bangkok? This pandemic doesn't really look like it's going anywhere, does it?'

'No, and you're right. The logistics would be pretty high risk, given the current state of travel. Let's think. My due date is mid-December, so, counting back from there, I would probably need to be in Bangkok in mid-November so they let me fly. And looking at the public holidays this year, it would probably make sense for me to start my maternity leave after the Thadingyut Festival. So, I would leave here in October, and then you would come over in November?'

'And what if they cancel flights and I can't get there? And what if Jen goes back to Aus? She might have to if she doesn't want to be stuck there on her own,' Dylan asked slowly.

I stared at him, processing the implications of being in Bangkok, alone, preparing to give birth and then afterwards, taking care of a newborn baby.

'Could you come with me in October? And work remotely for a month?' I floated.

'No. You know construction isn't easy to do remotely. And with all this estate management stuff, it would be too hard,' he said, making a face that told me not to pursue that idea further.

I looked back at my laptop and at all the luxurious, gold-plated interiors and shiny, happy faces on the Thai hospital websites. I looked at Dylan.

'Well then what are my options? I don't want to be there alone and I don't want to get stuck there. I don't want to go back to Jersey to my family because that's even further for you to travel when the baby comes and I don't want to be separated for months on opposite sides of the world. That's not even an option.'

'No, I agree. We don't want to be separated. Who knows how long the travel restrictions will be around? We should stay together.'

'Well, I suppose that only gives me one option. I have to give birth here in Yangon.' I said more decisively than I felt.

'Are you OK with that?' he asked gently.

I paused. 'Yeah, I think I am. While I always pictured having the baby in Bangkok, it just doesn't seem like it's a sensible idea right now. And when I think about the risks of travelling there and getting stuck, and without you, they outweigh my hesitation to give birth here.'

'I am sure we can get a good doctor here, someone who has dealt with foreigners before and has done a natural birth. I'll find out about rooms and packages through work.

At least the hospital is part of my company, so I can ask who we need to talk to,' Dylan added. Besides its construction business, for which Dylan had been hired a few years prior, the company he worked for also owned and ran hospitals, residential estates such as the one we lived in, restaurants, hotels and a bank.

'OK. Done. The baby will be born in Myanmar. Ha, phew. Do you know what? I feel hugely, hugely relieved with this decision. I was having nightmares about trying to settle into Bangkok on my own while heavily pregnant!'

We laughed. It felt kind of perfect for our story that our baby would be born in the place where we had met. Even if the medical system wasn't exactly up to international standards of technology, cleanliness or qualified staff, I had everything I needed for a normal pregnancy, which made me far more fortunate than most pregnant women in Myanmar. I found an obstetrician I trusted and who had trained abroad, had plenty of ultrasounds, and hoped above all that the baby wouldn't need any neo-natal care, because that was reportedly very limited.

'He'll forever have a Myanmar birth certificate, which will be a talking point for him in the future!' I laughed. 'One thing, though. I would want to stay much nearer to the hospital once we get closer to the due date. I don't want to be racing across the city after I go into labour. It's a two-hour journey in bad traffic and I don't want that stress.'

'Deal. I will find us an apartment on the other estate, near the hospital and we can call it a staycation for the month surrounding the due date.'

Knowing that I didn't need to travel for the birth was an enormous relief and it allowed me to relax and ride the very slow wave of what turned out to be a wonderfully boring and uneventful pregnancy.

We had moved out of the crowded, densely populated downtown Yangon and into our new home on a sprawling, half-empty residential and golf estate called Star City, on the outskirts of Yangon, just a few months before the pandemic began. I confess, we weren't roughing it. The estate boasted not one but two swimming pools, a football field, badminton courts, restaurants, cafes, a lush, riverside park, a nine-hole golf course and a doctor's clinic at which I did most of my tests and check-ups. Admittedly, the badminton courts were making temporary use of an outdoor car park which meant they were little more than a trio of nets where we would play what we referred to as 'extreme badminton'. Extreme badminton required players to adjust shot angles for cross winds and avoid drainage gutters that were dangerously close to the line markings. Throughout my pregnancy I swam almost daily and I played golf well into my second trimester, retiring my driver at six months, and abandoning all clubs in favour of a walk to accompany Dylan and Tony at seven months. I even shot my first, and possibly only, eagle at five months. The only thing the estate had against it, in fact, was its distance from the hospital where I would now be giving birth.

Tony had followed our lead in moving out of town and, while I wasn't quite ready to cohabit with my father-in-law, nor have him strolling between floors in his pyjamas whenever he pleased, we helped him to find a lovely apartment in the next tower. Tony was arguably more excited than we were about the approaching arrival of his grandson. On hearing that we would be staying at the other estate for a few weeks around the due date, he immediately invited himself to join us; an invitation we politely declined. We were supporting one another through the difficulties of pandemic protocols, but welcoming our baby into the world was something Dylan and I wanted to do alone.

At the very end of November, Dylan and I packed some bags and a newly acquired hand-me-down car seat, and set off for our staycation on the other side of the city. By this stage we knew that the baby would be born by caesarean section, as the little acrobat hadn't stopped spinning for weeks. What we didn't know until we arrived at the other estate and attended what would end up being our final doctor's appointment, was that he would need to be extracted sooner than expected for fear of the cord tangling. Dylan had decided to leave his job just before the birth, giving him an open-ended paternity leave to dive into first-time parenthood. With the news about the baby's arrival date being moved up, Dylan's leisurely week-long handover was condensed into a single day. My busy first week of maternity leave, during which I had lined up coffees, video calls and aquarobics classes with friends near and far, became one day of waiting and being monitored in a hospital bed before the surgery, lying to people about why I was cancelling our plans.

4

THE LITTLE GUY

Jasper arrived by scheduled caesarean section at the Pun Hlaing Hospital in Yangon on 2 December 2020 at 7.23am. Through the numbness of anaesthesia, his removal felt like a large bag of flour being pulled out of my abdomen, followed sometime later by a second large bag of what must have contained the placenta. Besides the clatter of scalpels and the collaborative murmuring of the obstetrician and her assistant, there wasn't a lot of noise in the operating theatre, and therein lay our problem: Jasper didn't cry. With the luxury of hindsight, we later saw that his first few moments of living, breathing consciousness were more indicative of his happy-go-lucky nature and casual acceptance of changing circumstances than of any underlying health concern. But the doctors had to do what they thought was best and, unfortunately, he wasn't quite ready to announce his presence with a belly laugh. Instead, he hesitated, mustered a not-very-reassuring gurgle and with that sealed his, Dylan's and my fates for the next thirty-odd hours.

In the context of the year that was to follow, those thirty hours were short, but in many ways, I have the trauma of Jasper's arrival into this world to thank for furnishing me with the resilience and humour I would need to weather the storm that whipped up as we went through 2021. Both my recollection of events and the way I experienced it at the time were undoubtedly affected by the intoxicating cocktail of painkillers, hormones and anxiety coursing through my mind and body.

Sometime after the alleviation of weight down near my pelvis, a small, blue burrito came floating over the medical sheet, out of which peeked a tiny, pale, slightly furry face. The paediatrician brought his impossibly soft cheek alongside mine. As our faces touched, I felt an involuntary tear roll down my face and decided on his name. Dylan and I had already narrowed our choices down to two and something told me that Jasper was the right one. Due to COVID protocols, Dylan hadn't been allowed in the room and due to old-fashioned thinking, I hadn't been allowed any skin-to-skin contact with Jasper. So, for now, it was just me and a bundle of blue blankets with an angelic little face.

It sounds cliché to say that everything else in the world faded away while I lay there, cheek to cheek with this diminutive creature, but it really did. In the absolute stillness I took in his smell, his warmth, the minute movements in his scrunched-up eyes and perfect cupid's bow from where he emitted barely audible grunts and snuffles. I saw wisps of gingery-blond hair escaping from under the snug blanket wrap. When he opened his eyes the tiniest amount, it felt as though he was sneakily sizing me up.

I could feel the tug of the stitching going on lower down my body and wished I had access to my arms to properly embrace Jasper. The tightness of his hospital-grade swaddle hid the floppiness of his limbs and head, as well as how small he was, and it wasn't until the following day, when I was finally allowed to unwrap him, that I fully appreciated how small and fragile a newborn baby is.

This intimate moment of mutual intrigue popped like a bubble. Jasper was whisked off for more checks and I was brought back to reality with the information that I was all closed up and was being transferred to the recovery room. For the previous hour, Dylan had been sitting alone on a blue plastic chair in the empty corridor outside the operating theatre, looking like he'd missed the last bus home. He later told me he felt as though he'd been transported back to the 1950s and how, if there were ever a moment to puff away on a pipe, that would have been it. From his look when I smiled drunkenly over at him from my gurney, I sensed something was wrong. I can't tell you where that sense came from as my usual centre of panic was still under heavy anaesthetic but I knew something wasn't right.

As Dylan slowly pushed open the door, he prefaced his supposedly reassuring speech by declaring, 'They have told me to tell you this as calmly as possible.'

'They are going to bring the baby in for you to try to feed,' he continued.

'Jasper,' I interrupted.

'So we're going with Jasper?'

'Yes - when I saw him, I just decided he's a Jasper.'

'They are going to bring Jasper in for you to try to feed, but then they want to take him to the children's hospital. They say not to worry, but they want to make sure there's no liquid on his lungs because they say he didn't cry out.' Dylan's speech was measured but his grip on my hand was like a vice.

My heart tightened as I took in what he had said. The children's hospital. On the other side of the city. Months earlier, Dylan had relayed the story of a colleague of his who had been required to accompany his own newborn in an ambulance to a children's hospital because this hospital we were in didn't have an NICU. We had commented at the time how stressful that must have been, and how mind-boggling it was for a hospital claiming international standards and delivering babies day and night not to have the necessary equipment to conduct at least basic monitoring. We had mused about how we might handle the same situation, but hadn't seriously considered it. I don't know whether to credit the drugs or the fact that my subconscious was already prepared for this impromptu father-son field trip but, as it was, I responded pragmatically, rather than emotionally. I requested a photo to look at in Jasper's absence, and agreed with Dylan that we would tell no one, not even Tony, until we knew where this little adventure was headed. Dylan had been invited momentarily to a viewing window to catch a glimpse of his son as Jasper was being measured and spruced, but father and son didn't formally meet until Jasper appeared for his feed, just moments before they were bundled into an ambulance together.

Those moments were all I had too. Lying flat on my bed, as I was strictly directed to remain for seven long hours, I made my first attempt at breastfeeding. It didn't go very well, but the nurse seemed encouraged by Jasper's effort and interest. As he tried to feed, I briefly forgot that he was about to be taken away to another hospital, but then our time was up and he disappeared. It made my heart ache to think that I didn't yet have a fixed image of him in my head. The photo I received from Dylan was overexposed and slightly blurred, a sign of the movement of the vehicle and possibly an unsteadiness in Dylan's hands. I must have looked at that photo a thousand times over the course of the day and night we were apart, wondering if that would be the last photo we'd have of our baby. I tried to stay positive, to reassure myself, but my thoughts often strayed to the darkest of places.

I drifted in and out of sleep and awoke to find myself

back in the suite where I had begun my day, still full of baby, hours earlier. I had selected the Deluxe Package from the hospital, which was a far cry from the luxury I had been ogling on the Bangkok hospital websites, but comfortable, by Myanmar standards. It included everything we thought we needed; the stay, the surgery, the drugs, three meals a day (plus snacks) delivered to the suite, all newborn tests, maternal monitoring and a family photograph. For a C-section, the stay was four nights and five days in a private suite for both the patient and their attendant. In a Myanmar hospital, private or public, in the absence of sufficient nursing staff, every patient needs an attendant; someone who is responsible for all nonmedical care, including but not limited to feeding, watering, bathing and wiping. Dylan was my attendant.

Rather foolishly, in our eagerness to keep Jasper's arrival and subsequent as-yet-undefined leave of absence a secret, Dylan and I completely overlooked the need to find me a new attendant. My big, strong, independent 'can-do' attitude told me I didn't need one anyway, so Dylan was reassigned to Jasper and off they went. Jasper was a tricky patient. Simultaneously under the care of two hospitals, he required an extended list of duties which included transport, logistics, financing and considerable paperwork.

Agitated by the quiet in my room I called Dylan for an update.

'Hi. Where are you? Do you know when you'll be back?' I asked.

'They want to keep him here overnight,' Dylan said flatly.

'Overnight?' It hadn't even occurred to me that they might be gone more than a few hours. 'But, why? What does that mean? Is something wrong?'

'No - they think he's alright. They have put a little tube

up his nose. I'll send you the photo they took. And he's breathing normally with no liquid on his lungs, but they would prefer to keep him overnight for monitoring.'

'But, then, what do I do? Do I just stay here?'

'Yes. I will stay here with him; I just have to find out where. And then if it's all still normal, he will be discharged tomorrow, I think. That's all I know for now. I am going to go and try to find someone who can speak more English and can give me more information.'

'The anaesthesia is starting to wear off. I feel so empty. And it hurts every time I move,' I told Dylan.

'I need to go and try to find a doctor and see if I can get more information,' Dylan continued distractedly. 'Can you call the driver and get him to bring the car? He'll have to come to me here to get the apartment key, and then go to the apartment to get the car keys, and some clothes for me, before coming back here with the car. Oh, and tell him to find my charger on my nightstand.'

'OK got it. Let me know if there is anything else I can do,' I offered, hoping it might at least give me something to think about other than the increasing pain in my abdomen.

'Let me know when you have a hotel and the car sorted.'

And so began my first twenty-four hours of motherhood; running back-office support for my husband and baby, alone in my oversized hospital suite. As I looked around the room again, I realised that admin was as good a distraction as any from the undeniable weirdness of my situation. In between administrative tasks, I continued to evade questions and calls from friends I had cancelled on. Every time a message popped up on my phone, I froze and in the momentary paralysis wondered if I should tell someone, just so that I had a confidante. Then as quickly as that thought had formed, another would crush it, reminding me that what little information I had would only lead to questions and I had neither the energy nor the inclination to be running comms too.

One message caught my eye, however. The contact was saved in my phone as Midwife Jess. Seeing her name pop up jolted me. Her message asked how I was, and if I had a date for the surgery. Partly in anticipation of being peddled some very outdated thinking around postpartum health and infant care, and partly out of envy for my pregnant friends in the UK with their NCT groups and nearby relatives to swap tips with, I had lined up Jess, a midwife from New Zealand, to be on call for me in the first few weeks of Jasper's life. She had recently looked after a friend of ours in Auckland and I decided that she was a worthy exception to our 'tell no one' rule. Within minutes of my having garbled a summary of my situation - baby is at another hospital, I can't move from my bed and I don't know what to do about milk - she had me confidently squeezing my boobs to trick them into thinking there was a baby nearby. I don't know if I was motivated more by the fear of failure to breastfeed or by the fear that not trying would give the universe a sign that I wasn't interested in getting my baby back. Either way, my boobs served as a pair of misshapen stress balls until Jasper's return the following day. Jess's shock over my situation and concern for my welfare and care made me realise that it was OK for me to be worried, and to feel as though this might not be what constituted a 'normal' birth experience.

I slept a lot during my first day as a mother, which I assume is rare. On waking from one of my many naps to see the sky outside dimming towards evening, I called Dylan again to give him an update on my progress.

'I'm not doing well on hotels,' I confessed. 'Everything

near the hospital is shut because of COVID. I was going to put you in the Governor's Residence, but even that's closed. I think the nearest might be Hotel G which is a good twenty minutes away. Is that OK?'

'Yeah - that'll be fine. I think they only need me nearby so I can pay for things. If he needs any tests or medicine, I will have to pay. I am trying to negotiate something with them now, so I don't need to keep coming back.' Dylan sounded weary.

'OK. I don't need to book, the hotel said. You can just show up. And is the car with you?'

'Yes, Johnny's here. He's helping to translate. What time is it, actually?'

I looked at the clock on the wall of my room, which I hadn't really noticed earlier.

'It's just gone 6pm,' I said.

'No wonder I am so hungry. I am going to go to the hotel as soon as I have sorted things here and order some dinner. I haven't eaten all day.'

'Do you know what? Nor have I,' I responded, with some confusion in my voice.

'What? Why not? Haven't they brought you any food? I thought it was all included in the package?'

Dylan sounded annoyed, which I understood. I was also annoyed now. I had requested some food a few times during the day, but now I thought about it, nothing had ever materialised. As soon as I ended my call with Dylan, I pressed my buzzer again, and again asked about some food.

I couldn't tell you if that night seemed long or short. I only know that it was painful. It was physically painful because every time I shifted my weight, I received a searing dart of pain across my abdomen. It was painful in other ways too.

The stream of people who came into the room seemed endless and, for the most part, I had no idea who there were. Very few of them seemed to be in uniform, so until they emptied a bin, checked my blood pressure or checked my wound, I had no idea what their job scope was. I suppose, in many ways, I still had no idea, even once they had performed whatever task they chose to undertake. I took to asking every one of them about food. Sometimes I was given a blank stare in response. Perhaps she was a cleaner who spoke no English. Sometimes I was treated to a flurry of apologies and promises that food would be found and brought. I recognised my obstetrician, of course, although I was more interested in pain medication from her, and I didn't want to bother her with my menu requests. The intrusions were relentless and every time, it felt as though I had only just fallen back to sleep after an interruption when I was woken up again for more checks.

With the delirium and disorientation of tiredness came sadness, and I remember spending much of that night fighting with tears. Such was the conflict within my mind that I couldn't quite allow myself to cry. Part of me feared the worst and that this separation could only lead to grief. The injustice of it all made me tearful, as well as the dread of how we would break bad news to our families. But another part of me felt as though I had nothing at all to cry about. After all, Jasper was alive and he was in the best possible care. Crying because I was all alone felt self-absorbed. Crying because I didn't know what was going on felt self-important. I wished I could wind back the clock to before the surgery. I wished I could get out of bed and go to the children's hospital. I wished I knew how it was all going to end: more than anything, I wished I knew that. The wait was torturous.

The next morning, I awoke to extreme hanger; I wasn't

angry *because* I was hungry, I was angry because of *why* I was so hungry. Overnight, during one of the many, many intrusions, I had established the reason for my starvation; the catering staff had dutifully delivered all my food to the living room, and nobody had thought to question whether I, with my debilitating abdominal wound, my IV, my catheter and my dangerously low blood pressure, would be able to reach any of it. Every time I had asked for food, the person checked the catering records which said I had been fed. Instead of coming back to address my apparent confusion, they had simply moved on to their next task. I can only assume they thought I was mad. And in many ways, I suppose I was.

My now seemingly permanent state of hunger strengthened my resolve to bring Dylan and Jasper back as quickly as possible. It was 7am when I called Dylan.

'Morning. How did you sleep?' I asked, more out of habit than actual interest.

'Yeah, you know. Not much,' he responded.

'What time can you go to the hospital?' I continued.

'They said 9am. At least, they said I can go at nine and they will tell me at that point if they can discharge him.' My heart sank. I must have misread the messages Dylan had sent me the evening before.

'Oh. I thought he was being discharged at 9am. When will he be discharged?' I pestered.

'I don't know. They only said to come at 9am. I am going to get some breakfast. I'll call you when I get to the hospital and can speak to someone.'

'OK. You know where I'll be! I still haven't had anything to eat, by the way. They've been delivering all the food to the room next door! So all my food has been delivered and then cleared away. I am so pissed off. And I'm still trying to find someone who will bring me some fried rice.'

'What? That's so stupid. Shall I call someone? Once I am back, I'll get you food. I can go to that restaurant in the hospital. I should be back in a couple of hours, I hope.'

Sometime after 9am we were told that Jasper was fine and that he was approved for discharge from the children's hospital. The trouble was, they had to wait for a discharge approval from my hospital before they could release him. The children's hospital had initially refused to discharge Jasper without seeing me feeding him. Luckily, Dylan argued his way out of that one on the basis that I couldn't move from my own hospital bed yet. But that didn't make the process go any faster.

Both Dylan and I had to sign forms. I had to locate, reserve and request dispatch of an ambulance, and apparently all the hospital staff with the authority to do these things were running late that day. It took another four hours of calls and messages and emails to get all our ducks in a row and for Dylan to confirm to me that he and Jasper had left the children's hospital. Finally, at 1.45pm on 3 December, thirty hours and twenty-two minutes after he had taken his first, quiet breath, Jasper made it back into my arms and Dylan unleashed an unprecedented fury on the hospital staff that, finally, secured me a plate of fried rice.

The remaining days left on our package went on forever. The nightly interruptions continued, as did my struggle to breastfeed even with the combined force of my remote midwife and the onsite maternity nurses, none of whom, I then realised, had checked in on me and my milk factory during the hours I had been separated from Jasper. At least now I had Dylan to commiserate with every time I was woken for blood-pressure checks and at least now I had Dylan to help me up out of bed to move around the room. I began those all-important first few days of motherhood feeling as though I was on the back foot. I hadn't done anything to prepare for Jasper's return during those horrible hours of separation and I felt as though, if anything, I had regressed in my preparation for taking care of a baby. My brain seemed to stall every time he made a noise and my body took a while to kick into action. I had been worrying about so many other things, besides how to change a nappy or how to burp him after feeding, and now he was here with me, I didn't have the time to watch tutorials or unpack his little bundle of clothes.

As soon as we felt settled and ready, Dylan and I decided it was time to start calling our families to let them know an abridged version of Jasper's origin story and to share the good news that he was here, and that we were all doing well. We had to call Tony last, despite him being the closest, because his reputation as family foghorn does not overstate his ability to ruin a surprise, and we wanted everyone to hear the news from us directly. When we did finally get to Tony, we could hear his car keys jangling as we spoke, and we had to break it to him that we wouldn't be accepting visitors for a few days. Not only was I disoriented from the anxiety of the first thirty odd hours of Jasper's life, but I was also exhausted just from making a few phone calls. The raw pain in my abdominal muscles made it hard to project my voice sufficiently to reach the phone microphone, let alone to reassure my family that I was my same, upbeat self despite Jasper and Dylan's little adventure. And then there was the fact that I was still clad in adult diapers and a hospital gown, turned the wrong way to allow easy access to Jasper's food. The last thing I needed in this state of mental and physical undress was a visitor.

Jasper lived for those hospital days on what looked like a tea trolley: a three-layered shelf unit on wheels with a shallow plastic tub at the top where he slept, in full burrito mode, and a floral net curtain laid across like an oversized doily protecting him from the unfortunate number of mosquitos who seemed to have gained access to the hospital. Below him were supplies for our ham-fisted attempts at nappy changes and various pairs of mittens to stop him scratching his beautiful little face. There were a few occasions on which I awoke from a very deep sleep to find the little tea trolley gone from my bedside. My heart would skip a beat and my mind would race until Dylan's voice would come from the recliner chair at the foot of my bed, uttering reassurances that Jasper had only gone for routine checks.

Finally, the day came for our release from the package and, for me, from the confines of the room in which I had been festering for four days. I woke, I showered, I dressed and then I remembered that nothing ever ran on time in the Myanmar medical system, especially not with two patients to assess and discharge. Then there was the matter of our family photo which had been promised as part of the package. We tried many times to say that we didn't need it, but the hospital insisted and kept trying to send the photographer in at the least convenient times. In his defence, it was hard to pinpoint the right time because everything in our morning schedule of checks and discharge signatures was running skew-whiff. The first time he appeared, I was having my wound checked. The second time, Dylan was outside with the hospital admin staff. The third time, Jasper was feeding, and I was hardly in the mood to be modest. On his fourth attempt, the stars aligned, and Dylan and I arranged ourselves with Jasper in my arms to be photographed. The resulting image has haunted and amused us in equal measure ever since. It so perfectly captures our weariness from the entire experience; the desperation we felt to leave the hospital: the stress and trauma of the previous few days: the irritation at being held against our will and the brave faces we were wearing as a cover.

As we emerged from the hospital into the warm, bright sunshine and cloudless sky of a perfect December day in Yangon, I felt a glimmer of the excitement I had felt five days earlier when I had dropped myself at the hospital on a golf buggy. A weight I didn't know I'd been shouldering for those few days evaporated, leaving me walking, albeit gingerly, as if on air. I am sure we had the nervous, jittery look of new parents setting off on the adventure of a lifetime, but I felt like a woman on a mission. After all that had gone before, I knew one thing for certain, I was going to mother the hell out of this baby.

5

BOYS' DAY OUT

It was two months before I heard the full story of Dylan and Jasper's field trip on 2 December. In part, this was because throughout the ordeal, Dylan was either fully engaged in trying to work out what was going on, or was left waiting for hours with no information. Once they had returned to me, Dylan then sensibly decided to keep the more worrying parts of the story from me until my hormones and, with them, my easily-activated emotions, had settled down. I think Dylan also needed some time to process the events for himself.

On that December morning, in the time it took for Jasper to hesitate before making a sound, Dylan's role in the birth changed from one of supporting cast to that of the leading man. Before he had even held Jasper, he had been told that he would need to accompany him in the ambulance to the children's hospital and, from that moment, Dylan had to assume all decision-making responsibilities alone. This was not something we had planned for.

Dylan relayed his adventure to some friends over a still relatively rare lunch out at a restaurant.

'OK, so what were you doing all this time while your

poor wife was lying alone and starving in her hospital bed?' our friend and fellow expat Tess asked, after I had shared my experience of Jasper's arrival.

'Ha. Do you know, Milla hasn't even heard this story yet,' Dylan started with a laugh.

'What? Haven't I? I was on the other end of the phone for most of it, wasn't I?' I countered.

'You were, but I didn't tell you everything,' Dylan said with a hint of a grimace. 'OK, where shall I start? I was bundled into an ambulance with Jasper and a nurse and told we were going to the children's hospital. I barely had time to grab my wallet and phone. When I say ambulance, I mean one of those flimsy little minibuses with the seats like benches on either side of the space at the back.'

'Where was Jasper? In a bed or a box or something?' I interrupted.

'No - he was just on the nurse's lap. It took us about forty-five minutes to get there; forty-five minutes of being bounced around in the back of the ambulance. That's when I sent you the photo, Milla. The hospital was somewhere in Ahlone township. The building we parked outside was one of those ominous, old institutions that's falling apart, with rain-stained walls, open corridors, stray dogs on the steps and betel-nut stains on the ground. The nurse didn't speak any English, so she just pointed to the building. I can't explain how bad this building was. I had to sign in on a betel-nut stand.'

'What do you mean?' Tess asked.

'There was no reception, just one of those folding tables that the betel sellers use on the street corners. I wrote my name in a book on one of those. The waiting area looked like a long-distance bus terminal. There were plastic chairs scattered in the middle of a big, concrete space, and everyone sitting on them was staring at us, of course. We were sent into a room to one side of where I'd signed in and, at this point, I am not joking, I thought it was game over. The room felt tired and forgotten. It *smelled* forgotten. It was dirty, the floor stained a kind of yellow, the walls peeling with mould and the windows didn't close properly in the frames. There were a couple of empty baby trolleys in the room, each with a big mosquito net over the top, and I could see why. The place was infested with the things. A doctor - or at least I assumed he was a doctor - had a look at Jasper and asked the nurse a few questions. I couldn't understand why we were there - this place made Pun Hlaing look like 5-star luxury. I'm serious when I say that I honestly thought that if this was where Jasper had to stay, there was not a chance he was going to survive.'

As Dylan recounted his story in his usual matter-of-fact manner, I stared over at Jasper, sleeping on a sofa close to the table and my heart felt tight in my chest. Dylan had been right not to share this detail at the time.

'And then the guy suddenly said 'OK, now we can admit you',' continued Dylan.

'Wait, what? Weren't you already admitted at the betel table?' asked Tess.

'No. It turned out, the building I needed to go to was round the back, thank god. We got back in the ambulance and drove a hundred metres further into the compound and there was another building. This one looked a lot better. There was a lift, but the lift-troll took one look at me and shook his head to say 'no lift', so I followed the nurse up four flights of stairs. At the top there was a proper, metal sign for the NICU. The doors opened and I was hit by a blast of air con - it was amazing. But they wouldn't let me in, so I watched Jasper disappear and then spent the next four hours waiting on a plastic chair outside. I had only really seen the reception desk, but I was so relieved to know that the NICU looked better than whatever building we were in before.'

'How? How is the NICU so much better than the rest of the hospital?' asked Tess's partner, Steve.

'Yeah, I asked the same thing. I am not sure, but I think someone donated it, or gave a large donation to it. So, it's free for everyone. They literally wouldn't accept payment. It's incredible. As soon as I saw that, I thought maybe everything would be alright. Before seeing it though, I mean, I was dreading calling Milla to let her know where Jasper was.' Dylan looked at me.

'I can see why you didn't tell me all this sooner. It didn't occur to me to look up what the hospital looked like. I'm so glad I didn't know,' I said.

'Yeah, I thought as much. Anyway,' continued Dylan, 'I sat there, sweating my ass off. No air con in the corridors still. Finally someone came to talk to me, and that's when I spoke to you, Milla, after the doctor came and told me that Jasper was fine, but they wanted to keep him there overnight. That was when I realised, I needed the car and some of my stuff.'

'And that was when I started running logistics from my hospital bed.' I laughed. 'It kept me busy at least!'

'The stupidest thing was that they needed me to stay there, but they wouldn't let me stay there,' said Dylan.

'What do you mean? Why did they need you and why didn't they let you stay there?' asked Tess, with understandable confusion.

'The rooms they have there are only for the mothers,' said Dylan bluntly.

'But, what if ...' Tess started.

'Don't,' said Dylan with his hand up and a bemused smile on his face. 'It's not worth trying to find the logic. They said they had rooms but only for the mothers. And if a father needed to stay, then he usually slept on the chairs or in the car. The reason they needed me there was because while the hospital is free, the pharmacy isn't. So, if Jasper needed any tests or medication during his stay there, I needed to be available to collect the sample from the NICU, carry it downstairs to the pharmacy for testing, pay for it, and then take the results and any medicines back upstairs to the NICU again. Basically they needed me as a courier and they needed my wallet.'

Dylan sped through the next part to pre-empt the questions that he could already see forming on Tess's lips.

'No, I couldn't pay in advance. No, I couldn't pay after. No, they wouldn't let me open a tab. I tried everything. Finally, they agreed that someone could be the runner for us, and they accepted a bunch of cash. Whatever wasn't used for Jasper's treatment was our very generous donation to the hospital. I mean, I would have made a donation anyway, but they did pretty well out of us. I had no idea what they might need so I just emptied my wallet!'

'Whatever it took, right? At that point, you would have emptied your bank account, surely?' said Steve, joking.

'Pretty much,' agreed Dylan. 'So, then I just waited there until our driver arrived, and then after I spoke to you, Milla, we headed to the hotel. The doctor, the only one who spoke English, told me to come back the next morning at 9am because that's when he did his rounds, and at that point he would decide if Jasper was OK to discharge. I wasn't allowed to see Jasper at all after he went through those doors, so I don't really know what they did to him - an X-ray, I think. They did tell me the next day they had fed him a little formula, which I assumed was fine ...' he trailed off, shrugging at me in query.

'They told me that in the hospital when he got back too.

Obviously, that was fine. I would have said yes to anything they advised I think. Poor little hungry baby,' I said.

'That was a weird night,' Dylan reflected with half a laugh. 'Knowing that my son was in one hospital, my wife in another and I was staying in a hotel with the driver - in the middle of COVID! The next morning, the driver and I had a romantic breakfast, and then I went back at nine, like they said. Except, typical Yangon, the doctor hadn't arrived yet. He got there at about nine thirty or something, and said Jasper was OK to discharge. Actually, no, he didn't say he could discharge Jasper to begin with, because he wanted to see the mother breastfeeding,' continued Dylan.

'What does that mean?' I asked. 'Didn't they know I was in the other hospital, unable to get out of bed?'

'They knew that. I had to fight hard to get the doctor to accept the logic that you couldn't come there. He wanted you to be brought to the children's hospital so he could see you try to breastfeed. I don't know. It must be some policy they have, but I wasn't having a bar of it. I just said no,' said Dylan, apparently irritated by the memory of the discussion.

'But I thought you said they didn't get back till after lunch, Milla? What took so long?' asked Tess.

'Eurgh, yeah. Admin,' grunted Dylan. 'Trying to coordinate the two hospitals was the most painful thing ever. The children's hospital approved the discharge, but it took them forever to align with Pun Hlaing Hospital, and then, once they were finally both OK with it, we found out that we had to arrange our own ambulance. Milla was trying to do that while I was waiting for Jasper to come out. I guess we should have brought him back in the car, but, as we left the hospital in an ambulance, we just assumed that we would be driven back in one.'

'Assumed, hey? More fool you guys,' said Steve, with an

eye roll of someone who has been on the wrong side of Myanmar's administrative chaos more than once.

'Yeah. We realise that now,' said Dylan. 'The ambulance took about an hour to come, and only then was I allowed inside the NICU to collect Jasper. It was incredible in there. There must have been hundreds of babies, all in those little boxes enjoying the air-conditioning, with no mosquito nets needed. At least now I know what it looks like, I wouldn't be so worried if he had to go back, although we hope he doesn't need it. I took Jasper, the only little blond baby in the place, and finally we headed back to Milla. And then I went absolutely nuts at the hospital staff for having not fed her!'

Dylan paused, as though to reflect on the story he had just told for the first time.

'I honestly can't even express how I felt when I saw that first bit of the hospital. I really thought that was it. Because I didn't know if Jasper had something seriously wrong, all I knew was that we were going to the children's hospital because he didn't cry out. Thank god it turned out to be nothing. Do you know the funny thing? I barely even thought about Milla. I mean, I guess I knew where she was, and that she had doctors and people to look after her, but I was so stressed about the little guy and what I had to do for him.'

'Milla's a big girl, she can take care of herself,' said Tess joking. 'So, Jasper's all good, nothing to worry about?' she continued.

'Yes, it turns out he's a normal, healthy baby,' I said.

'Well, cheers to that!' toasted Tess, raising a glass. 'To Jasper, a normal baby.'

'Cheers,' Steve, Dylan and I repeated. 'To a normal baby.'

'One thing, though, Dylan,' said Steve with some contemplation. 'You work for the company that owns the hospital ... couldn't you have called in a favour to get Milla some food earlier?'

'Worked, Steve. Worked. I no longer work there. But yes, had I thought about it, I probably could have been a little more help. But like I said, I pretty much forgot she existed for the twenty-four hours I was out with the little guy.'

6

WELCOME TO MOTHERHOOD

PARENTING a newborn is like jet lag. It's disorienting, but full of promise. For the first few days after Jasper was born and we were released from the hospital, I felt as though I had travelled two and a half times around the world, emptying the drinks trolley along the way. I felt nauseous and off-balance. I struggled to keep track of what time of day or night it was, and I never had any idea what meal I should be eating, if I was even hungry. One cup of coffee perked me up, but a second would have given me the jitters. Sleeping as much as Jasper would have been too much, but not sleeping as much as him felt like too little. I wished I had read more guide books before arriving in this new, unfamiliar world. It didn't help that we weren't at home, either. While nice enough, our staycation apartment wasn't as comfortable as our usual one and not having all my home comforts around me added to my befuddlement.

I had underestimated the volume and variety of decisions that Dylan and I had to make now that we had a dependent. I kept wondering if I didn't have any maternal instinct, because nothing seemed to come naturally to me, but after a few days, I realised that it was simply hidden under mountains of rational judgement. I was second guessing myself on everything. I didn't know if this was because I was worried about what other people might think, or because I had too many conflicting advice apps on the go. Perhaps because of sleep deprivation or because I was scared I might fail this defenceless, squirmy little thing I could now see and touch. For whatever reason, I found that decisions I could make for myself in a matter of seconds drove me to confused paralysis when I was making them for Jasper.

Take bathing, for example.

'Do I need a bath?' I could ask myself. 'Sure, that would be nice. I'll quickly hop in the shower.'

'Does Jasper need a bath?' I don't know. Does he? His first bath. Or perhaps it's not. He has probably already had one during his little out-of-hours adventure, so perhaps it's OK to give him one if all the vernix and other goodness has already been sponged off? Or maybe we shouldn't? After all, he hasn't exactly had a chance to get dirty. Weren't there some celebrities who admitted they only bathed their kids if they were visibly dirty. I can't remember if the internet public were pleased or outraged by that, though, now I think of it. It's been five days since he was born. Maybe he'd enjoy the sensation of it? After all, we don't want a baby who is scared of water. But what if he is scared of water and then we add to the fear by doing something terrible like dropping him in it? I am not even sure I have assembled the bath correctly. Maybe I should ask Dylan to look at it. And the baby wash. Did they say we could use it this soon, or maybe wait until we know if he has sensitive skin? But I suppose we'll never know how sensitive his skin might be unless we try him with some products.

'Hellooo ... are you OK?' Dylan's voice cut through my internal monologue. 'You seem to have zoned out there.'

'Huh? Oh. Yes. I was wondering if we should give Jasper a bath today. What do you think?'

'You've asked Jasper's nanny to come in tomorrow, right? Maybe we wait until she arrives and she can help us?' suggested Dylan.

'Oh that's a good idea,' I said with relief. 'Are you sure it's OK to ask her to come in so soon? Shouldn't we be doing this on our own until I go back to work?'

The decision to bring in Jasper's nanny, Wai Wai, who we had hired a few weeks before he was born, was not one that I took lightly. I tore myself up with worry about whether Jasper would ever bond with me if I were to introduce a secondary carer so early on, especially given that we had been separated for the first day of his life. I was embarrassed by the idea that I couldn't cope with a bit of tiredness. I was worried about how I would develop my own style of parenting if I was taking my lead from someone with more experience. And I felt as though it was lazy to allow someone else to watch and change my baby so that I could sleep in the middle of the day.

'Of course, it's OK,' Dylan reassured me. 'What is the point in making it harder for ourselves than it needs to be? We have Wai Wai, hired and ready to help. Jasper's not going to forget who his mother is. You are going to be here too. You should try to sleep while he does. I'm sure you'll find it much easier to rest knowing that there is someone else around to listen out for him. You have your own recovery to think about anyway.'

'But what if Wai Wai does things in a way that I don't like?'

'Well, then you talk to her about how you'd like her to do it. She'll be happy to work with you. I think it'll help having someone to learn from. You have to remember that in more normal circumstances we might have asked your mum or one of your sisters to come to Bangkok. It's because of COVID that you don't have any of your family around to support you, and that they won't even get to meet the little guy until he's almost not a baby anymore!'

'You're right, you're right. I just worry about so many things.'

'I know you do,' comforted Dylan. 'And that's how I know you're going to be an amazing mum.'

Wai Wai was an angel. She was a gentle, calming presence who brought with her years of experience in looking after infants, although never one quite as fresh as our six-day-old hamster. With Wai Wai around to placate me, Dylan was free to pop out and run errands. The apartment had a serious mosquito issue, so Dylan's first mission was to procure a mosquito net. And while he searched, Wai Wai gave Jasper a bath.

I watched as closely as I could without giving her a complex, in the same way I watched her change him and burp him after a feed. I asked her for her views on how Jasper was feeding, and for her help in getting him to latch on. Breastfeeding still wasn't going very well. I was feeling angry and disheartened. I had enjoyed such an easy pregnancy that I had naively assumed that biology was on my side, and that motherhood would continue in the same way. Some feeds were taking over an hour, which didn't seem quite right, based on what my mother and all my friends had told me when I had called and messaged in desperation.

'I don't understand why it doesn't work!' I snapped at Dylan one evening. 'The lactation consultant showed us, we did what she said and he still can't latch. Bring up the video again - what are we doing wrong?'

I was ready to give up. Except I couldn't. I felt pressured by our circumstances to do everything in my power to breastfeed. Living in a developing country with limited healthcare and volatile supply chains meant that I wanted to avoid the stress of being reliant on milk formula. I searched online for advice and enlisted Dylan and Wai Wai's help in stuffing my increasingly loathsome nipples into Jasper's increasingly agitated mouth. We were all thumbs and elbows and the more we tried, the more frustrated I felt.

'Why not try to use the pump?' suggested Dylan one day, after Jasper's mouth disconnected for the umpteenth time. 'See if anything comes out. We can try to put it in the bottle for him to drink.'

'But I shouldn't have to! I have boobs, I have nipples. Why aren't they working? Why can't he get it straight from here? It seems so stupid that I have to use a piece of equipment to do what's supposed to be the most natural thing in the world,' I said with irritation.

'I know. But maybe you just need some help to start with. And then once he's a bit bigger he'll be able to feed normally,' Dylan persisted.

'Fine. Whatever. But it probably won't work. These stupid, useless boobs don't work.'

The first time I used the pump was horrifying. With one squeeze of the lever, my nipple blew up into an inch long cocktail sausage and ejected a yellowish-cream goo into the funnel. Taking in the strange out-of-body phenomenon I had witnessed, I expected to feel some pain, but I didn't. If anything, I felt some relief. I squeezed again.

'It's working!' I cried excitedly. 'How much do I do?'

'The internet says he only needs a teaspoonful or so, so stop when you think you have that?' Dylan said.

'Maybe once I am done, the nipples will stay the same shape and Jasper can latch?'

'Maybe, but let's focus on one thing at a time. When you

are done, we'll see if he can drink from the teat of the bottle.'

To my tremendous disappointment at the time, but my enormous relief eventually, my nipples did not retain the shape they adopted during pumping sessions. Inspired by the positive results from the pump, I next explored nipple shields, which acted like straws for Jasper. In the end, it was three months before I was able to ditch the shields and have Jasper latch directly, but by that point, Dylan, Wai Wai and I had just about perfected our shield management system: use, wash, sterilise, store, use, wash, sterilise, store. All day and all night.

For these first few days, we had continued to keep Tony at arm's length, delaying his visit until we felt a little more settled into a routine. Tony, impatient as ever, had checked into the hotel on the estate where we were temporarily renting our staycation apartment, so that he was on hand should we have any further emergencies. Anyone who spends more than five minutes with Tony will hear the story of how he convinced Dylan to move to Myanmar to set up a business with him, which led to Dylan meeting me and, ultimately, to Jasper being born. He takes a lot of credit for Jasper's existence and the moment we gave him the green light, he appeared at our door.

Silence from Tony is a rare thing, but the second he laid eyes on Jasper, he fell into a trance. I don't think Tony breathed for the entire time he was holding a deeply sleeping Jasper in his arms like a fragile, glass vase. Watching them, my heart softened and I realised that I should have called Tony to come and be my replacement attendant in the hospital, but our decision to protect our privacy, until we knew if Jasper was going to be alright, had overridden logic. In the same moment, I could see Tony's own irritation at having been side-lined had melted away. He was completely and utterly lovestruck.

We cut short our staycation in the end, moving home in time for Christmas. I had enjoyed the change of scenery and had enjoyed making daily walks to the poolside coffee shop where we had caught up with friends and Dylan's old colleagues, all of whom had heard rumours of our nightmarish first twenty-four hours as parents. They had all expressed their disbelief and solidarity, and many of them had proceeded to share their own horror stories from the same hospital. Stories of which, thankfully, I was unaware at the time of our own ordeal.

Our driver, Johnny, was under strict instructions to drive as slowly as required not to disturb our sleepy, precious cargo, and the journey home took much longer than usual. I could swear Yangon looked different somehow. Nothing had changed, and yet I felt as though I was seeing it for the first time. I hadn't left the estate for three weeks and, during that time had been handed a baby, had the baby taken away again, been handed the same baby again a day later and had stumbled tentatively into motherhood. It had been a rollercoaster and an exhausting one at that, but I felt calm as we drove back through the gates to Star City. I felt incredibly grateful for Dylan, without whose cool head and practical approach to all the changes in our so-called plan, I might have taken myself through some very rough terrain, emotionally.

While Dylan lugged our belongings indoors, I introduced Jasper to our helper, Lin, who fell instantly in love and immediately adopted him as her own baby brother. Having help around the house is very common in Myanmar, especially within the expat community, and some helpers very quickly become like a member of the extended family.

Lin's excitement for the baby's arrival had rivalled Tony's in the weeks running up to the birth.

This was the first time I had seen Jasper's cot constructed in his room, having not wanted to tempt fate by having a ready nursery before I left for the hospital. I took in the new look and feel of the room where I had spent so many hours working from home during COVID. Now my former desk was the changing table.

'Where did the play mat come from?' I asked Dylan.

'The Skippers. When I went to collect their old buggy and travel cot, they gave me a few extra things. Thank goodness for people getting rid of old baby items. Without them, and the Hills, we would have had to buy everything new, and I honestly don't know how we would have done that with the travel restrictions.'

'We haven't done too badly, have we?' I reflected. 'Choosing to have the baby in Yangon, not having any serious complications around the birth, baby adventure aside, and being able to get all the baby stuff we needed secondhand.'

'True. And having decided to stay together. Just imagine if you'd gone somewhere else for the birth. You'd be stuck there indefinitely now. Even with all the drama, staying here was the right decision. I think we can pretty much handle anything if we do it together. We are a team. A three-person team now.'

7
THE HAPPIEST OF NEW YEARS

THE START of 2021 really was the happiest of New Years. I felt as though I was on top of the world. I can't be sure if the credit goes to Dylan and me as the parents, or to Jasper as the baby, but between us, we seemed to be doing alright. When I bumped into a friend in the supermarket and they asked how it was going, I could answer with genuine enthusiasm that it seemed to be going very well. Jasper was sleeping well, growing well and we seemed to be colic and reflux free, which was a huge relief after hearing nightmarish stories about those two ailments from other battle-hardened parents. I owed a lot to the enormous help that I had from Jasper's nanny, our helper (who seemed to arrive at work earlier and earlier each day to maximise her time with Jasper), an unemployed husband and a doting grandfather, but that didn't take away from the fact that I was truly and deeply happy with the way things were going.

Star City was the perfect place to rehabilitate after my surgery, and the perfect hideaway from COVID and the trail of economic sadness that it left in its wake. Despite having filled up considerably since the start of the pandemic, as people realised that inner-city living no longer offered the same benefits now that almost everything was shut, Star City still felt empty. The master plan foresaw thousands more apartments and condos than had been built, which meant wide, almost car-free roads, barely used facilities as well as restaurants and shops without even a short wait. I very rarely had an excuse to leave Star City but never felt in any way confined. When Dylan and I had moved into our apartment, we were the sole occupants of a 28-storey tower. We gained the odd neighbour over the years, but never enough to bump into someone in the lift, and they were all gone. Jasper rode around the estate in his buggy every day, taking in the trees; the birds; the smattering of cars and motorbikes; the odd stray dog who had escaped capture and eviction, blissfully unaware that we lived in a city.

Dylan, Jasper and I rang in the 2021 New Year three times; catching the Sydney Harbour Bridge hurrah on TV as we headed to bed, conducting Jasper's well-timed midnight feast from the balcony while watching the Yangon sky light up with fireworks, and then rounding off with the London display over morning coffees the next day. Celebrations may have been muted the world over, due to the continued drag of the pandemic, but with a newborn baby, that didn't bother us. Before New Year, we celebrated Christmas twice. Having had such a good time on Christmas Day and having far too much food leftover, we went for a rerun on Boxing Day, minus the present opening. I love Christmas and the entire festive period. I obsess over decorations and traditions and gift giving, ignoring the practicalities of then having to store a household's worth of festive nick-nacks for the other eleven months of the year. I am a snob about mince pies and insist on making my own shortcrust pastry, and I disapprove of any deviation from the traditional turkey-with-all-the-trimmings lunchtime meal. For me, it is the ultimate festival of togetherness and, despite only having one available invitee outside of our newly minted family, I was extremely excited about hosting my first Rae family Christmas. Tony joined us for a breakfast of mince pies and a Full English and then the four of us wandered around the estate, wasting time while we awaited delivery of our turkey, which was being roasted by a local chef whose oven was considerably larger than ours.

Lunch was very much a team effort: I was in charge of mince pies and a packet of Paxo stuffing: Tony was on vegetables and roasties: Dylan was responsible for making sure the baby didn't disappear under the mountain of gifts or discarded wrapping paper. The previous year, Dylan and I had been on our honeymoon over Christmas, and I had carted his stocking and several small presents to the middle of the Namibian desert to ensure the festive spirit joined us there too. This year, given far simpler logistics and COVID-improved delivery systems, both Dylan and I had gone overboard on the gifting front. The risk of losing a three-week-old baby under a present was very real.

What further solidified my feelings of utter joy in January 2021 was the weather. December and January in Yangon are an annual masterclass in cloudless, azure skies and sparkling sunshine. It's hard, as a Brit especially, to feel anything other than uplifted when there is absolutely nothing in the weather worth complaining about. I often wondered why they even bothered reporting the weather for those two months when the only status was 'perfect'. Again. Day after day in January I took advantage of the climate and my situation to focus on my physical recovery; I walked the golf course daily while Dylan and Tony played and I swam in the pool. Milk factory policy dictated that I could only be away from Jasper for short periods of time, but that was more than enough to stretch my legs or clear my mind.

I met with a personal trainer to begin rehabilitating my abdomen and even managed to visit the hairdresser. I travelled alone into the city, to the trainer's house, where I completed an assessment and short training session and made it home with minutes to spare before breastmilk burst out of my overfilled boobs. My personal trainer had also been my antenatal class teacher. She was a Dutch expat with two children of her own who worked for an NGO and had started giving antenatal sessions in the absence of any up-to-date motherhood advice being shared by the local hospitals. I was excited to start my rehab because I wanted to get back to golf, tennis, running and anything else I could use as an excuse to spend time outside and because it was enjoyable to interact with someone outside my very small day-to-day circle.

Another solo expedition I made was to the third party passport and visa application centre known as VFS Global to submit an application for Jasper's British passport. I was relieved to discover that I was only required to submit copies of the necessary documents which included our marriage certificate and Jasper's Myanmar birth certificate. Even before COVID, the postal system in Myanmar was near non-existent and even the more reliable courier companies had been hit hard by COVID-related staff shortages globally which meant that delivery speeds were no longer guaranteed. I only needed to show the original documents to the VFS Global clerk in order that he could verify the copies and send them to Her Majesty's Passport Office in the UK for processing. I left the office with a receipt and assurances from the clerk that the process would take 'up to ten weeks', and that they would call me when the passport was ready to collect. I calculated that we should have Jasper's passport by the end of March which would open up the possibility of introducing Jasper to family in either the UK or Australia at Easter, if COVID allowed.

By mid-January, I was comfortably sharing Jasper's care with his nanny, Wai Wai. The division of responsibility required a huge amount of trust, as well as a certain level of management. I found the trust came very easily, thanks to Wai Wai's innately caring nature as well as the glowing reference I had from the friend who had lent us Wai Wai while she was out of the country. Several families had left Myanmar during COVID with a view to returning after the pandemic and we were fortunate to have borrowed Wai Wai from one such family while we searched for a suitable permanent nanny of our own. The management took a little more trial and error to establish, but was soon running smoothly with the help of a series of colour-coded, check-box-style spreadsheets which satisfied my inner organisation nerd immensely. By management, I mean collectively monitoring what went into Jasper, what came out of Jasper and how long he slept for.

From the outset, I had grand visions of mastering sleep training. Despite the lactation consultant having warned me that 'you don't train your baby, your baby trains you', I printed off sleep schedules from an app and talked them through with Wai Wai. As I did so, I realised just how all-consuming the schedules were, with fifteen-minute power naps, endless 'if not this, then this or this or this' alternatives to choose from, troubleshooting advice that went on for pages and a need to become a human stopwatch to meet all the wake windows, nap lengths, nappy changes and feeding times dotted throughout the regime. It was overwhelming. Little did I know as I was trying to assert my authority over Jasper's sleep needs, but Wai Wai was a sleep magician. After a few days of humouring my schedules and listening to me ramble on about how on earth we should follow one, she quietly suggested that we simply aim for four naps a day, and see how he did. Within a couple of days, Jasper was a world-class sleeper. I gave full credit to Wai Wai whenever anyone commented on how unlike overtired new parents Dylan and I suddenly looked, and studied Wai Wai's techniques hard, out of fear for the day when she might have to return to her original employer.

I had no idea, before becoming a mother, just how much attention is paid to baby poop; the frequency, the colour, the smell, the viscosity and the volume. To save Wai Wai and I exchanging photos of every defecation, my spreadsheet included a handy set of checkboxes in a spectrum of poopy colours. Dylan was less enthusiastic about studying the finer nuances of Jasper's poop palette, but I found that as far as motherhood was concerned, the more I was cognisant of the tiny details, the more confident I felt about the bigger picture. Monitoring what came out of Jasper went hand in hand with monitoring what went into him and, as far as getting things into him was concerned, it became apparent very early on that even with the nipple shields, breastfeeding wasn't going very well. Jasper's resistance, manifested as twisting and wriggling and turning his head away, was leading to physical and emotional distress on both our parts. I clocked in and out of every feed and logged left and right boob on my spreadsheet in lieu of leveraging my short-term memory, which appeared to have taken a leave of absence. On some occasions I would spend an hour wrestling with him, only for the pain in my boobs and the hunger cues from Jasper to indicate that he hadn't really consumed anything. Sometimes he would drain one boob followed hungrily by the other. Other times, he would drink half of one and show no interest in the other, leaving me unbalanced and uncomfortable. I had to concede that I would have to try a hybrid approach - pumping and feeding.

It still made me feel angry and inadequate that I couldn't feed him naturally, and I was bitter towards the pump to begin with, but once I realised that Jasper was happily consuming a healthy volume of breastmilk from a bottle each day, I relaxed and signed over half of the milk delivery responsibility to Wai Wai.

Feeding issues aside, Jasper was such a good baby. He slept, he ate, he grew and he watched. Oh, how he watched. As his eyes began to spend more time open, they grew in intensity of both colour and expression. I lost count of the number of people who, totally independent of one another, exclaimed, 'Wow, he's taking it all in, isn't he?'

Friends who came to visit would start to shift nervously in their seats while Jasper subjected them to an extended stare down over the course of several, long minutes. For those who didn't mind being stared at, however, Jasper was a very relaxed, very welcoming baby. He was quickly comfortable around new faces and very rarely cried. His modus operandi from the outset was to sit quietly and observe.

At five weeks old, we took Jasper for his first swim, which he took to like the proverbial duck. Inept parents that we were, Dylan and I forgot that he owned a swimsuit, and so for his first dip in a sun-drenched pool, his pearly white little body was clad only in a swimming nappy. It was only when we shared proud photos back to our families and Dylan's mother questioned his lack of sun protection that we remembered she had sent over a swimsuit set from Australia. At the same time, Tony lamented his lack of invitation, so we did the whole thing again the following day; with sunscreen, with swimsuit, with sun hat and with grandfather. Swimming quickly became a daily activity. With his bobbing head the only part of his body visible above the surface of the water, Jasper floated around the pool using his inflatable neck ring: his expression curious, eyes alert and little legs starting to explore their weightless freedom below the surface. As the child of two parents who grew up near to the sea, there was no way Jasper was going to be allowed to bypass the basics of water survival skills, even if he was a city baby. And besides, the underwater bicycling seemed to help his digestive system process some of the more stubborn blockages.

Despite global COVID case numbers soaring into the start of the new year, Myanmar was still yet to succumb to a major wave of the virus, which meant that life wasn't far from normal for us, in our tower on an estate out of town. There were still restrictions on travel, and anyone found to be COVID positive while trying to fly was still immediately and unceremoniously being thrown in a government-run quarantine centre, but the restaurants and shops which had survived the extended lockdowns and closures of the previous year were beginning to trade again.

We started to venture out for lunches with Jasper in tow, and to socialise again. Jasper and Wai Wai would entertain themselves appreciating the art on the walls or the flowers in the gardens and then Jasper would nap quietly on a sofa while we caught up with friends. I never quite felt comfortable breastfeeding in public. The idea of maintaining eye contact and conversation with anyone other than Dylan while I fed Jasper, even if the intimate bits were covered in a shroud, made me feel very odd, so on the rare occasion that he was hungrier than the milk I had expressed for him, Jasper and I convened in a private corner until he was satisfied.

Had the year continued as it started, I would count myself among the luckiest mothers in the world with a good-natured baby, a comfortable home environment, a supportive team of people around and a job to which I was excited to return at the end of my maternity leave. As events unfolded, however, this utopia was simply the calm before the storm. By the very end of January, rumblings of a potential military coup were beginning to gather velocity and volume. We joined our friends Tess and Steve for lunch in a recently reopened brasserie on 30 January 2021 and talked of almost nothing else.

'It's never going to happen,' announced Steve with considerable confidence.

'Aren't there armed battalions lining up outside the cities?' I asked. 'I heard that they're bringing in truckloads of soldiers to clutter the streets of Yangon.'

'Nah. My mate says it's all just posturing. A flex by the military to remind everyone that they still hold all the power,' said Steve.

'We used to joke that we would leave when our future child needed a more competitive sporting environment or if we saw tanks rolling down the streets of Yangon. Suddenly the latter seems more likely,' I said darkly.

'Nah. It's just a power play. The new parliament is due to form in Naypyitaw the day after tomorrow, so it's all just a dance in the lead up to that. My mate knows a guy who says it's not going to happen,' said Steve, fighting his corner with resolve.

'I mean, I guess if they did want to coup - is that what we say, to coup? If they do want to stage a coup,' said Tess, 'now would be the time. All the politicians will be in one place, so it's pretty easy to find them all.'

We finished our lunch fairly well convinced that a coup is out of the question. But, as we bade one another farewell, we did so with a send-off of 'see you on the other side'.

PART II

8
A-COO

By mid-morning, Monday 1 February 2021 already feels like it has been a long day. With Dylan safely back from the supermarket and our nappy stock replenished, we sit, Dylan, Jasper and I, in a strange state of suspension - waiting. It has been several hours since we found out that the rumblings of a potential coup have become the rumblings of military vehicles on the streets of Yangon. We are outwardly calm about the situation; expat life has a way of keeping us on our toes and being guests in the country affords us the privilege of feeling more like observers than participants. Instinct tells me that waiting to see what happens next is undoubtedly the right thing to do but that doesn't stop me from bouncing between gallows humour and blind panic and back again. One minute I am telling myself that it will all blow over, the next I am mentally packing our bags.

I let my family know what is going on, sending a message that they will read when they wake up.

'It does rather look like we have a coup,' I message, understating it somewhat.

On reading my message, my mother switches on the TV

at her home in Jersey and sees the now infamous video of an Instagrammer performing a dance aerobics class in the middle of Naypyitaw's eight-lane highway, while armoured vehicles assemble behind her. Not long after this, the international news outlets are all covering the breaking news of Myanmar's military coup. My family are worried, despite my trying to reassure them that, so far, nothing has changed in our lives and that as a result, we have no plans to leave. The news is saying that phone and internet coverage is limited which confirms to us that our unaffected internet connection is precious and explains why we aren't hearing much from anyone locally. Friends and acquaintances back home begin to check in on how we are and how much we are affected by what they are seeing on the news. In some cases it feels like genuine concern, but in others, especially when I haven't spoken to the person in several years, I think they just want in on the action.

'Is your phone working?' I ask Dylan, as I finish up feeding Jasper.

'Yes, I've still got reception,' he says, pulling his phone from his pocket.

'Call Tess and Steve. I want to hear what Steve has to say about his guy who knows a guy ...'

'Ha - you're right! What happened to his inside man who *knew* there wouldn't be a coup? OK I'm calling him.'

We wait for a response.

'So, I'm guessing you've heard about the coup,' comes the greeting.

'Oh, we have, Steve, we have. And we want to know how your guy got it so wrong! What happened to there's no way there is going to be a coup?' asks Dylan with a laugh.

'Yeah. So, I guess he was wrong,' Steve laughs back. 'How are you guys? How's the wee man?'

'We're good. He's good. He's probably wondering why

he's got these two chumps looking after him.' Dylan says. 'Star City closed the gates to outsiders so we have no nanny and no helper.'

'Oof, poor little guy,' says Tess joking. 'So what have you been doing since the internet went dark?'

'Actually, we still have internet! We have no idea how or why. We've been watching the same news report on the BBC on repeat which probably isn't healthy. Milla sent me down to City Mart for nappies. There was a line there, but otherwise it just seems eerily quiet here. But you know Star City, we're in a bubble. How's your township? Anything exciting happening?'

Tess and Steve live in a particularly bustling part of Yangon where the buildings are close together and the roads are a clutter of cars, cyclos (three wheeled pedal taxis), potholes, stray dogs and market stalls. Sanchaung township has a vibrant energy to it and its narrow streets are lined with popular beer stations, restaurants and general stores. The apartments there have a lot more character than our sparkly new one in Star City, but that character comes with no lifts, uneven staircases, regular power cuts, the odd plague of hatching locusts and little or no access for cars. With our new baby and all his logistical paraphernalia, we are thankful that we live somewhere less crowded.

'Nothing yet. We're thinking we'll lie low for most of the day, but we're meant to be having dinner with some friends, so we might venture out later. Unless something happens, like, I don't know, tanks or something, we assume we can just continue as usual. We don't really know what to expect,' comes Tess's typically practical response.

'That's exactly where we are too. We're waiting to see what happens over the next few days,' I say in agreement. 'That said, I feel kind of twitchy. I don't quite know what we're supposed to do while we wait. We feel very out of it here, which is both good and bad, I guess.'

'We'll send you an hourly 'hello' to check we're all still connected and to report any action,' says Tess. I am surprised at how reassured I feel by this.

As we plod through the day, I am immensely grateful for Jasper and his control over the structure of it. Even broken into three-hourly cycles of feeding, changing, settling and waking, time seems to be passing very slowly. For a couple of hours we lose our phone connections, something I only notice when I miss my 'hello' from Tess, but at some point we are reconnected. As the sunlight fades into the grey-blue of evening, I see a message, forwarded by a member of a WhatsApp group I am a part of. It sends a chill through me. It is mostly written in what I assume is aviation code, but the part that's recognisable I understand clearly: *All Airfield in Myanmar Closed from 01.FEB 2021 to 31.May 2021.*

I have spent the entire day telling people that we are safe, that we are content with waiting to see what happens next and that we have no intention of leaving, but the moment this option is taken off the table, all I can think about is how we can get out of here. I think of all the possible reasons that we might *need* to leave (none of which are good) and my lungs start to feel too small for my breath. I am sitting comfortably in my own home, where I have been all day, but suddenly I feel trapped. Regular commercial flights in and out of Myanmar have officially been suspended since the start of the pandemic, but there were still what were known as 'relief flights' to neighbouring transit hubs like Bangkok, Singapore and Kuala Lumpur operating almost daily. This message suggests that even the relief flights will now stop.

I show the message to Dylan who immediately puts the breaks on my escalating panic. I focus intently on a milk stain on Jasper's sleep suit as Dylan reminds me that nothing has changed since before I saw this message. Our plan, so much as we can make one, should still be to wait and see what happens in the coming days. We have to expect more restrictions on communications and movement but as we keep telling our friends and families back home, we also have to try not to worry.

In the days which follow the coup, the internet (including our fibre connection) comes and goes and we quickly start to lose major messaging platforms like WhatsApp, Facebook and Viber. I move my family WhatsApp group to Signal, a less-popular platform which remains unblocked. A week into the coup, we lose all communication for twenty-four hours. A popular theory is that the Chinese have been brought in to help install spyware and firewalls on the telecom networks. The Chinese Embassy's claim that the flow of cargo planes in and out of Myanmar is due to seafood imports entertains Myanmar's netizens for a short period of time (those tech savvy enough to use VPNs to get around the blocks on the various apps) with memes about Chinese prawns momentarily overtaking bitterness towards the coup. Other apps and websites follow the messaging platforms and, while some broadband connections are available, mobile data shows no sign of being reinstated. The only way to stay connected is to stay home, or to send an SMS.

The military claims that these blocking and control measures are to prevent the spread of misinformation, but for me it prevents access to parenting advice. On the days when there is no internet at all, not being able to Google skin rashes or poop colours alerts me to my heavy reliance on the internet for all things Jasper-related. I don't own a single parenting book, either. Even before the coup or COVID, there were no real international book stores and there was no Amazon through which to order something niche like a parenting book. Soon the internet is shut down entirely every night. Not being able to chat with UK-based friends and family during overnight feeds makes me feel isolated. There is an uncertainty to just about everything, which I find very wearing.

Just a few days in, Jasper is due his first round of vaccinations. We are lucky that the clinic in the complex is open because the doctors live onsite. The clinic is a small outpost of the hospital in which Jasper was born and is therefore owned by the same local conglomerate as the Star City estate. Many businesses are closed, either because their staff are unable to get to work due to roadblocks or because the owners are hesitant to continue trading under such extraordinary circumstances - fearing either a run on their produce or, worse, aggression for having continued as though nothing has changed. When we arrive at the clinic I see the sign asking us to pay in cash, rather than by card or mobile money. With no mobile data available, the clinic's card machines aren't working.

'OK, so today we are doing three immunisations for Jasper,' says the doctor calmly.

I grimace. 'Yes, I think so.'

Dylan, a self-confessed hater of needles, is hiding outside the examination room, staring at the floor, missing his usual YouTubing.

'It's alright, I will do it very quickly and he'll barely feel a thing,' reassures the doctor. 'Before we start, I need to let you know that we are running low on some of these vaccinations, so are you planning to stay in Myanmar? If you are I will keep some back for Jasper, so I can do his boosters in a couple of months. I can't say how the supplies of medicines will be now that ... well, you know. Since 1 February, things are unsure.'

'Oh, thank you. Yes, we are planning to stay. We don't really have anywhere else to go!' I say, only half-joking.

'I hope things will stay peaceful,' says the doctor.

'Me too. At least here in Star City we are in a bubble, away from what's happening outside,' I say.

The doctor jabs Jasper so quickly that he doesn't even have a chance to register the pain before it is all over. I handover some precious cash while Dylan pops Jasper back in his stroller and we set off back to our building.

'He asked me if we are planning to stay,' I tell Dylan.

'And what did you say?'

'I said yes. He needed to know in case the medicines start to run out. He's going to keep some back for Jasper's boosters.'

We walk in silence for a few strides.

'I guess we will need to decide what we are going to do, at some point,' I think out loud.

'Yeah, at some point. But not yet. It's only been a few days and nothing has really happened yet, besides the increased restrictions. I thought we agreed we would wait to see how things play out?' says Dylan with characteristic logic.

'I know. And I agree. I just feel a bit uneasy. If we had Jasper's passport already it would be easier to leave in a hurry, but who knows how long that will take. As soon as the airports open again, I am sure lots of people will leave. I don't want to, but it would be nice to know that we could, if we needed to.'

'I know it's getting to you. But as you say, we can't do much until we have Jasper's passport anyway. Where do you think we'd go, if we did leave?' asks Dylan.

'I guess the UK? Australia is closed to visitors. So, I

suppose we would have to go to the UK and then decide from there? Ooh - shall we go past the ATM and see if it's stocked?'

'Sure. I don't have high hopes, but let's see. We can see if the bakery has baguettes for lunch too.'

The ATM is empty of cash, as it has been since that first morning of the coup when Dylan decided not to join the queue, and the bakery is shut. The supermarket is open, but the fresh food hasn't been restocked so we leave empty-handed. At home, Dylan takes Jasper to sit on the sofa while I make some lunch, deep in thought. It is quiet and still in the apartment. Neither Wai Wai, nor our helper, Lin, have been able to come to work for a few days now, because our residential estate closed its gates to outsiders in the wake of the coup and has yet to relax those restrictions. That might explain the empty shelves and unstocked ATM too, I realise.

As I lay the table, which is stationed directly behind the sofa, something catches my eye. Peeking up over the back of the oversized cushions is Jasper's tiny, almost perfectly spherical little head. At only two months old, he isn't doing this himself. His head is lolling slightly from side to side, his little tongue poking through between his lips and his arms are sticking out in front of him as though he is leaning on a lectern. I can't help but smile.

'Oh hello,' I say with a laugh.

'Hello Mummy,' comes Dylan's very poor attempt at a voice for Jasper.

I laugh and rush over to scoop Jasper up and smother him in kisses. Dylan sits up from where he is slumped as Jasper's hidden puppeteer. He smiles.

'I know you're worried and I know you don't like the uncertainty of it all. But we have the little guy! Look at him. How can you feel sad with him around? He's so cuddly and small. He just wants to love you.'

'I know. He's the best baby. He's like an emotional support animal,' I say. 'Oh no, wait! Emotional support baby! That's what he is. My little Emotional Support Baby. I *do* feel better when he's around. And you're right. We just have to keep waiting and see how things play out. That seems to be what everyone is doing.'

While we wait, life continues to be unpredictable. Gossip starts to circulate about demonetisation of certain cash notes, which only exacerbates the run on the few functioning ATMs and banks as people scramble to withdraw their money. It doesn't matter if it's a rumour I hear, or an official statement from the military, they weigh about the same when they land on my shoulders. I start to look at our home situation to make sure we have sufficient provisions should even stricter movement rules be brought in, or supply chains break down entirely.

We already have well-stocked food reserves in our apartment, bought in preparation for the 2020 COVID lockdowns, which never fully materialised. Luckily for us, Tony went one step further and purchased a chest freezer some months earlier. It is currently stuffed with enough frozen meat, vegetables and ice cream to last us well past Jasper's first birthday. Having miscalculated a pre-Christmas purchase of brussels sprouts, Tony is about halfway through a twenty-kilo bag of the things, so if all else fails, we will survive on a diet of experimental sprout dishes for at least another month. I hope the bacon supply doesn't fail us. Tony's favourite 'sprouts with bacon and balsamic vinegar' side dish has morphed into 'balsamic bacon with blink-and-you'll-miss-it solo sprout' to better suit his palette, which might explain why the sprouts just keep on coming. It's a relief that Jasper has his private milk factory which, despite continued challenges with latching, balancing supply and demand and the resulting clogs, is fully operational. We have loo roll, but also the last-gasp backup of the 'bum gun': a bidet hose that comes as standard on any Myanmar toilet. We have some very basic cloth nappies for emergencies, although we have absolutely no idea how to tie one and no nappy pins. Our building has a backup generator, in the event the military starts tampering with power supplies, and our car has petrol. As photos of long, winding queues at ATMs and banks continue to proliferate on Facebook, we count our cash reserves and agree we are lucky that Dylan lives by the motto of 'always have enough cash to get yourself out of trouble or out of the country'. The issue we face is that trouble and country are the same now. Furthermore, even if we all had passports, and if there were flights out of Myanmar, the world is as good as closed due to COVID.

Every conversation we have with anyone in the days and weeks which follow the coup is about the coup: the peaceful protests by the people; the increasing (and unjustified) force of the military's response: the effect the situation is having on cash availability: the unclear rules about how and when we are allowed to move around the city: the nightly chorus of pots and pans being banged by residents to 'drive out the evil spirits': safety on the streets: when the next blackout might be coming and, for us, whether there are still enough nappies in the supermarket. I admit, my obsession with nappies comes from a place of self-preservation, rather than from some instinctive, maternal desire to put Jasper's needs before my own. It really doesn't matter how the coup plays out; we need protection from Jasper's volatile little bottom, regardless. Shocked at how quickly a pack of disposable nappies can disappear, I have ordered some reusable ones online, but they are coming from China and I anticipate that the change in leadership isn't going to be good for delivery timelines. I am learning that there is a very fine line between under-buying and over-buying nappies. If I hoard too many, Jasper will inevitably have a growth spurt, forcing me to donate and replace weeks of supplies, but buy too few, and I might find myself days away from an uncontained poonami sweeping through our apartment.

For a few weeks, I don't leave the estate where we live. Anecdotal COVID numbers are trickling through on an ad hoc basis, despite official testing having pretty much ground to a halt, and they seem to be higher than ever before, tipping over one hundred thousand for the first time. This makes sense given the mass protests that are happening across the country, almost on a daily basis. Despite the military's attempts to hinder communications and to thwart organisation of these protests, the will and strength of the Myanmar people is evident. They refuse to accept military rule. They spent decades suffocating under the military's brutal restrictions, they have lived under the consequences of a failed revolution in 1988 and they are not about to let history repeat itself.

The protests are peaceful and highly creative, involving large numbers of people operating within the law to cause disruption on the streets and to hamper the aggressive door-to-door raids the military is conducting to round up suspected dissidents - or their relatives, neighbours or someone who is simply in the wrong place at the wrong time. One day, hundreds of pedestrians simultaneously stop in the middle of the road to tie their shoelaces, made funnier by the fact that most people in Myanmar wear only flip flops. Another day, hundreds of vehicles experience engine trouble at the exact same moment, resulting in long lines of cars all with the bonnets up blocking bridges, intersections and main roads. On a separate occasion, foot traffic around wet markets flows endlessly back and forth over pedestrian crossings, with shoppers accidentally dropping onions and other round, rolling produce that need to be slowly chased down and accidentally dropped again. I am impressed by the bravery behind the coordination of these protests, because anyone caught posting pro-democracy or anti-military content on social media or messaging apps is being hunted down and arrested. But the protests also worry me. The distance between where we live and the hospital where Jasper was born is significant, even in good traffic, and it makes me uneasy to think of how disrupted our route is now that there are military checkpoints and protest hotspots all along it. My COVID-conditioned brain looks at the images of thousands of people, shoulder to shoulder, singing and shouting as one voice and sees a ticking time bomb. These people have made the choice that the fight for their freedom is worth the risk of a wave of COVID, but with a two-month old baby at home, I am not willing to take that risk. Despite data from the UK and elsewhere suggesting that babies and children aren't as susceptible to serious COVID symptoms as adults, I am very protective of Jasper and won't let anyone near him. I give Tony the cold shoulder for several days after he confesses that some of his employees have been out protesting on the days they are not in the office.

As well as marching on the streets, many people are protesting by joining the growing Civil Disobedience Movement (CDM). The CDM began as a strike by government workers, teachers and medical professionals as a way of showing that they did not accept, nor want to work for, the incoming military authority. Before long, employees from all sectors are CDM-ing or 'doing CDM' as it is known and, as the movement gathers momentum, anyone who doesn't join it risks becoming a victim of 'social shaming'. This means photos and personal information, such as contact details and home addresses, being splashed across social media to scare the person into ceasing work and joining the movement. Without people, particularly frontline staff, many businesses can't function; hospitals close, banks close, shops close. February is my last month of my three month statutory maternity leave and, as I build up to my return to work, I talk to colleagues about who is and isn't doing CDM. I can sense the strain that the decision puts on people, whichever way they choose to go. The idea of putting themselves and their families at risk of social shaming by working is terrifying, but joining the movement is also dangerous.

February is such a short month but this year it feels as though it has gone on forever. In messages and calls to family I try to sound upbeat, downplaying the severity of the situation and quashing some of the media rumours about things escalating. I don't really know if it's them I am trying to convince - or myself. As we near the end of February, I realise that it has been six weeks since I submitted Jasper's passport application but that we have heard nothing. The lack of passport is a convincing reason as to why we have not given much thought to leaving Myanmar but I am concerned that I haven't heard *anything* at all from the passport office - not even an email confirming that the application has been received in the UK.

At the end of the month, the first round of expat departures starts, with some international companies pulling their employees out and sending them elsewhere in South East Asia until the situation in Myanmar stabilises. Two families from our residential estate hold a leaving party at the golf course cafe. Dylan joins the farewell round of golf before, and Jasper and I walk over for the social part afterwards. It is the first time we have seen many of the attendees since Jasper was born, with most of them being based elsewhere in the city, and it is the first time I have taken Jasper to any sort of gathering. The estate reopened its gates to visitors a week or so after the coup, but there are now stringent ID, temperature and sometimes military checks at the entrance. I am still strict about keeping physical contact to a minimum, for myself as well as for Jasper, but decide to make an exception this time. The guests are mainly expats, too, none of whom have been out protesting over the past few weeks. Over beers and BBQ on the sun-bleached grass off the back of the final green, every conversation opens with the same question.

'So, what are you thinking of doing? Will you stay?'

To which most of our friends respond, 'I will stay, for now at least. I am just waiting to see how it plays out.' I find this reassuring.

Chatter then turns to the situation in the different townships where people live, to the nightly pot-banging, to raids and arrests, to the creativity of the protests, to the unofficial COVID numbers, to the cash situation and then to Jasper. Everyone wants to see him, to hear the story of his newborn adventure and to gaze into his bright blue eyes. Jasper, in response, wants to watch and study these new faces and nothing makes him happier than getting a reaction to his new party trick.

'What happened at the start of February, Jasper?' I prompt.

'A-coo, a-cooooooo', he replies earnestly.

'Did he just say a coup?' our friends exclaim incredulously. Jasper revels in the resulting laughter and applause. He is quick to learn that this reaction is for him and the more his audience cheers the more he performs.

'A-coo, a-coo, a-coo' he babbles over and over.

The laughter is good for all of us. As Dylan, Jasper and I walk home that evening, in the heat of the setting sun, I realise just how lucky we are. Compared to most people here and compared to many people across the world. We have each other, which we are thankful for each day. As expats, we can leave the country while its people have to navigate the inevitable period of dark uncertainty. We are stable financially and I am still employed. Even through COVID we were lucky that neither of us was furloughed or required to take significant pay cuts. We live in a quiet, self-contained estate which so far hasn't seen any trouble. And above all, we have a genius baby who, at not quite three months old, has already made his conversational debut.

9

THE NEW, NEW NORMAL

By March, the running joke is that COVID upped and left Myanmar on 1 February. Testing has stopped, reporting has stopped, quarantine centres are being packed up and there is no sign of the vaccination program promised by the previous government. Despite vanishing without a trace, however, COVID has already done much of the heavy lifting insofar as preparing us all for the *new*, new normal.

This new, new normal is far more ominous and is defined by three things: COVID, coup and cash. These three Cs are a troublesome trifecta. If we aren't worried about one, we are worried about the others. With the military messing around with internet connectivity, digital payment systems lose their way and the value, and appeal, of physical cash soars as it once again becomes the only dependable currency. The black market for cash booms and, despite the support I am receiving from my employer, we struggle with liquidity. To help our domestic staff afford the extortionate fees that agents are charging for cash withdrawals of their salaries (which we still pay through the mobile wallet, to help our own cash crunch), we increase their salaries by ten percent. We call ahead before going anywhere to check what cashless payment options they will accept, and only choose restaurants and shops that accept my mobile wallet or have their card machine connected to the internet. When Dylan suddenly needs a root canal treatment, we have to ask a friend to make the payment on our behalf, because the only reputable dentist accepts a mobile wallet that we don't have (and which is incompatible for transfers with the one we do have), and it isn't really something that we can put off until a later date.

I find the lack of cash by far the most worrying. It is a leveller. Even those of us who might have the luxury of living away from likely COVID or protest hotspots and who have the means to leave the country can't ignore the sense of panic that rises as our cash reserves deplete. I fear not being able to pay for essentials such as drinking water, food, nappies or inoculations for Jasper, and this fear chips away at my ability to adapt to the other changes brought about by this new, new normal.

We live with a curfew which, although apt to change with little warning or communication, mostly sees us banned from leaving the house between the hours of 10pm and 4am. While having a small baby means that we don't *plan* to leave the house between those hours, it adds a layer of fear knowing that we would not be able to even in an emergency. We also live with the regular news of raids on homes and businesses suspected of being pro-Aung San Suu Kyi and her NLD party. These raids stir up a collective paranoia that hangs in the air above the city. It isn't long before neighbours turn on one another and we learn the word 'dalan' - informant. We hear stories of people whose names have made it onto military 'wanted' lists being betrayed by their own communities, and then of the retaliation against these military informers from others. The city in which we always felt so safe is barely identifiable behind this new mask of vigilante justice and distrust.

The local media is muzzled, but using a VPN we are still able to stay connected with the outside world. Since the very first day of the coup when all TV broadcasters began to experience 'technical difficulties', media licenses have been arbitrarily revoked and media offices raided with violence extending to both people and equipment. We watch an armed convoy roll into Star City one day to raid a media outlet whose offices are in the compound and whose broadcasts are not 'on message'. Tony, Dylan and I are minding our own business devouring Tony's speciality lamb shanks eighteen storeys up and are at least partially hidden behind some net curtains, but we feel momentarily very exposed. It's moments like this that make me wonder about the long term effects of living under these conditions; I worry I will become hardened to the horrors I hear of daily and that I will end up normalising events which should never be considered normal.

Friends and colleagues in downtown Yangon live with blockades constructed at the ends of their streets, manned by members of the community who are doing their bit to protect their own from the targeted raids and arrests. One of my male colleagues, the gentlest, most non-confrontational member of our team, is out on the street every night manning the barricade on his road together with all the other men in his community. The images he shares on the group chat are like something straight out of *Les Miserables*. When he repeatedly apologises for missing the morning meetings due to being exhausted from a terrifying night out on the street, it seems as though he is straddling two parallel worlds.

The once lively streets around Tess and Steve's home are eerily quiet at night and they take to keeping golf clubs at the front door in case anyone should try to break in at night. And this in a city in which we all felt safer than in our home countries only months before. Tess is about as likely to use a golf club as a weapon as she is to play golf with it, but she says it makes her sleep easier knowing it is there if she needs it.

What really brings the reality of the coup right into our living room is when our helper, Lin, is caught up in a raid at her home. It surprises me to see her name pop up on my phone as an incoming call on the morning of her day off.

'Hi Lin!' I breeze. 'What's up? Is everything OK?'

There is a pause, during which I hear her breathing unsteadily before she coughs to clear her throat.

'No.' Her voice falters.

'No, everything's not OK?'

'No. They came. They came to my house. In the night. The soldiers.'

I am walking back from the supermarket with Dylan and Jasper, and I stop dead in my tracks.

'Lin? What happened? Where are you? Are you OK?'

'Yes. I am OK. I am at a friend's home. They looked for the owner, but she has gone. I saw a man in the street. They shot him. The back of his head opened.'

Lin is 20 years old, working in her first job with us at home. Ethnically a mix of two different minorities, and with her immediate family living in armed conflict regions elsewhere in Myanmar, she is no stranger to stories of military brutality, but she is audibly shaken. I feel queasy hearing the panic in her voice. The place where she is living with her aunt is a sort of hostel above a cafe in the village only ten minutes' walk from our residential estate. We often hear gun fire from the village and recently have seen the smoke from burning barricades and arson attacks. Only days before this incident, Lin rushed to fetch Jasper to the window of our bedroom to see his first rainbow; a rainbow into which pillars of smoke were melting as they rose up from the streets around her home. These are sights and sounds that this new, new normal has made, well, normal. But this is different. This is someone I feel responsible for. She has directly witnessed something horrific, and she is terrified.

'And your aunt?' I ask.

'She has gone. She went in the night, with the owner. They are hiding.'

'OK, Lin. You should come and stay with us. Do you have any clothes? Can you go back to your house to pack some?'

'I can't go there now. I will come now to your home, and go back later.'

A short while later she arrives at our apartment and I give her a hug. Her matchstick frame crumples as she begins to cry. Not for long though. After a couple of minutes she pulls away and looks at me with a bemused expression.

'They took ladies' dresses,' she says.

'Who did? The soldiers?' I ask, wondering where she is going with this.

'Yes. I asked my friend; he told me other people also said the same thing. The soldiers, when they come, they take money and gold and ladies' dresses.'

We look at one another, processing this very strange information, and then Lin begins to laugh. 'We don't understand them,' she concludes.

I couldn't agree more. Not long after this incident,

Jasper's nanny Wai Wai, decides that she is no longer comfortable travelling for work every day, from her home in Golden Valley, where her husband is a caretaker. Since working for us, she has been taking taxis to and from work, to avoid having to pile onto a crowded bus during COVID. What worries her is that there have been several stories of taxis being fired upon by soldiers and of passengers being arrested randomly. We only have one spare room but Tony is the sole occupant of his sprawling three-bedroom place, so Lin and Wai Wai become Tony's new housemates. Tony, Dylan and I make light of the situation in private, joking that Tony is now running a hostel, but when Lin and Wai Wai are around, the fear and gratitude they wear on their faces is heartbreaking. Sometimes I know I am laughing to avoid crying as the injustice of the coup reaches its long tentacles into our lives.

Lin and Wai Wai absolutely dote on Jasper. We call them his two-person entertainment committee and I am forever in awe of their creativity playing with what is essentially a hungry, gassy, human potato. Wai Wai is as caring of me as she is of Jasper, and shows me just how positive an impact Jasper's routine can have on my own life. She genuinely wants nothing but the best for Jasper and for our family. Lin is a free spirit, incredibly astute but somehow clumsy and absent minded at the same time. One day she makes us an apple pie for dinner. Only an apple pie. When I ask her about it, she says that she forgot that it was in the desserts section of her recipe book and she just felt like making a pie. Once she moves in with Tony, Lin takes it upon herself to look after him too, stating 'in our culture, we take care of the old people'. Tony, at sixty-six years old, wisely chooses not to take offence at this label, and instead takes full advantage of a live-in sous chef. Between them, Lin and Tony turn out weekly roast dinners and finally finish off the sprouts.

We all grow very used to the intermittent internet blackouts and we assume we are being monitored. There are some days where there is no internet at all, and others where there is fibre broadband but no mobile data. The days when the entire internet is switched off are like time warps. There we are, sitting at our same kitchen table in our same apartment, only we are in the nineties. I can win an argument about the status of some celebrity couple's marriage or the lyrics of a song without anyone being able to prove me wrong. Dylan merrily makes up his own 'official rules' of Scrabble without me being able to double check his point system. We can be entirely present in our own lives without feeling guilty about not sending enough photos and videos of Jasper to our families back home. What we can't do, however, is listen to a song spontaneously, or enjoy a new Netflix show. We cannot look up a recipe to combine the strange selection of foods we have sitting in our fridge, or make payments using anything other than much-sought-after cash. It turns out we cannot contact half our friends, who we only have Facebook profiles for or international WhatsApp numbers. We take to keeping a pen and paper on the table for when we return to the present day and need to make full and efficient use of the internet to fill the knowledge gaps we identify while we are in the dark. We are lucky to have our fibre connection which is rarely disrupted - most people in Myanmar only have their mobile phones (no Wi-Fi or computers at home) which means they are stuck in one of these time warps, without news or information, day after day.

In early March, I return to work. My first day back coincides with International Women's Day and, as I set up my laptop at the kitchen table the night before (my former desk having been commandeered as Jasper's changing table), I feel excited and empowered. In my impatience to return, I have already drafted an email that will let colleagues know that I am back and available to be brought into active projects. But I never send it. When the internet comes on at half six the next morning, marking the start of the connected day, a message from my line manager appears. It tells me that under no circumstances am I to send any emails, make any calls, or set up any meetings until I have spoken to him. He is in the UK (six and a half hours behind me) which leaves me with a long wait for more information. I call a friend in my team and she is emphatic in her support of our manager's advice. In the past few days, a colleague of ours has been named, shamed and abused online for having sent an email to her team. The fact that she is a foreigner adds fuel to the fire already fanned by the fact that she is working rather than joining the Civil Disobedience Movement; half the voices online want her to leave the country while the other half defend the contribution she is undoubtedly making by staying. I catch my breath as I imagine what it must feel like to be singled out in such a volatile climate of finger-pointing.

Dylan and I choose not to participate in any acts that can be construed as visual or verbal rebellion. We don't follow any social media groups, 'like' any posts or apply any frames to our profile photos. We certainly don't attend any marches or rallies. We don't even join the nightly banging of pots and pans, which is a symbolic effort by the people to drive away evil, and which naturally angers the increasingly impatient military forces who have yet to gain something which in any way resembles control. We are intent on flying under the radar to protect the safety of our home and family.

I sit at my desk, nervously filing old emails that I have missed while out on maternity leave and await a call from my manager. He confirms that the suggestion that I lay low is for my own protection; to protect my identity and the sanctuary of my home life. He asks me to help with some simple communications tasks, but mostly encourages me to enjoy the slow pace of my return. This is how I spend day after day after day in my first few weeks back at work. Unable to send emails or to join meetings (another colleague fell victim to similar social shaming when his voice was recorded during a group call and shared online), I wait expectantly for my manager to call me with a request to review the English version of an SMS text or to re-word a poster before it goes to print. The clunky, analogue nature of the work is a far cry from the frenetic, overlapping digital marketing campaigns I was leading before Jasper was born. Being micro-managed feels a long way from the autonomy I had in overseeing my own team of twenty-five people before my maternity leave too. I expected an adjustment on my return, but I never imagined this. I feel like a fraud, sitting there, passively, waiting for information and requests to come to me, rather than actively reaching out to make myself useful.

Returning to work plugs me back into daily updates on the cash situation and the status of protests and arrests. Colleagues translate and summarise the broadcasts on the state-owned TV channels too. Being privy to this kind of information is a double-edged sword. On the one hand, I enjoy feeling informed. I can plan for eventualities I might not have foreseen and am happy to be back in regular contact with people who can help me navigate issues which might arise. But, on the other hand, it adds to my mounting pile of worries. The more I know, the more I have to think about. And as the work slowly increases, the pressure I feel isn't from its volume, but from its gravity. There is no sugar-coating, we are operating in unprecedented depths of crisis management. At the end of each working day, often signified by a sudden disconnection of the internet, I close my laptop, take a deep breath, rise slowly from my chair and go to find Jasper.

Playing with him, cuddling him and laughing with him helps me unwind from my day and brings my focus back to a far more pleasant place. But in some ways, my version of motherhood (against this backdrop) feels like a form of crisis management too, as I try to stay one step ahead of problems, such as Jasper growing out of all his clothes, and the mystery of why, after over two months, we have still heard nothing about his passport.

I consider giving up on the British passport and going for an Australian one, but there we are thwarted by our disreputable circle of friends. The list of acceptable professions for someone who is allowed to countersign a true-likeness photo is one of pillars of society - doctors, judges, service personnel, teachers and the like - all of whom must have known the parents for at least two years. COVID and the coup cleared out any Yangon-based Aussies who meet these criteria.

As the British parent, I am the one who is chasing the passport. As the working parent, I am the one who has to split my focus between my job and Jasper each day. As a breastfeeding mother, I am the one who has to carve out time to pump or feed. As the default parent, I am the one who keeps track of Jasper's mealtimes, milestones and check-ups. And as the family worrier, I am the one who feels as though I am absorbing all the stress. As hard as I try to shrug the pressure off, I feel it starting to affect my behaviour. It doesn't take much to make me angry; not being able to find a particular item of clothing when I need it, an empty tube of toothpaste that hasn't been replaced, forgetting to drink my tea while it's hot. My outbursts are short but explicit and though the sound comes from my mouth, the emotion courses through my every fibre and explodes out of my every pore. I am frustrated that Dylan doesn't seem to feel the same pressure that I do. He continues as though he hasn't a care in the world and I resent that as much as I am starting to resent the situation we are in.

I am not getting what I need from Dylan. I want him to tell me that, yes, our situation is less than ideal, but that in spite of things, I am doing a good job with Jasper. I want him to tell me that he also has days where he feels lost. I want him to tell me that the news of escalating violence around Yangon worries him. I want him to show me that he's stressed over the cash situation. But he has his own way of handling pressure, and it's certainly not to talk things through.

At the end of March, I start to write a journal. Putting it all into words on a page not only helps to create some space in my head, but it also helps me find some distance from the events which are unfolding. And with that distance, comes objectivity. I don't know why it took me so long to start writing about the surreal situation we find ourselves in; almost four months into the life of our funny, happy little baby Jasper but at the same time surrounded by what feels like a rapid implosion of everything good in Myanmar under a violent military coup. I chat to my journal like I would chat to an old friend and it helps me to accept the absurdity of the situation I am in and to forgive myself a little for not knowing how to handle it all.

As I write about the internet outages, the loss of TV channels, the cash situation, the raids, my return to work,

Tony's new housemates and the strength of the resistance, I realise just how many terrible things we have already normalised. And as I write about a recent morning on the golf course when we heard gunshots and flash bangs (the soundtrack to clashes between civilians and military patrols) from miles away across the river, it really hits me how utterly terrifying it must be to live in downtown Yangon.

10

NO ORDINARY CIRCUMSTANCES

On 1 April the internet is switched on later than usual which does nothing to quell rumours that we are headed for a ten-day blackout, ten days from now, over the upcoming Myanmar New Year holiday, or Thingyan Festival, as it is known. The thought of ten days with no communication with the outside world frightens me for two main reasons: firstly, we don't even want to imagine what the military might be capable of under cover of ten days' information darkness, and, secondly, we still haven't heard anything about Jasper's passport and I suspect something has gone wrong with the application process. Ten days without the internet would be ten days when I am unable to search for an answer as to what is holding things up. The ten days of the Myanmar New Year holiday is also, traditionally, ten days of office closure which means that, even if the passport arrives in Myanmar, the local visa and passport office (VFS Global) will be closed and I will be unable to collect it. I feel a rush of adrenalin as I realise I am chasing down information against the clock.

I search for a phone number for the VFS office in Yangon. And then when they don't know any more than I do, I search for a phone number to call the passport office in the UK directly. I don't seem to have any of the application reference numbers that they ask for, or a proper receipt to show that I submitted the application and this makes me feel angrier and more frustrated than I already am. I try to remain calm while I speak to the representative but I am sure that I sound unhinged and borderline hysterical. I push and push for help on their end to work out what has happened and where my application has gone. They agree to do some digging and I agree to call back the next day for an update. At last I feel as though I am getting somewhere.

This cycle of calling and waiting and calling back and waiting some more continues day after day. My call is passed through various different teams, all of whom try and fail to tell me what exactly is going on. We establish that the application has stalled somewhere in the process but, as I count down to the possible communications blackout, I can feel my fuse burning closer and closer to an emotional outburst.

There is one thing which prises me away from my home internet connection for a few hours and makes me skip my daily call to the passport office, however, and that is the opportunity to be vaccinated. COVID has taken a back seat to the coup since February and the last I heard about a vaccination program was that there wasn't one - at least, not for civilians.

'Keep this to yourself,' a friend says, when he calls me out of the blue. 'But we can get the COVID vaccine, if we'd like it. Family members too. I just need you to send me the names, passport numbers and ages of anyone who wants the jab.'

'Oh wow - I didn't realise there was a vaccine program any more,' I say. 'This is amazing news. It'll be me, Dylan and Dylan's father, then. I'll send you the info. Where do we go?'

'You know the quarantine centre near the Inya Lake hotel? It's in there. When you get there, call the number I'll send you and someone will come to meet you. It's all a bit hush hush, to be honest.'

'And when will it be?' I ask.

'Tomorrow,' comes the reply. Short notice is something that six years in Myanmar has trained me for, but despite being used to it, my first instinct is still to try and push back and reschedule. Luckily, reason gets the better of me and I remember that this is no situation for a lecture on time management.

We dutifully follow the instructions given and Dylan, Tony and I set off for the convention-turned-quarantine-turned-vaccine centre. I hate to leave Jasper even for a couple of hours, but I decide that it is preferable to bringing him when I don't really know what we are heading into. That there are two frequently-disrupted bridges between me at the vaccine centre and Jasper in Star City puts me on edge and the length of time we expect to be out means my boobs will likely be agony by the time we get home.

The convention centre is in the grounds of one of Yangon's popular, up-market hotels which sits on a sprawling plot overlooking the city's even more popular Inya Lake. We once played a tennis tournament at this hotel, enjoyed several boozy Sunday brunches here and frequented a small deli in the same grounds, which was the only place in Yangon (and maybe the whole of Myanmar) where it was possible to buy a Lincolnshire sausage. It feels almost eerie to be back here in such different circumstances.

After a few wrong turns and some head shaking from various armed security guards, we find the right entrance to the centre. We are let in through a side door, and directed into the vast convention hall which I had last seen photographed as a quarantine centre – then, filled with rows of beds and medical equipment. Now, it is filled with a ghostly silence, but for the echo of our footsteps. Some men are lining up oxygen bottles near the door through which we have just entered, and as I look back, I see that they are loading them into a small truck outside. I wonder where they will end up.

We walk through a wide, empty corridor which has been created by pushing the equipment and cubicle dividers to the two ends of the hall. Dylan pops his head around a screen wall to see if the beds are still there. They are, but with no mattresses and no sign of the medical equipment. If we weren't here for our COVID jabs, it would be easy to imagine that COVID was well and truly over.

We reach a small room on the other side of the hall. My friend is there, and a handful of others - mostly expats. We greet one another jovially, with some of us interacting in person for the first time in over a year. We joke about whether the vaccines are real, whether they have been stored correctly, whether they are still within their expiry dates. We are cocky and insensitive considering the armed guard outside and the fact that we do not deserve to be the first in line.

There are not enough vaccines for the entire Burmese population to have even their first one. There are only a million doses, donated by India, which means only roughly one in a hundred people stand a chance of being fully vaccinated. We are incredibly lucky to be offered not one but two doses - the second a month after this first one. Some of the local people are being invited for the vaccine but they are too scared to sign up. Such is the climate of fear that the idea of filling their name and address in a form stirs their paranoia about how this information might be used. They would rather take their chances with COVID.

We fill in our forms with barely a second thought, accept the paracetamol and water we are handed for after the jab and then we are led in silent, single file through some airport-style security scanners. As we emerge from our VIP room out into the public area, the other vaccine recipients look as surprised as we are suddenly sheepish. They look every bit as old and vulnerable as their 'high risk' categorisation suggests as they shuffle or are wheeled towards their assigned cubicle. I want to leave as quickly as possible afterwards, before the guilt at having taken a dose from someone more needy or the anxiety (and pain) from having left Jasper for so long catches up with me. As we arrive home from our field trip, however, I realise I am reassured by how uneventful it was; we saw no explosions, we weren't stopped and none of the roads we needed were blocked. We did see the remnants of earlier barricades and scorch marks on some roads, but it wasn't as bad as I was expecting.

Other foreigners who we know, including Tess and Steve, start to search for vaccines through contacts at embassies, chambers of commerce and large private businesses. Dylan and I stay very quiet in these conversations - there is no advantage in people knowing how and where we had ours because the channel is not available to them. Elsewhere in the world the 'anti-vaxxer' movement is gaining momentum and news reports about it make me want to scream at the imbalance of it all. For me, the vaccine might be the difference between being able to travel or not travel when the time comes to leave Myanmar. For many people in Myanmar, it might be the difference between life and death given the lack of any appropriate medical support in the country. That people elsewhere in the world have the self-centricity to refuse something so fundamental to other peoples' survival sickens me. If they could only feel the desperation and fear of the people in Myanmar, I doubt so many of them would have the heart to take such a strong stance against saving lives.

I spend the next few days preparing for life without the internet. I download recipes, parenting advice, Spotify playlists and Netflix shows. I send an 'if you don't hear from us' email to my family giving them our phone numbers and asking them to call every day to make sure that we are alright. I ask them to continue my calls to the passport office in my stead and give them all the necessary security information that they will need in order to reach the case officer. I give them the links to the COVID travel declaration forms from neighbouring countries, in case we have to make an emergency departure from Myanmar and are unable to fill in the necessary travel forms due to having no internet. And lastly, I remind them not to believe all of what they read in the news, because despite what they see in the reportage, there are still areas of Yangon where life is relatively calm.

On 10 April, the first day of the holiday period, we awake to find that we still have the internet. We rejoice for a few seconds before we see the news that there has been a huge clash between civilians and the military in a town called Bago not far from Yangon; more than sixty people are dead. Selfishly, I hope that this incident, and the Myanmar people's reaction to it, won't trigger a delayed implementation of the rumoured internet shutdown. I still haven't quite got to the bottom of where Jasper's passport application is stuck, although my daily calls (on which I give unsolicited anecdotal situation updates) do seem to be helping to push my case up the chain of command. I also hope that news of this battle will have reached international media and will add clout to my anecdotes.

Lin tells me that, as part of their hunt for the protest leaders, the military are printing out Facebook profile pages and hanging them up like wanted posters. I also hear that township authorities are collecting census-like records of who is living where, in order to keep tabs on their citizens. In jarring contrast to this, I start to see photos of friends who have taken the opportunity of a ten day break from work to go to the beach. I am bitterly jealous. But then a few minutes later, I am judgemental. And then after a few more minutes, I realise I don't care. Ordinarily I would be the first person to choose a sun-soaked trip to the seaside over a city staycation, but this year my feet have entirely lost their itch. It didn't even occur to me to look at travel; I assumed there were no domestic flights and I didn't fancy dealing with checkpoints on a long drive. Perhaps because of our ever-changing Jasper too, I don't crave a change of scenery as I have in other years.

With renewed fervour, I continue my daily calls to the passport office. I am not aware just how much I am hoping for good news until I receive the opposite; the clerk at VFS Global in Yangon didn't stamp my documents correctly. Worse than that - he didn't stamp the copied documents *at all* to show that he had both seen the originals and verified the copies as true. Without verification, the application cannot even be submitted into the system in the UK, let alone processed. The application stalled months ago, before it began, but nobody noticed. This is why I don't yet have an application reference number or any updates in the system.

I rage like a tornado - spitting expletives and gesturing wildly. And then I collapse in a desolate heap of tears. April *should* have been be the month when we traveled to introduce Jasper to one of our families. We *should* have had the passport by now and we *should* have had the freedom to travel (or to leave) if we wanted to. And now April is as good as gone and we are no closer to any of these things than we were in January.

In order to reactivate the application, I have to resubmit the original documents - something which is far easier demanded than actioned. The VFS office is closed for the Thingyan holiday period so I can't show the originals and resubmit copies for another week at least (and that's if the office reopens at the end of the holiday which seems unlikely due to the threats from both COVID and violence). The courier companies are also closed (indefinitely) and even if they were operational, I am not willing to let Jasper's birth certificate out of my sight. It is his only formal piece of documentation and it was not easy to come by in the first place.

* * *

Weeks before Jasper was born, I asked how much support the hospital would give in getting the new baby properly documented. They said, 'The hospital will give you a birth certificate.'

This was surprising because official birth certificates are usually issued by an official authority, not by an admin team at a private hospital. I asked again, while I was lounging around in my suite a day before my surgery, and this time the response was, 'The hospital doesn't give the birth certificate.'

'Ah. You see, I was told the opposite last time I asked,' I explained politely. 'How do I get a birth certificate?'

'The hospital will give you a hospital certificate and then your country will give the birth certificate.'

'Hmm, I don't think that's quite right either. To get a British passport for Jasper, I will need to submit a local birth certificate with the application. So, it can't be something from the UK.'

'You can use the hospital certificate.'

'Oh OK. So, it's a proper certificate? It looks like a Myanmar birth certificate?'

'No, he can't have a Myanmar birth certificate. He is a foreigner.'

'Yes, I know that he's a foreigner, but he will be born here. So, he will still need a local birth certificate.'

'Yes. From the hospital.'

I stared at the twenty-something standing at my bedside, who was clearly hoping her strong command of English would mask her complete lack of relevant knowledge.

'Perhaps you could check with your colleagues, or call the authorities and get more information for me?' I asked, stepping off the merry-go-round of a conversation.

After Jasper was born, in our complaint to the management of the hospital at the end of our 24-hour separation ordeal, we again raised the question of the birth certificate. This time, the answer was different again.

'Tell us what you want it to say and we will make it for you', came the response. In normal circumstances I would fully support an attitude of 'if in doubt, show willing', but this didn't feel like a situation where enthusiasm would overrule regulation.

'Fine. Dylan will fill in the form,' I snapped. And then, to Dylan, 'Can you fill in whatever they need? I am guessing it's just all our names and addresses spelled correctly.'

'Can we have multiple copies of the birth certificate?' Dylan asked. We had spent a long time discussing the perils of Jasper having a birth certificate from a country with limited digital document control. To pre-empt any challenges in Jasper's future, if he or we were to lose his original Myanmar birth certificate, we had decided we would try to get a second copy of it up front.

Off Dylan went. He was pointed to the reception desk and the computer on it. He was directed to type the information into a Word document. It was only when the first wonky, faded sheet of paper fell out of the tired, monochrome printer that it struck Dylan that we were still talking at cross-purposes with the hospital about the definition of a birth certificate. They offered to stamp each flimsy copy with an ink chop, which of course we accepted, but our hearts sank. This couldn't possibly be an official birth certificate. In our desperation to leave the hospital, we grabbed what we were given and ran, before one of us committed a murder.

Out of some freakish good fortune, there were three foreign babies due at the hospital within a day of one another and we mothers all lived in Star City. While I wasn't close with either of the other mothers, there is a solidarity in expat life that enabled me to ask them for advice on how they were handling birth certificates and passports. A brief exchange with one of them led us to a local township administration office, not far from our home, for an official birth certificate, and to a public notary for translation and notarisation. This certificate is a not-quite-square shiny, white card, printed with tiny, red, Burmese letters. Jasper's details are handwritten in spidery English capitals in blue biro. On one edge, there are the telltale dots of a perforation. It was just our luck that Jasper's was the last birth certificate in the book, so our hopes of having a copy were swept away with the book of stubs, which I imagine is lying in the corner of the office since the coup led to its closure.

* * *

My sadness at not yet having the freedom to travel dissipates, but my anger does not. The Thingyan holiday period comes to an end but neither the VFS Global office nor the courier companies show any signs of reinstating their services. I continue to call the passport office in the UK almost daily, pleading with them to find a more creative way for me to show the documents to someone in a position of authority, given the extraordinary situation I am in. I am unable to resubmit the documents at VFS and I am unable to courier them. But the passport office is unable to offer me any other option. This means I have to wait. It is infuriating; I know what needs to be done, but through no fault of my own, I am physically unable to do it. It doesn't help my mood to know that a UN special envoy for Myanmar is reported as using phrases like 'failed state' and 'imminent bloodbath' in a discussion about the state of the country. This news causes my family to increase the volume and frequency with which they ask us to consider leaving. When I explain to them about my stalemate with the passport office, I then absorb their frustration and disbelief at the inflexibility of the system on top of my own.

While I wait, a military checkpoint appears and then disappears at the entrance to Star City, a directive is issued by the regime that all companies must bring striking employees back to work and more expats leave Myanmar. Fortunately, the supposed closure of all ports until the end of May never really came into effect so flights are still running, albeit on very reduced schedules and with manifests being checked and approved by the military, several days before the flight is due to leave. I envy those who leave, not because I want to say goodbye to Myanmar but because once they are out, they all speak of an invisible weight having been lifted off their shoulders. To make myself feel better, I try to convince myself that they left unnecessarily soon; the Thingyan holiday period passed quite uneventfully in the end (after the initial shock of the Bago incident) and, on the whole, despite many businesses remaining closed, things are starting to feel more settled. I try to distract myself by doing ordinary things in as ordinary a way as I can, but ordinary these circumstances are not.

11

HANGING IN THERE

MINE IS the first appointment on the day that the VFS office re-opens. I storm in, documenting every move the clerk makes as he checks the original documents and stamps the new set of copies I have brought. The first time he tries to use the stamp, the impression it leaves is barely visible, so I demand that he go and find more ink to try again.

Despite the fact that there are fewer mass protests and clashes between civilians and military haven't escalated in recent weeks, I am now obsessed with obtaining Jasper's passport. There is another way we can gain permission to travel and that is by applying for an Emergency Travel Document (ETD) for Jasper. In fact, the British Embassy sends out regular emails to British citizens still in Myanmar, encouraging the take up of services, such as Emergency Travel Document issuance, while they are still available. I toy with the idea of getting an ETD, but the more I look into it, the more I see that it won't work for us as a family. An ETD is an official letter which allows a passenger to travel to a named destination on a specified date, without a passport. The journey must be exactly as is stated on the letter. We plan to head to the UK. At this time in early May, the UK government is developing its traffic light system for categorising countries onto red, amber and green lists according to their COVID risk. The problem with an ETD is that, in between us booking our travel and us arriving in the UK weeks later, Myanmar could have moved from the amber list to the red list. Travel from a red-listed country to the UK is heavily restricted and only possible for British citizens and residents. No foreigner is allowed to enter the UK within fourteen days of visiting a red-listed country. Dylan is a foreigner. He has no visa or right to reside in the UK, despite being married to me. I have visions of us stuck in a transit airport like Tom Hanks in *The Terminal*, unable to continue our journey to the UK as a family because of Dylan's foreigner status, but also unable to change our plans and make a two-week detour due to Jasper's Emergency Travel Document.

We decide that it is safer to wait for Jasper's passport, however long that takes, but this doesn't make the waiting any less tense. Our families are urging us to leave. Our friends too. Even the lactation consultant tells me to leave, when she checks in on me, out of the blue, to discuss my plans for Jasper's upcoming weaning journey.

Jasper's appetite and curiosity are starting to outgrow his monotonous milk diet. The contract I made with myself, based on WHO guidelines, was only to breastfeed for six months. I am nearly there. I long to ditch my front-access tops and my stained maternity bras. I dream of going out for longer than a few hours without Jasper, not because I need to, but because I can. He is increasingly feisty at feeding time, fighting me all the way, which is not only miserable for both of us, but it's causing me some physical discomfort. I have noticed a tremor in my neck and, while I can't be sure it's entirely Jasper's fault, given the intensity of the environment in which we find ourselves, it's certainly aggravated by the strain of trying to keep him on the boob. On more than one occasion Dylan takes my involuntarily shaking head as a no to a question I most definitely mean to answer with a yes. Miscommunication with my husband is not something I need to add to my stress load, especially not when he's offering me coffee.

With the end in sight, I start looking into available milk formula brands and read up on how best to transition to the bottle during the early stages of weaning. I am all set, with a cut-off date identified and a celebratory bottle of bubbly in the fridge. That is, until the lactation consultant messages unexpectedly, asking for a call. I haven't spoken to her for months and the time she proposes tells me she is no longer in Myanmar.

'You're not still in Myanmar, are you?' she asks abruptly, without so much as a hello.

'Yes, we are,' I say.

'Why?' she says with equal parts horror and criticism.

I feel myself bristle. It is a valid question, but I don't enjoy the judgement in her voice.

'This is our home,' I say. And then, realising that it's a lot more complicated than that, I continue. 'We're still waiting for Jasper's passport, which has taken longer than expected, and the situation where we are in Star City isn't dangerous. I'm still working at my job here and we don't really know where to go. We might leave later this year, but for now, we're staying put.' I hope that I sound a little more convinced than I feel with the stream of excuses.

'You can leave with an Emergency Travel Document for Jasper. You should get out of there. It's not safe. Not safe for a baby. Did you know that the children's hospitals are all closed? All the doctors are doing CDM. There are no doctors, so no hospitals.'

I didn't know that for sure. I knew that most hospitals

were closed and, by extension, I supposed that included the children's hospitals, but until she said it, it hadn't felt important.

'I didn't know that,' I confess.

'You should leave,' she says again.

'Maybe, but for now, we're staying,' I repeat with a bit more bite in my voice. Whenever I hear someone suggest that we need to leave (be it a family member, a friend or an old acquaintance who has popped up on social media looking for some insight into what they've seen on the news), I feel sick. And with the sickness comes a wave of dread. My deepest fear is that I am making the wrong decision and that this wrong decision will jeopardise Jasper's life. When I talk to Dylan about it, we agree that we are waiting until we have the passport before making a decision about leaving, but that in itself is a decision; the decision to wait. Motherhood is made up of endless decisions - some tiny, some bigger and others huge. I don't fear making one huge wrong decision, because at least I would be able to pinpoint that one as the mistake. I fear that I am making many, many tiny decisions which at some point will amount to having done the wrong thing. And I dread having to look back through my pile of tiny decisions to work out at what point I should have taken someone's advice.

'So, how is breastfeeding going?' asks the lactation consultant.

'It's going OK. Still not easy, but it works,' I say. 'I'm thinking of switching to formula soon, because he's almost six months old and we are about to start weaning. He's happy with a bottle and we have introduced a little formula in the last few weeks so he will drink it.'

'You shouldn't stop breastfeeding,' she says decisively. 'You can't stop.'

'Wha ... why?' I stammer, confused. It was this very lady

who told me that if I make it to six months, I am doing a good job. 'But I thought at six months I could stop?'

'Ordinarily, yes. Six months would be very good. But you are about to introduce new bacteria with food. And the season is changing into monsoon, which is when people get sick. And there is COVID. And remember, there is no children's hospital. Like I said, you should leave. And if you leave, you can stop breastfeeding. But if you stay, you must continue.'

We chat some more about weaning and the importance of breastfeeding, and then the call ends.

'Fuuuuuuck,' I say loudly.

'What's wrong?' says Dylan, coming to where I am supposedly working, surprised by my use of such a potent swear word.

'The lactation consultant says I can't stop breastfeeding. Eurgh. I am so ready to stop. I had already started reducing my feeds and now I have to crank back up to full production.'

I stare blankly at Dylan as I let the idea of continuing to breastfeed sink in. I want to scream. I don't, because there is a sleeping baby next door, but I very much want to. The lactation consultant is right, of course, and, on top of her very good reasons, there is also the disrupted supply chain to consider. Since the coup, imported produce is slowly vanishing from the supermarket shelves, leaving shoppers with fewer choices. On a work call one day, after everyone has given their daily bomb report for their neighbourhood, a colleague bitterly remembers the soap which defined her childhood in the nineties: a locally produced, one-soap-washes-all bar. It was the only thing available to wash hands, hair, clothes, dishes, the lot. As liquid detergents and scented hand washes disappear, she wonders when we'll all be forced back into the trusty care of the wonder soap. That will be her tipping point and her trigger to think about moving abroad.

'Well, that's my dream of stopping breastfeeding over,' I say to Dylan. 'Might as well accept it and move on. I'll never forgive myself if something happens to Jasper and I know I've ignored someone's advice.'

'On another note,' I say to Dylan after a while, 'I've booked us into that first aid course. It's a zoom call next weekend. It's just the basics of newborn first aid, like choking and stuff. I want to do it before we start Jasper on solids.'

'OK great. And are you doing that yoga class you wanted to go to? The one in town? When is that?' Dylan asks.

'Eurgh. No. It's the same day , but in the morning,' I say.

'Why not? You should go. Didn't you say it's the last one before the yoga people leave?' Dylan says encouragingly. 'I thought Jasper and I were going to come and join you after for a coffee.'

'It is, I think. But I only want to do yoga when I can lie on my stomach without my boobs hurting. I thought I would be finished with breastfeeding, so I thought it might be good. But now, I just feel like it'll be uncomfortable. And if I book it, something will probably go wrong on the day.'

'Milla, don't let yourself fall into a funk. I know you want to finish breastfeeding,and you know that you still can, by the way. We'll deal with whatever we have to deal with in terms of formula and things if you decide to stop. You can't let the situation we're in get you down. Otherwise, we'll just be so miserable. Book the yoga class. It's silly not to plan things because you're worried they won't go ahead. If you start thinking like that, you'll end up never doing anything at all!'

'I know, I know. But today I *feel* like being in a funk. It's all very well for you, you're not the one who has to continue being a human milk factory for the foreseeable future. Maybe tomorrow I'll book the class.'

I do book it, and then I go back to waiting impatiently for news about Jasper's passport application and trying not to think too much about how many miles may be left on my breastfeeding marathon. I look ahead at my empty calendar for May, June, July and beyond and wonder how I can make the time pass more quickly. Our second COVID jab makes for a nice excuse for Tony, Dylan and I to leave Star City and this time we even take the opportunity to go out for lunch. While the cash situation continues to go from bad to worse, with banks lowering the ATM withdrawal limits with alarming regularity, 3G and 4G mobile internet has now been restored for a few whitelisted payment apps and websites. We duly select one of the few restaurants which will accept a mobile payment and comment on how this feels like the first positive step in a while. Over lunch we admire our vaccination certificates, which we weren't sure we would get and which reinforce just how incredibly lucky we are to have been vaccinated. We return home buoyed by our luck and by another uneventful trip into the city and I give myself a pep talk about staying positive and trying to enjoy our extended stay in Myanmar as much as possible.

I am jolted out of my new-found optimism just two days later when my salary information is suddenly splashed all over social media. My blood runs cold and my breath catches in my throat when I see the message that my colleague sends me. She is the first to alert me to what's happened, but more messages and calls follow as other friends and colleagues make sure I know about the privacy breach and check that I am OK. Of course, my imagination rushes straight to the worst case scenario: social shaming. If someone has access to my name and salary information and is bold enough to share that online, surely they also have access to my home address and are willing to hand that over to the general public (or the authorities). I fear for Jasper first, being separated from his food supply. And then I fear for my wellbeing if I were to be detained. I am also a little ashamed at how much I earn compared to my local counterparts. I am not the only member of staff whose salary has been leaked - four other foreigners join me on the list. A good friend is also on there and he calls to assure me that since the perpetrator (a member of the finance team) has been identified and fired, there will be no further repercussions. I try to mirror his nonchalance, brushing the incident off with more bravado than I feel inside. I brace myself as I read the comments below the original post on Facebook, terrified that I'll witness real-time formation of an angry mob ready to protest how much foreigners are earning amidst the current turmoil. To my surprise, the comments almost unanimously direct anger at the person who wrote the post, express embarrassment at how someone could act so unprofessionally as to leak confidential information, and sadness at the fact that there are so few foreigners left in the country, sharing their expertise with people who are keen to learn. After reading the comments, I no longer fear for the safety of our family, but I still feel shaken and exposed. I feel jumpier than I have in weeks.

Dylan suggests that we go to the Japanese restaurant in Star City for an afternoon beer and some snacks. I am initially reluctant to leave the apartment, but, once outside, I enjoy the sunshine and the walk. We are on our way back when we pass a navy truck propping up a lackadaisical, flip-flop-shod officer and his weapon. It is highly unusual for a military vehicle to be inside Star City and I feel a rush of panic, undoubtedly fuelled by my peculiar morning. Ignoring the alarm beating fast in my chest and resisting the urge to grab Jasper and run, I make a comment about his dozy appearance and we joke about why he has chosen that location to take a standing nap. With barely a second glance at the man and his gun, we continue walking and our conversation winds its way back to whether it feels hot for this time of year.

We find out later that the rest of his team were, at that time, raiding an apartment in the building behind. A raid that resulted in thirteen arrests and one death by jumping from a fifth-floor balcony. This tragedy is not the first time that someone has chosen to take their own life over the alternative of capture and inevitable torture at the hands of the ruthless, cruel regime. But it is disturbing that this happened so close to home. Suddenly I don't feel as safe in Star City.

It is a sign of the extraordinary circumstances in which we are living that I stop thinking about this experience in a matter of days, and return to feeling cocooned and removed from the violence that others in Yangon witness on a daily basis. I wonder if I am unable to dwell on it because it seems too real, or if it seems to too *sur*real. Or because I simply can't allow thoughts of brutality to mingle in the same brain that is filled with the wonder of watching Jasper grow.

The following weekend, I do not attend my much-anticipated yoga class. I am thwarted in my ambition to go and attend a normal class in a room full of normal people and eat a delicious normal smoothie bowl afterwards by rumours of bombs and attacks in the downtown area, which is precisely where the yoga class is. In the end, nothing transpires, leaving me enraged by a lack of explosions.

In the early afternoon, Dylan and I put Jasper down for his nap and perch ourselves on the edge of the sofa, to join our online first aid lesson. It is taught by Daisy First Aid and our jolly trainer is teaching us from her home in London. It is as terrifying as it is useful. Learning about how to respond in an emergency alerts me to the myriad ways in which there could *be* an emergency. We are most interested in what to do in the event of Jasper choking on food. We listen carefully, make a few notes and practise the baby choking manoeuvres on a toy elephant. It is the second time the trainer says 'and then, as soon as you are able, call 999 for an ambulance' that I raise my hand. I have a question.

'I am wondering, what should I do if I need to get the baby to a doctor or clinic, but there is no emergency service and no ambulance? For example, am I best to run with the baby and hope the jiggling dislodges whatever is stuck, or best to put him in the car and keep him as still as possible?' As I ask my question, I am mentally mapping out both my running and driving routes from our tower block to the clinic.

'You should run through the initial checks and then you should call 999 for an ambulance. Or the appropriate number for where you are,' she says, remembering that we said we weren't in the UK at the start of the call.

'I understand that, but there is no emergency service where we are. There are no ambulances and no hospitals. But we have a clinic nearby. It's about a seven-minute run, or a three-minute car journey. I am wondering what is the best way to transport a choking baby,' I say. Even as the words come out of my mouth, I realise just how incomprehensible our situation must seem to people who are not here.

I watch as the other couples in the call try to hide their 'who are these weirdos?' faces and their 'what are they doing with a small baby in a country with no ambulance service?' mutterings. If the shoe were on the other foot, I would question our choices too.

'Oh. I suppose, in that case, you are best to drive. Lie the baby on its side, in the car and drive to the clinic,' says the trainer. 'But, just to be clear, for everyone else, you are best to call 999.'

Feeling almost less confident than before the class, we go ahead and start the solids. Jasper doesn't choke and he doesn't get sick from the food or the change in the weather. Of course, I'll never know if this is because his immune system is bolstered by the breastmilk, but I decide that it's probably worth the sacrifice to enjoy a drama-free weaning journey.

12

TO STAY OR TO GO

Sometime in early June, when we can put it off no longer, we hold a family 'Coup Response Strategy' session. The attendees are Dylan and me, while Jasper takes a nap. I am a marketing and comms strategist by trade, and Dylan works in project management for construction so, between us, we feel confidently qualified to define and articulate a strategic approach to any sudden changes in our predictably unpredictable circumstances. And, if it comes to it, to execute an action plan against a tight timeline. We also own more than enough Post-It notes and highlighter pens to get us started. I open the meeting.

'I think we need to agree on some absolute triggers for getting out of here, so that if, or when, one of them happens, we don't waste any time thinking about it. We just leave.'

'Agreed,' says Dylan.

In a short but productive meeting, we agree on two things; whether our departure from Myanmar will be permanent or temporary (until things stabilise), and what will make us leave.

We also realise simultaneously that we have absolutely

no idea what our departure would, could or should look like, given the state of international travel.

TO STAY OR TO GO?

Departure: temporary or permanent?

Fundamental considerations:
- Plan to be in UK for <u>Dec</u>
- Apartment lease ends in <u>Nov</u>
- Milla contract ends in <u>Oct</u>
- Dylan visa expires <u>Sept</u>
- Don't have Jasper's passport

> Other option for Jasper: Emergency Travel Doc. But then can't deviate from travel plan if entry rules change. 12 weeks to start new passport application. Wasted months here.

When we leave, we leave for good.
(If still don't have it, have to head somewhere to get Jasper passport)

What would make us leave? → When cons outweigh pros

Pros of staying:
- Milla job
- Dylan golf
- Lifestyle - <u>under constant review</u>
- This is home
- Possible it will resolve?

Cons of staying:
- Cash situation
- Internet issues
- Stress
- COVID situation
- No friends/ no travel (lifestyle)
- Families want to meet Jasper

Tony?!
Will he leave?
Wife in aus, biz in Myanmar.
Aus closed

One of absolute triggers OR

★ Loss of medical care for Jasper
★ Immediate threat to our lives
★ All-out civil war in Yangon

When do we leave?
September at latest

STILL TO DECIDE - where to and how?

How? Relief flight - check routes
Where to? Aus closed, so UK?!

<u>Do we continue to be expats?!</u>

ACTIONS:
Milla: Jasper's passport + work out route, flights + documentation
Dylan: golf handicap to single digits, talk to Tony about leaving

As soon as we have worked it through and written it down, we see clearly that we *are* going to leave Myanmar, that it will be before September and that it will be for good. It is just a case of when, and the more complicated question of how. Even though our plan doesn't extend much beyond leaving Myanmar and arriving in the UK, we are fairly convinced that our expat lives may be over. The post-COVID world seems to have far less need for expats in interesting roles - and we have lost some of our enthusiasm for living abroad.

We know plenty of expats who left Myanmar in the early days of the coup, or at least, as many as could get a seat on one of the infrequent relief flights. Some returned home to stay with family while others decamped to Bangkok from where they could continue to work from an adjacent time zone, with the expectation of returning to Myanmar once things 'settled down'. Even more left during COVID, for what they hoped would be a temporary stay somewhere with better transport links and a higher quality of medical care. Their belongings gather dust and mould in hundreds of empty apartments around the city. One such family very kindly invites us to go and raid their home for toys and books, which they have imported over the years. The haul we come away with is certainly more than enough to tide Jasper over until we leave. Picking through someone else's abandoned belongings confirms to us that our decision to leave for good is the right one; we don't want to find ourselves in a similar situation further down the line.

Those who are presently unable to leave, or who have decided to stay on in Yangon, rally together with a bleak resolve to make the most of the situation we are in by trying to continue as normally as we can. We make plans to see one another and to get out of our homes as much as seems sensible, but everything always comes with the caveat 'depending on the situation on the day'. It is like checking the weather on the day of a picnic, except it's not high winds or rain we are looking out for, it's roadblocks and explosives.

One day we manage to meet one of our few remaining expat friends for lunch. She is mother to a half-Dutch, half-Burmese baby not much older than Jasper. She and her son arrive in the restaurant after us and, with a nonchalance we would all have baulked a few weeks earlier, she explains that she had to wait for a barricade on her street to be moved for their taxi to bring them to the restaurant.

'It's nice to get out, to be honest,' she continues. 'Our whole apartment smells of smoke from the flash bangs and homemade explosives that have been going off in the next street over. There's been a lot of activity in our neighbourhood.'

My eyes flit from her to her son and then to Jasper as my eyebrows twitch. I am unable to hide my horror.

'I know,' she says. 'Don't worry, we are leaving. Even though my husband's family are here, we just can't stay. It doesn't feel right to take the risk.'

'I know,' I say quietly, avoiding eye contact with Dylan. He will know how hard I will take the news of yet another friend making the decision to leave, especially one with even stronger, familial ties to Myanmar than our emotional ones. I benchmark our own decision not to leave yet against other people almost daily - justifying the fact that we are still here by telling myself that there are other expats with small children who have decided it's safe enough to stay. I know that in the car on the way home he will ask me how I feel and that I will tell him that I want to leave as soon as possible but that, deep down, I know that the sensible thing is to wait for Jasper's passport. This is what I will say. But what I will feel is my heart beating fast and heavy in my chest, my breath growing shallow and uneven despite my attempts to inhale deeply, a tightness in my neck, an emptiness in my stomach and a desperate need to hold Jasper.

Lunch is enjoyable but sombre and at the end we say what might be our goodbyes, given that our friend leaves within the month. Her son is Jasper's only little friend and I feel sad that he no longer has another similarly sized companion to swim or roll around on the floor with. However, Jasper does benefit from his friend's departure when we inherit a timely pile of his outgrown clothes. At nearly six months of age, Jasper is almost too big for the clothes my family sent over (at my request) before he was born. Assuming that we would have been able to travel in April and visit shops in either the UK or Australia I only thought to buy clothes for his first six months. Not only are there are no shops selling baby basics in Yangon, but there are also no courier services to enable my family to send over the next size up.

We decide that we would like to rent an apartment in Star City for Lin and Wai Wai. They have been staying with Tony for a little over two months now and Lin could undoubtedly do with a day off from being Tony's sous-chef. We find a nice, furnished apartment for them and help them to move in. At first, they are nervous to be two women staying alone in a large residential estate and they take some time to settle in. I have learned that this is normal for Myanmar people, who tend to enjoy close communal living with large extended families. On business trips I took over the years, my female colleagues would always choose to share rooms with one another and were fascinated by my preference to have my own.

They arrive at our apartment earlier and earlier each day, because they love Jasper and because they are not sure how to pass the time, alone in their quiet apartment. Lin continues to take care of Tony too, trotting over to his apartment every other day to help with his laundry and cleaning. We tell them that the apartment is theirs until the end of the year, even if we are no longer in Myanmar, but we know from their reactions that as soon as we leave, they will return to their families.

Tragically, Wai Wai loses her mother to what the village doctor records as 'not COVID, but a respiratory illness' a few days after they move into the apartment. She is at work when she receives the news, rushes from Jasper's room with an anguished cry and then shuts herself away in our bathroom for a few minutes while agony pours out of her in uncontrollable sobbing. When she finally emerges and allows me to comfort her, I am overwhelmed by anger towards a regime which has not only prevented a mother and daughter from meeting for months with their military checkpoints along routes to ethnic minority areas (where Wai Wai is from), but also for the lies they are spreading about the cause of this and other recent deaths to mask their own failure to bring COVID under control. I ask Wai Wai if she would like to go home now, to grieve with her sister, but she says no. I ask if she'd like to go to her husband in downtown Yangon. She says no to that too. She says that Jasper is the only joy in her life for now and so she chooses to stay. Wai Wai tells me that she and her husband prefer to remain in the city as long as they can. She says that if they both lose their jobs, they might be forced to return to their village to keep chickens. She is old enough to remember the impact of the unrest in the eighties, when the loss of jobs in the cities caused by the political turmoil and economic crisis again forced many people back to rural life. There is a hopelessness in her eyes as she describes how she felt back then, and how her recent years in the city will make the transition even harder this time around. Lin is too young to know the disappointment of being led down a new, exciting road to a better future only to have all the gates slam on you half way along, but she too has lost family back home for whom she has yet to formally grieve. In her case, it was a brother whose name she identified on a Facebook post which listed those who had recently lost their lives in fighting between an ethnic armed group and the Myanmar military. She came to work in pieces that day, but she too said she preferred to stay with us and Jasper rather than make the long and undeniably dangerous journey back to her village.

Finally, in mid-June, a month after I resubmitted the documents, an email arrives from the passport office in the UK, inviting me for an interview. I am unsure what to expect from this interview, but I suspect it is to validate that I am who I say I am. I am oddly nervous about being tested on details from my own life and wonder if my increasingly traumatised memory is going to fail me. My first appointment comes and goes without the call I am promised ever coming into my phone. I wait an hour before I decide that something must have gone wrong with the scheduling. I call the passport office to demand to know why they didn't bother honouring the appointment and the response is that they tried - fifteen times. A cartoon lightbulb might as well illuminate over my hot head. Months ago, in the early days of the coup, there was a rumour that some kind of spyware was being applied to the Myanmar telco networks. The passport office tells me that they need a secure line and that, if it doesn't connect immediately, the call fails. I realise that the rumour must be true and that's why the call failed. I request an alternative way to conduct the interview, which they provide.

Two days later, the interview takes place, by video, with a lovely old man somewhere in the north of England, who, by coincidence, was planning a cruise to Myanmar, (this was postponed due to COVID, and is now cancelled due to the coup).

After some initial niceties, my interviewer asks me, 'What can you see out of the window?'

I look at him. And then look from the window of our eighteenth-floor apartment, over the river towards Yangon. I briefly wonder if he is asking me to describe what he will miss, due to his cancelled holiday. I fight back the tears as I start to speak. 'I am in my apartment, in an estate called Star City. We live on the eighteenth floor. I can see the river which runs alongside the estate. We watch sunset over it every night from our balcony. We used to attend boat parties on the river and we also did some cycle tours which took us through the countryside just a short boat ride from downtown Yangon. It's dotted with naval patrol boats now. I can see the bridge which connects us to the rest of the city. It's narrow, just one lane in each direction. I used to commute over there before COVID put a stop to office-based work. It's been blocked a few times lately, by barricades and military blockades which have been repeatedly built and destroyed. It scares me to think the bridge might get blocked. It's our only way to reach the airport, the hospital where my son was born and our few remaining friends still in Yangon. I've barely been over the bridge since the coup, to be honest, but I used to love going into town. It had such a buzz to it. There is actually a second bridge, but it adds an extra hour to any journey and I imagine it's been blocked too. Next to the bridge is the abandoned site of what would have been its replacement. It was a huge project, using Japanese money, but I doubt it will ever be finished now the companies have all pulled out of Myanmar. So many businesses are pulling out now. It's just not a viable market any more. My father-in-law will lose everything he has worked to build here if his last project stops."

The interviewer is nodding and making notes. 'What else do you see?'

I sigh and squint a little further away. 'On the other side of the river, I can see the Yangon Waterboom. It was a water park built at the height of international investment here. It was fun - I went a few times, but it never really took off because the prices were prohibitive for the local community. Everyone I visited it with has left now. We would have left too, had we not had this hiccup with Jasper's passport.'

'Is there anything else?'

'I can't see anything burning today, but there's been a lot of violence in the past few months, and a lot of clashes between the people and the military. That's why we are so desperate to leave. I can see the golf course where I used to play with my husband and father-in-law. And if I really crane my neck, I can just see the tip of Shwedagon Pagoda. Dylan and I had our pre-wedding shoot near there. That's a very Myanmar thing. We were sweating like crazy in a ball-gown and dinner jacket in thirty-five-degree heat!'

I smile, thinking about how the make-up artist painted one of my eyebrows black and the other dark brown (after I objected to the black with my fair colouring), and how glad I was when most of it melted off.

'Just below our apartment tower I can see a few farmers and fishermen, and then there's the rest of the city in the background.'

The light of the evening sun breaking through the monsoon clouds gives the room a sudden romantic, yellow glow, under which everything looks beautiful and peaceful. I glaze over, thinking of how mesmerised I was by the tropical skies when I first arrived in Yangon, and of how many 'perfect' sunset photos I have tried and failed to capture over the years. Now, it feels like I probably haven't taken enough. In my mind's eye, I can see the life that I had in Myanmar and it breaks my heart to think that it is nearly over.

'I have heard about the difficulties you've had with this process,' comes the old man's voice, slicing through my daydream. 'We just have some formalities to finish up and then, hopefully, we'll be able to get this application moving again.'

As I say goodbye to my interviewer, I realise I am also saying goodbye to Yangon.

I feel appreciation for the wait for Jasper's passport; despite the frustration it has also been something of a blessing. It has given us more time in Myanmar and, as is easy to say during a lull in violence and with still relatively little impact from COVID, that is something I am ultimately grateful for. I am sad that Jasper will never have a chance to know and love Yangon as we have, and as we hoped he would when he was born just a few months ago. I question whether we are making the right decision by leaving.

Once my interview concludes and I release myself from my compliant locked room, I gather Jasper in my arms. As I look at him and hold him close, I remember that despite that momentary flicker of doubt which the nostalgia of the interview triggered, my priority remains to do what is right for Jasper and for our family - sadly, that is to say goodbye to Myanmar.

13

COVID

You know something's afoot when you find yourself rifling through your business card box at nine o'clock on a Friday night, wondering if you still have that card belonging to the guy you sat next to at that black tie dinner one time. The guy who repatriates bodies.

Since the start of the pandemic, there have been tiny ripples of COVID in Myanmar, but never a wave. Not until June 2021 when, suddenly, everyone is shouting from the rooftops about how they have COVID, what symptoms they have and where they think they might have caught it. Compared to the hushed whispers of closed-door COVID confessions prior to this, it is a veritable chorus. I think there are two reasons that people are so excited to share the news of their contagion. Firstly, the quarantine centres into which the previous year's positive cases were being rounded up and thrown are now closed, so 'home-Q' as it is called, is where they get to spend their fourteen days of isolation. And secondly, having caught it means that they have been in contact with someone and that means that they have socialised. With friends! Or colleagues. Or neighbours. Whoever they are, they are people with whom these newly infected socialites have interacted in close enough proximity to exchange illness.

News of positive cases spreads mostly by word of mouth, in the absence of any official testing and reporting. We hear about friends, and friends of friends, who have it, and about their housemates or partners who have become live-in nursemaids to those who are sick, and glorified errand boys to those who are just milking the attention. Most hospitals are still closed and the handful which are both open *and* willing to treat COVID patients are full. These hospitals are also not equipped to treat even a few seriously ill patients and so most families prefer to care for their loved ones at home if they are unwell. Through my team at work, I hear about elderly family members who need oxygen and of the queues wherever oxygen tanks are being sold or refilled. The situation takes a very dark turn when we start to hear reports of soldiers shooting into crowds of desperate relatives who are lining up for oxygen at refilling stations. We feel so sorry for the people for whom the risk of being shot is worth the reward of keeping a family member alive, and we think of our own relatives back home, all of whom have avoided the virus so far miraculously. We buy ourselves an oximeter to monitor our own oxygen levels, as is the hottest trend in Yangon, and we flinch whenever anyone coughs within two metres of Jasper.

I try to impress COVID protocols onto Dylan, Tony and our helpers. I insist on everyone eating more fruit, taking vitamins and on obsessive hand-washing when we come indoors. We stop short of hoarding eggs, as advised by an influential local doctor, whose social media posts advising consumption of eggs as a way to prevent COVID cause an egg shortage, and see egg prices double. In response to the upsurge in demand for eggs, the Ministry of Health and Sports then prints a special Public Notice in one of the few remaining newspapers to inform people of 'the nutritional value of the egg-substitute food when the price goes up'. Lentils, peanuts, bean curd and bananas are among those foods to have their media moment, although the public notice seems to do nothing to dim the spotlight on eggs.

I have no social life to speak of, but I seclude further, banning Tony from the house on the weeks he goes into the office and asking Jasper's nanny and our helper not to leave the Star City compound without telling us.

The day Wai Wai comes to work with a tickle in her throat, I send her home again and ask her not to come back until she feels better. I also ask Lin to stop visiting Tony for a few days. Before Wai Wai can return to work, and before Tony notices Lin's absence, Jasper is suddenly engulfed in mucus, his body hot to the touch.

This is the first time Jasper has fallen ill. It is our first experience of him having a fever and it is frightening. He is like a human geyser, hot and oozing snot for two full days. I watch him like a hawk: monitoring his fluid intake, his foods, his poops and his energy levels vigilantly. I am terrified of his condition worsening and him needing medical care. I don't sleep or smile properly until he recovers. If I had thought there was a lot of snot when it was just Jasper, then we are swimming in the stuff once Dylan and I get sick. It seems odd to us that we should both get sick in the same way, at the same time. Ordinarily, when a cold does the rounds, I get a momentary sore throat and passing cough, a couple of days before Dylan is floored by an all-encompassing, record-breaking, hitherto unimagined, worst-ever bout of man-flu. This time, however, our symptoms are identical and seem to progress in parallel.

While Dylan and I are fighting over the tissue box, thankfully Jasper recovers as quickly as he deteriorated. This leads us to believe it is merely a forty-eight-hour bug and we assume Dylan and I will have the same luck. That is, until Dylan starts to say that he can't taste or smell things. Naturally, I don't believe him at first. On previous occasions when he has been at death's door with a common cold, he has claimed not to be able to taste anything due to the extreme, and almost certainly deadly, congestion in his sinuses. Unwilling to take his word, I want proof. I send him round the house to sniff Marmite jars, poopy nappies, toilet bleach and coffee beans. It is only when he eats a tablespoonful of Colman's Hot English Mustard without so much as a wince that I start to wonder if he might indeed be telling the truth. The following morning, I awake to a draughty emptiness in my nose and, realising I almost certainly can't smell anything, dutifully stick my face in the coffee jar. I can feel Dylan hovering behind me, with his 'I told you so' and a spoonful of Colman's at the ready. I scowl, dodge the mustard and accept the telling off but not without taking the opportunity to point out that perhaps Dylan is not the superhuman typhoid survivor he thought he was after all. I trudge my way back to bed to consider my choices. While it seems obvious that what we have is COVID, I decide again that I want hard evidence. I take my chances with one of the Lateral Flow Test pedlars I have seen doing the rounds in Signal groups and Facebook posts, and await a delivery of tests, to find out for certain if we have the lurgy. I also put off answering several calls from Tony, begging for company and carrot cake at the end of his long, lonely day working from home.

In my opinion, not enough is written about the dangers of cooking while unable to smell. On more than one occasion during my week without smell or taste, I turn apples that I am steaming for Jasper into caramel by wandering off to do something else while they are cooking and remembering them only minutes short of a stove-top fire. During an attempt to cook a hearty bolognese, I burn all the onions, not realising how much I rely on my nose to alert me to their readiness while my back is turned to chop other veg. With a second batch of onions carefully babysat as they brown, I am quite sure that the bolognese is the best I have ever made. It looks vibrant and thick and textured as I add a dash of red wine, a slosh of Lee & Perrin's Worcester Sauce and toss in some fresh herbs. It is a feast - but only for my eyes.

Having established that cooking with only sixty percent of my senses is genuinely dangerous, I am certainly not about to attempt a carrot cake for Tony. Furthermore, we don't want to give him COVID if he doesn't already have it, so I make up some excuse why he isn't allowed to visit. I make Dylan take the first COVID test as soon as the delivery arrives and the result is as expected. We stare down fourteen long days of nanny and helper-free isolation with a seven-month-old Jasper-no-naps who is almost certainly going through a developmental leap and the resulting sleep regression. He is already pushing the boundaries of our creativity, devising entertainment for a baby who is frustrated by his view of the ceiling and yet unimpressed by our attempts to prop him up. Without the option of nature walks around the estate, swims or driving range excursions, our apartment is starting to look smaller and less entertaining by the minute. As we work out a duty roster and baby entertainment shift schedule, my phone rings.

'Hello?' I say, looking at the vaguely familiar Yangon number on the screen.

'Hello. I am calling from VFS Yangon office. Your passport has arrived. You must collect in one hour. We are closing the office due to current COVID wave,' comes the breathy, garbled response.

'Wait, what? One hour? You can't do that. It will take me

at least two hours to get there. Please, please, please, say you can hold the office open until I get there,' I beg.

I know I have COVID, and I feel guilty at what I am about to do, but that passport is our ticket out of Myanmar; the long-awaited puzzle piece that will allow us to travel as freely as COVID allows, and to change our plans if needed. I scramble the driver who scoots his way from his village to our car in one of the heaviest rainstorms we have seen all monsoon. As I pace the car park waiting for him to arrive, I worry that he has crashed and fallen off his bike in his hurry to reach me. I almost consider driving myself but, despite knowing how, I don't have a local licence, or the guts to drive on the wrong side of the road in a country with few discernible road rules through townships under martial law and via a route which might be littered with military checkpoints. The idea that the driver might have fallen makes me feel worse about the fact that I have COVID and more panicked about time.

I am double masked and I try not to touch anything that he might touch as we race off towards the VFS office. I barely keep my cool as I snatch the passport out of the clerk's hand, check it and speed back out of the VFS office, rushing to get back home before Jasper's next meal. Having left home in a hurry, I have missed a feed and the pressure in my boobs is rising along with my stress level. As soon as we pull into the car park again, I thank the driver, run up the stairs to the lobby and manically stab at the button to call the lift. Once upstairs, I burst through the door of our apartment, waving the passport above my head.

'We got it! We can leave whenever we want. Start looking at flights and things while I feed Jasper,' I shout, wild with exhilaration.

As I fit myself into my personal groove in the sofa, my

phone reconnects to the wi-fi after two hours outside and off grid. My emails and messages load. One catches my eye.

'Oh god,' I say.

'What's wrong?' asks Dylan.

'It's a travel alert from the UK Government. Myanmar just went onto the UK's red list. You're no longer allowed to enter, because you're a foreigner.'

We look at one another, as I stuff my aching boob into a parched Jasper's mouth. Dylan starts to laugh. One of those maniacal laughs that descends quickly into hysteria. There is no joy in this laugh, only incredulity.

'So, we have the passport we've been waiting months for. But we have COVID so we can't fly and now we can't travel to the UK because I'm a foreigner. What *exactly* does that mean, I'm not allowed to enter?'

'It means you can't go straight from Myanmar to the UK because you can't enter from a red list country. You're not even allowed to do hotel quarantine there. So, yep - that about sums it up,' I say. 'Shit. Should we tell Tony? I've already shared photos of the passport with my family, but we haven't told anyone we have COVID yet. I guess now is the time to let Tony know why we've been avoiding him!'

We listen as Tony takes a quick ride on the same emotional rollercoaster we have just disembarked, taking in all the news we have to share. He is ecstatic about the passport, shocked by the news that we have COVID and furious to hear that there are no extenuating circumstances under which Dylan can enter the UK.

'You seem to have a bit of a cold, Tony. Are you feeling OK?' asks Dylan.

'Oh yeah, it's nothing. Just a bit of a cough stuck in my throat. I'll be right in a day or so,' Tony replies.

'I'll bring you over a COVID test anyway,' says Dylan.

'Better to know, especially if you are still planning to go to work this week.'

'But you're not allowed out.'

'I'll come later when it's quiet. Or you could come and get it?'

'Why would I come and get it? I don't need it. It'll be nothing. I don't have COVID. I'm not weak, like you guys,' Tony says with his usual blustering, mildly offensive optimism.

A few hours later, Dylan sneaks out to deliver the lateral flow test kit to Tony's apartment door. Tony rubs it in our faces that he has tested negative. Until a couple of days later, on Friday night, when Dylan's phone starts going mad with calls and messages from his family back in Australia. The message is the same on every channel and from every person 'Go and see Tony. Go and see Dad. Something is wrong.'

We look out over our balcony at all the people from the compound doing their evening exercise at the foot of our tower.

'We can't go out.' I say. 'Everyone knows we have COVID and if someone sees us, we'll be in so much trouble.' I am not scared of a telling-off from the estate management, nor of some judgemental looks from the neighbours, but I am worried about someone using our blatant flouting of COVID protocols to accuse us of higher crimes.

'I'm calling him,' says Dylan. 'You see if the clinic is still open or if you can call Jasper's doctor. But call Jen first. Find out what they are worried about. We spoke to Tony this morning and he was fine. He was ranting about The Open'

'The Open?' I ask.

'The Open Championship golf tournament in Europe. Surely, you've known Tony long enough to know how much he loves to watch golf?' says Dylan.

My hands are shaking as I follow my instructions and I have one ear open for when Tony answers the phone to Dylan.

'Tony,' says Dylan. 'Tony, are you there?'

There is a series of grunts and shuffles as Tony rearranges himself on what we know to be his faux-leather recliner.

'Yeah. Yallo. Hello.' Tony's voice is sludgier than usual and he sounds more patient.

'Tony, what's going on? Who have you spoken to back home? They are worried about you.'

'Oh. Oh, nothing. Yeah. I suppose.'

'Tony. Tell me about the golf. Are you watching the golf? Tell me about it.' If there is anything that is going to get Tony forming sentences, it is a golf major; his favourite series of events to watch and then discuss ad infinitum, every year.

'They, uh, they. Um. They just need to, uh, get the wheelbarrow.'

I stop mid-dial to Jen, Tony's wife who is back in Australia and stare at Dylan.

'I'll call the doctor first and see if he can go round there now. The clinic closes soon. Something is really wrong.'

I know it is against all protocols, and hugely selfish, to ask the only doctor serving the entire community to do us this favour, but I have Tony's negative COVID test on my side and something is clearly very, very wrong. The doctor, exhausted from his shift, agrees to make this one house call. He tells me he is taking a nurse with him. We hover in the middle of our living room motionless, but for the freshly bathed and quickly tiring Jasper wriggling in my arms. We wait for the doctor to call back with news. While we wait, Dylan speaks to his brother, his sister and his stepmother

Jen. All sound panicked and some close to tears. After a while, the doctor calls me back.

'He has COVID. And he is weak from having not eaten for a few days. And he's been reclined on his chair which is not good for his breathing. His oxygen level is low and he needs oxygen. You will need to find it somehow. Tonight, if possible. Please call me tomorrow to update me. I have sat him up and told him to eat something. Has he been vaccinated?'

'Yes, yes!' I shout with a joy that surprises the doctor and me. If I was grateful for access to the vaccine before, there are no words for how I feel now. Tony is seriously unwell but if he hadn't been vaccinated, the doctor believes he wouldn't have survived the past twenty-four hours.

It is past curfew. There are no hospitals. Oxygen refill centres are being shot up by soldiers. We have COVID. And now Tony is dying. Great. It is past Jasper's bedtime and his tiredness is doing nothing for my nerves. I leave Dylan working out what to do about oxygen and go to settle Jasper down for the night. Dylan is at least now able to partially reassure the Australian family with the news that we have identified what is wrong with Tony, even if we have no way to do anything about it. Sitting in the dark while Jasper has his last feed, I listen to Dylan trying to explain to his family why we can't break curfew, even to help Tony, and why there aren't any hospitals open. It strikes me that to anyone not living through the coup, it is for us hard to paint an accurate picture of how volatile things are on the ground in Yangon, especially given that from photos, our lives appear to be filled with golf and swimming, not bombs and barricades. My sister has said how hard it is to reconcile the horrific images they see on the news with the photos we share of Jasper.

'The welding station!' Dylan exclaims.

'What?' I stage whisper from the door of Jasper's room, still holding an almost-asleep Jasper.

'The welding station on Tony's site. That will have an oxygen canister.'

I stare at him, incredulous, as he comes closer. Unbelievably, he is right. Tony's team can't risk curfew to retrieve it tonight, but they are prepped and ready to go to site tomorrow when curfew lifts at 4am. Jasper in his cot, I finally find the business card for the corpse repatriator, giving us what we agree is a solid Plan B, and with that we clamber into bed.

As soon as Jasper wakes us the next morning, Dylan says quietly, 'Let's call Tony to see if he's alive.' It is a joke we will make every morning until we leave Myanmar, six weeks later, but that morning it cuts a little too close to the bone.

Tony is weak, but alive. He has already seen his team who have retrieved and delivered the oxygen bottle, and have somehow come by a concentrator for it. Tony has eaten some toast. He has made it from the bed to the toaster and to an upright chair in one piece. He promises us that he will eat some fried rice later if we order it to his apartment. He also promises not to have the TV so loud he can't hear the doorbell. He understands that if he doesn't open the door, we will think he is dead.

For a week we conduct spontaneous remote check-ins on Tony and, with every day that passes, it becomes apparent that he is thoroughly enjoying his new breathing apparatus. 'It's amazing,' he raves. 'I feel a little dizzy in the mornings, but thirty minutes on this, and I'm right as rain!'

This COVID experience is one punch too many for me to roll with. I can no longer pretend that everything is alright. I can no longer stand the wait. I don't even know what we are waiting for anymore (besides recovery from COVID so that we can fly). I don't like feeling responsible for both Jasper and Tony. Tony almost died and it gave me a glimpse of the regret I would feel if something were to happen to any one of us because we stayed too long. I can no longer sit still and do nothing. With very little research or thought beyond getting out of Myanmar, I book some flights. The earliest date on which there are available seats is six weeks from now, at the end of August, and the only flight I can find is from Yangon to Seoul (which takes us further away from the UK). Dylan tells me that we can't leave before Tony does and I know he's right. We are now fully responsible for him. I cry, I shout, I spend long periods sitting on our balcony in silence, feeding Jasper, deep in thought. I want nothing more than to leave Myanmar, immediately. Even though I know that's not possible, I tell Dylan over and over that I'm done. We need to leave. And Dylan, ever the rational thinker, reminds me gently that we will leave, and we can leave now that we have Jasper's passport but that there are still six weeks between now and the flight which I have booked.

I am permanently on edge. I jump at the smallest sound and panic at the slightest disruption to my day's plans. I try to distract myself with work, but all I can think about is how trapped we are. Netflix releases a new show called *How to Become a Tyrant,* which Dylan and I hope will offer some comedic insight into what's going on around us. Despite its happy-go-lucky tone, by the third episode I am forced to stop watching. As the voiceover sums up Idi Amin's successful use of violence to control his people with the statement 'when people fear you, you are in control of them', I can't breathe. It's too real and too accurate. And it feels too hopeless to imagine the lengths the military might go to in order to gain control over the Myanmar people and their brave resistance. We already have martial law in many townships across Yangon, which gives soldiers the power to arrest and oppress. The initial glimmer of hope that the General who is the driving force behind the coup might be overthrown from within his own network has faded. He has crushed his rivals by putting them all in jail. The next logical step, according to the TV series, is more violence. And I don't have space in my overloaded heart to consider the effects of yet more violence.

As soon as Dylan and I are freed from our own quarantine period, we head over to see the patient in all his oxygenated glory. He is a little slimmer, which even he agrees is no bad thing, and he is bored. But he is alive.

Having regained our taste and smell after a little over a week, Dylan and I, and possibly Jasper, are hankering after a roast dinner, so we celebrate our survival in style. We also discuss exit plans. Despite his near-miss, Tony is still not convinced that it is time to pack up; his business in Myanmar has stalled but not quite closed and he can't go home to Australia because their borders are completely shut, even to citizens. Furthermore, he thinks there is no urgent reason to leave. The way he sees it, now that we have all had COVID the worst is over.

I see things differently. As bad as we felt knowing that Tony was sick, I can't bear to think about how it would feel if it had been Jasper who needed oxygen. I feel negligent, as though I am not taking my responsibility to Jasper seriously enough.

'It was too close a call for my liking,' I say to Tony. 'I don't think any of us wants to stick around long enough for something else to happen. Even you can't deny that we have to leave. We've had COVID but there are plenty of other things that could go wrong. And, we don't even know where we got COVID from, so how can we protect against other things. We don't really know if it was Wai Wai, you or Jasper who was patient zero.'

'She's right,' agrees Dylan. 'We've been meaning to ask you, Tony. Were you sick during that week that we didn't see you?'

'No. I was fine. You said Wai Wai had a cough first,' deflects Tony.

'Wai Wai had a cough, but then Jasper got sick very quickly after. We don't know which of them had it first. Maybe you had it before them and gave it to Wai Wai and Jasper when they came to visit you? Who knows. And who cares to be honest. We all survived. Some of us with more help than others,' I say, mocking gently.

'You really scared us, Tony. Imagine if we hadn't been vaccinated,' says Dylan. 'We have already booked a flight out, Tony, at the end of August, but you need to agree to leave before us. We can't take the risk of leaving you here.'

There is a momentary silence.

'Yeah. I'll leave. I was really crook there for a minute,' concedes Tony.

14

WHERE TO?

I LONG FOR the days when travel planning was fun. I am quite sure that I have lost entire days, if not weeks of my life, pouring over a map of the world or a globe or, more realistically in recent years, a laptop, to find an exciting new holiday destination. Never before, however, have I embarked on a travel plan that is so all-consuming as trying to work out how to leave Myanmar and where on earth on the planet to go. I have a to-do list of around forty items which grows longer every time I speak to someone whose own exit plans alert me to something I have overlooked. Under normal circumstances, our options for how to reach either the UK or Australia from Yangon were via the Middle East or via a neighbouring South East Asian transit hub such as Bangkok, Singapore or Kuala Lumpur. In July 2021, none of the usual routes are available to us. And nor is Australia. Our target is the UK, or Jersey, to be more specific.

For starters, our route needs to meet some very strict criteria. Firstly, the transit hub (or hubs) must be open to passengers with a recent travel history that includes Myanmar. Secondly, the final transit hub must be on the UK's amber or green list. And thirdly, this last stopover must be somewhere that allows Australian and British tourists to stay, visa free for two weeks. Our target is the UK because Australia is closed. Once safely in the UK, we will work out what to do next, with a fall-back plan of moving to Australia as soon as they open their borders. We assume we will both be unemployed for some time and will need to scrounge off my family in Jersey for a few months, and then will continue to do the same with Dylan's family in Australia until we find our feet. We are banking on Jasper's status as the first grandchild on my side of the family and the newest grandchild on Dylan's side, to open the doors for us. Neither of us wants to say it out loud, but we are both questioning our old plan to be expats for another ten years, and we both repeatedly allude to being ready to giving up that dream in favour of stability and normalcy.

With Myanmar being on the UK's red list, we need to hide somewhere for two weeks to push it off our recent travel history. We toy very briefly with the idea of dividing and conquering, with Jasper and I heading to the UK where, as Brits, we are more than welcome to waste a couple of thousand pounds and fourteen days on a soulless hotel quarantine, and Dylan heading somewhere else to wait out the two weeks lag he needs to gain entry. But this goes against our guiding principle and what we consider our greatest pandemic decision – whatever we do, we do it together. I shudder thinking about where we might be had I gone to Bangkok for Jasper's birth. Separating, however temporarily, is an absolute last resort for us.

As well as the three non-negotiable criteria that the transit hub needs to meet, there are other considerations for which route we take, such as the length and comfort of the layover, and the overall value for money. I am already in possession of tickets from Yangon to Seoul, but I quickly realise that this route is going to mean a layover of a minimum of twenty-four hours, no matter where we go from there. The airport hotel is fully booked for the dates in question, too. There are two other routes out of Yangon which I had overlooked in my panic purchase of our Seoul tickets: one to Dubai and one to Paris. The Paris flights come up at very short notice and are ludicrously expensive. The Dubai flight leaves a week later than the Seoul one and it takes Dylan a while to talk me round to delaying our departure even by a few days. I am finally convinced by the wider range of connecting flights, the abundance of space in their very comfortable airport hotel and, as a bonus, the restaurants being open on the concourse. I book the Dubai tickets, but I keep hold of my Seoul ones too - just in case.

As far as value for money is concerned, we are hoping to avoid spending two weeks' worth of time and money climbing the walls of a hotel room, if possible. Having our first flight to Dubai booked gives us a timeline: we have six weeks to pack up and get out. We also have to help Tony navigate his own travel nightmare, as he too is unable to enter Australia where he would like to go to be reunited with his wife for the first time in almost two years. His backup plan is to go to Thailand, but their borders are closed to anyone not from the ASEAN region and tourist visas are not being issued. As luck would have it, Tony has a special APEC card, which allows him to travel freely around South East Asia, thanks to having travelled extensively in the region during the nineties and early two-thousands. This turns out to be his golden ticket into Thailand, giving him somewhere familiar and safe to wait until Australia reopens.

Dylan and I spend nearly two weeks looking at every country in the world; we assess its entry qualifications and quarantine requirements and then cross-reference that with the ever-changing UK traffic light list. We eventually narrow our options down to the US, which is very expensive, and Morocco, which is somewhat unpredictable as far as flights to the UK go, when the time comes. In the process, we study and reject some or all of the 'Stans, Georgia, South Africa, Singapore, Malaysia, Thailand, UAE, Qatar, Germany, The Netherlands, Greece where we have a wedding to attend, France, Croatia, Korea, Japan, Turkey and Scotland. During a more heated discussion around our options, I threaten to waste a private jet's worth of savings on a Hail Mary charter flight, only to be scuppered (or saved, depending on how you look at it) because even charters aren't allowed to fly freely in and out of Myanmar. Our friends Tess and Steve are going to the US where they can get a vaccination on arrival (having been unsuccessful in their hunt for one here in Myanmar) and where they have accommodating acquaintances with space to take in a couple of homeless vagrants. We thank the universe that we are vaccinated because, without that, even more of the world would be closed to us. They are booked on the same Dubai flight as us and I admit it is tempting just to follow their plan to save myself the brain juice involved in making my own, and to take advantage of their babysitting abilities en route. I am halfway down a wormhole of accommodation and transport in and around LA, with only about four weeks to go until wheels up on our Dubai flight, when I remember a conversation I had with Tess about Ireland.

'What about Ireland?' I shout to Dylan, who is sitting opposite me looking at flights and connections back from the US to the UK.

'There's no need to shout, I'm right here!' he scolds. 'What about Ireland?'

'Didn't Tess say her friend had gone there with his partner? A foreigner. Filipino maybe? They're not even married and I think they were both allowed in and did hotel quarantine there. I remember she said their quarantine hotel room had natural light, a window that opened and they were given an hour a day outside!'

'I vaguely remember this,' says Dylan.

'See if there are flights from Dubai to Dublin. Because d'you know what the best part is? Ireland is considered part of the UK for the UK's COVID travel restrictions. So, once we are into Ireland, we are into the UK! It's something called the Common Travel Area.'

The Common Travel Area refers to a long-standing arrangement between the UK, the Crown Dependencies (the Channel Islands and the Isle of Man) and Ireland. Within the Common Travel Area, the borders are open, and travel within this zone does not count as international. For the purposes of the COVID traffic light system, movement within the Common Travel Area is still permitted and some testing and quarantine protocols are less stringent. Once we are cleared by one country within the Common Travel Area, we are cleared by all. For me, in my desperation to reach Jersey, anything which makes the journey appear less risky in terms of getting stuck somewhere feels like a lifeline. In this case, the idea of reaching Ireland and knowing that from there we will be allowed to travel freely to Jersey (even if Ireland were to see a sudden surge in COVID numbers) is like a warm hug - a secret one. I feel as though I have found a loop-hole in the system.

'Well, that would certainly save us a lot of stress,' says Dylan.

'Let's hope the plan works. You get onto flights to Dublin and I'll check the immigration requirements. Also, as soon as we get something booked, I really need you to start selling some of our stuff. Our apartment still looks the same and we are leaving in a month.'

Given that he isn't working, Dylan is inexplicably dragging his feet on some of the organisational tasks that need to be done for us to leave. I feel as though I am trying to push open the door to our departure while he is leaning on it from the other side. I don't know if he's in denial about us having to leave, or if he believes that we might not have to. He tells me that when the time comes, he will fly into action and everything which needs doing will be done within days, but waiting for him to decide that it's time is adding to my stress load. I am working full time, Monday to Friday, and while I am not exactly busy, I have other things on my mind besides travel planning. I am anxious about the journey itself, however long and convoluted that might turn out to be. I am unsure about what to prepare and pack for Jasper, given that we don't know where we will be or for how long. I am both stressed and depressed that I have to ramp the milk factory up to full boob-to-mouth production in anticipation of the journey itself and also the two weeks that follow, during which I don't want to be lugging around a bottle steriliser.

I am dreading packing up the apartment. I have a spreadsheet categorising all our items to donate, sell or take; a spreadsheet which Dylan has so far not even looked at. I plan as though our final destination is Australia, somewhere we are unlikely to have the luxury of so much space, and so I am ruthless in my cull. I decide that we should sell most of our furniture, give away most household and kitchen items to friends, and donate superfluous clothes to those who need them. We will still have some items which we will need to ship, but we don't know exactly where to or when. It seems likely that our shipment might spend months at the port in Yangon before we are finally able to give a green light and an address, and I have low expectations of the standard of care there. I have photographed everything that is up for grabs, but I need help managing the sale of it all.

I have no idea how I will continue to work from a different time zone, without Jasper's nanny or our helper to support me. I am in complete denial about saying goodbye to them. Since we told them of our plan to leave at the end of August, I have witnessed each of them, on numerous occasions, sobbing quietly into Jasper's hair as they hug him tightly. I see now that he isn't only my Emotional Support Baby, he has been supporting all of us without even knowing it. I find some comfort in knowing that, however difficult the coming weeks and months are going to be, at least Jasper will be with me.

Work will be difficult to find for both Lin and Wai Wai. Most foreigners have left and most local families won't be in a position to pay the salaries our helpers deserve for the skills they have learned with us. A Myanmar family needs a helper with English language skills about as much as they need an apple pie for dinner. I am relieved that their apartment in Star City gave them access to the estate's vaccine program. I only wish there was more that I could do to help them stay safe and find new jobs.

I feel guilty about leaving my team at work too. They have been pushing me to take Jasper somewhere safer for months on account of the state of the medical system. At the start of August, the United Nations Population Fund (UNFPA) and the UN Women releases a joint statement expressing their deep concern for women, especially pregnant women, in Myanmar due to the instability of the political situation. Their statement being that of the estimated 685,000 pregnant women nationwide, 'nearly 250 preventable maternal deaths may occur in the next month alone if they are not able to access appropriate emergency obstetric care'. This shakes me up for days. Jasper was born by cesarean section for his safety and mine. The thought that had he been born just two months later he would not have had the emergency support he needed at birth, and the knowledge that the health and well-being of thousands of women is being jeopardised by 'the collapsed health system, [...] attacks on hospitals, financial barriers and movement restrictions' has me choking back tears of relief for me, and tears of devastation for the women of Myanmar.

Three of my closest colleagues are young, married women who might ordinarily have been thinking about having children in the not-too–distant future. On a call one day, one of them volunteers the fact that she 'will not have a baby until democracy is restored,' while another says she doesn't 'feel safe enough to get pregnant under the current circumstances'. It is heartbreaking to think that they might be denied the chance to be wonderful mothers. I find the myriad, deep personal impacts the coup is having on my friends and colleagues far more upsetting than anything covered in the media. I want to express my sincere empathy for their situation, but I immediately feel ashamed to say anything in the same breath as I break it to them that I am leaving Myanmar. Their initial reaction is relief that I am heeding their advice and taking Jasper somewhere safe, but when they learn that not long after leaving the country, I will also be leaving the company, I realise that they were hoping I would continue in my role remotely. It feels so selfish that I am abandoning them.

I pull my mind back to the task at hand, scouring Ireland's immigration website for rules to follow and forms to fill.

'There's something I need to tell you,' Dylan says after a few minutes of what I assume is flight searching. 'I have an interview tomorrow.'

15

CHANGE OF PLAN

'An interview? For a job here?' I feel my heart rate and my voice rising in synchrony. My breathing too starts to join the racket in my ears. 'I thought we'd agreed there wasn't any point in pursuing jobs here? We have a flight booked less than four weeks from now, what are you doing looking at jobs? Is this why you haven't sold any of our stuff? Is this why you are dragging your feet?'

'It's not for here,' Dylan says quietly.

'Oh.' I settle myself down and sit back in my chair. 'Where then? Aus?'

'It's in Mumbai.'

I am stunned. I feel my chest contract and my face go slack. I have so many thoughts racing around in my head that I struggle to pull them together into questions.

'Mumbai? Why? When did you apply for this?'

'I gave my CV to someone back in March but I didn't think it would come to anything,' Dylan explains. 'But now it has. The client wants to interview me tomorrow.'

'What kind of job? Did you know it was in India?' I am trying to make sense of such a huge potential change to our (barely formed) plans so late in the game.

'It's a project management role on a massive, super-high rise. It's a good project, but yeah, I knew it was in India.'

'Why didn't you tell me earlier?' I ask.

Dylan makes a face that tells me I already know the answer. 'I think you had enough to worry about, without wondering about whether or not I was going to be offered a job in a country with one of the world's highest COVID death rates.'

He's right. India is still reeling from its second wave of COVID, which infected millions of people and killed hundreds of thousands in only a few months. Stories we heard from India were not dissimilar to what we witnessed in Myanmar, with long queues for oxygen and a shortage of oximeters, except, with a far larger, far more densely packed population, the devastation was far worse.

The mother in me wishes that we weren't even having this conversation and remains focused on what is necessary in the coming weeks. The wife in me thinks it sounds like an incredible opportunity for Dylan and prompts the professional in me to experience a tiny ripple of excitement at the idea of working in such a vibrant market. The long-silenced, lurking adventurer in me stirs, with her interest suddenly piqued.

'OK.' I say. 'What time is the interview?'

'I don't know yet. But when I do know, I'll need your desk and I'll need it to be quiet in the house.'

'Sure. OK. I can work out here for a bit.' I motion to the kitchen table, littered with scraps of paper scribbled with country names and travel routes, our laptops, passports, vaccine certificates and other travel-planning debris. 'Wow. OK. India. Never even considered that!'

'It probably won't come to anything still. It's just an interview,' shrugs Dylan.

'But ... it might. So ... what does this mean for our plans?'

'Like I said, it might not come to anything. So, let's wait until after tomorrow. And don't mention it to anyone.'

The interview goes badly, according to Dylan. So, it is a huge surprise to both of us when, a few days later, an offer arrives in his inbox. This time it is my turn to laugh like a woman possessed, my brain fizzing as he tries to tell me the details of the offer.

'I have to get back to them in twenty-four hours,' he concludes, snapping me back into the conversation.

'Wait ... what? What do you mean? We can't make a decision that quickly.' I suddenly feel as though I am a character in a movie or a contestant on a game show, being forced to answer an impossible question under unreasonable time pressure. Except this isn't a movie or a game show, it's our life.

'How would it work?' I say finally. 'I want to go to the UK. I need to go to the UK. My family is expecting us. I can't go from here to India. I think it'll break me.'

'I know. We can't get to India from here anyway, I don't think,' says Dylan. 'I'm not sure exactly, but I think we go to Ireland, and then to Jersey, and then from there to India.'

I consider this. 'When does the job start? January or something?'

'No. I would have to be in India by 1 October.'

Suddenly I am angry. 'What? No. That's unreasonable! Do they know where you are now? What if you had a notice period? They can't possibly expect someone to be available that quickly!'

'If I can't get there by 1 October, there's no job,' Dylan says. 'And that's partly why I have to decide so quickly. Not that we have much time to be indecisive here anyway. As you say, we leave in a month and we still have an apartment full of stuff.'

'But that means we have to split up.' The words hang in the air. They are big and ugly.

'Right?' I push. 'If I want to be in Jersey but you have to go to India, that means we have to separate. I don't really see any other way.'

'Yeah. I think we do,' says Dylan sadly. 'You need to spend some time in Jersey. I can see how much you need some normality and stability around you and Jasper.'

Over the next twenty-four hours we have a lot of half-conversations about India. We discuss bits and pieces, like we whether we have visited before (I have, Dylan hasn't), whether we like the food (Dylan does, I am less enthusiastic), how far India is from each of our home countries (pretty much equidistant, similar to Myanmar) and whether we think it's safe (acknowledging that our perspective on safe is wildly different now from what it might have been a few months ago). The project sounds like a great challenge for Dylan, but neither of us is sure if we are really looking for a challenge right now. Not once do we mention how long we will be apart and I think that, deep down, each of us wishes the other will make the final call. I ask Jasper what he thinks of the idea as we watch sunset over the river that night. He gurgles and wriggles in response, which is just as helpful as anything Dylan or I have said.

'I say we do it,' I declare the next morning, as the clock ticks closer to Dylan's deadline. I sound more convinced than I am.

'Do you mean that?' asks Dylan.

'I think I do,' I say. 'We don't really want to give up being expats, do we? And we don't really have a plan for once we reach Australia. We also don't *really* want to be both unemployed and sponging off our parents for a few months, do we? So ... even if India isn't somewhere we've ever considered before, and even if it's not exactly ideal given how badly it has suffered with the pandemic, I think that, right now, it might actually be our best option.'

It's a round about way to make a decision, I realise, but as I say it out loud, I think it sounds almost sensible.

'What's the worst that can happen?' I am smiling. 'Oh, that's right ... we could get stuck in a military coup in the middle of a pandemic with a newborn baby. Lightning doesn't strike twice.'

'If you really mean it then, thank you,' says Dylan. 'I didn't want to say how much I want this job because I know you just want to go home and get some stability around you before we make any big decisions. But I really think this is good for us. It's better than giving up and going home, I think.'

'Don't get me wrong, I would prefer to make this decision from the UK and I really wish we didn't have to split up but ... divide and conquer, as they say. Our families are going to think we've gone mad. I'm not looking forward to telling my mum that we're moving to India. She'll think I've lost the plot entirely.'

Dylan laughs. 'So, we're moving to India.'

'Looks like it,' I say. 'On one condition though ... we don't let ourselves get emotionally attached. We take a furnished place and we don't invest financially or emotionally in Mumbai. I don't care if it's a democracy, I don't want to get too comfortable there. I don't think I could take this heartbreak all over again.'

'Deal,' says Dylan. 'Although we'll be there five years, at least.'

I stare at him. 'Five years?'

'That's how long the project is,' he says. 'Does that change anything?'

I don't know what I was expecting. We have been in Myanmar for longer than that and I know that construction projects take time. But hearing Dylan say that it's a five year commitment gives me momentary cause to wonder if perhaps we are taking the decision too lightly. Five years is a long time in Jasper's life. I think back to when I arrived in Yangon and I wonder what I might have done differently had I known that I would be here for so long. I realise that the only difference might have been that I wouldn't have explored the country with such eagerness in my early months, and I make a mental note not to put off travelling around India on the basis of there being time later.

'No,' I say to Dylan finally. 'I guess not.'

We relish the relief of having a final, final destination in hand for the shortest of minutes, before thudding back down to the reality of our immediate situation. We are in Myanmar, sitting in an apartment full of things, with only one flight booked as far as Dubai.

'Well, let's get it all booked then,' I say. 'I'll do hotel quarantine in Ireland and work out what forms we need to fill in for immigration. You do connecting flights from Dubai to Dublin and look at how we get to Jersey once we are released. We can book your India flights from Ireland, once you have a contract, I guess.'

And then, finally, the dominoes begin to fall.

16

PACK

FOR A LITTLE OVER TWO WEEKS, we have a revolving door at our apartment, through which bargain hunters and new homeowners pour, to take advantage of our flash sale of items which I have carefully curated and collected over six years. From my home office, I have to keep one eye on Dylan after I catch him almost agreeing to sell some paintings of mine which were a thirtieth birthday present, commissioned by my mother and painted by a friend. I give him a proper talking to after he pops in to ask if I am willing to sell a six-foot sneezewood giraffe sculpture we brought back as a souvenir from our honeymoon in southern Africa.

He gives me the slip the day he sells my beloved DeLonghi toaster and kettle, leaving me with no way to make tea for a week. I am trying to pull my weight as a salesman too, in between work calls, feeding sessions, packing and farewells. On one occasion I sell my nearly-new bespoke dresser to a neighbour who sends round some lifter-shifters to lug it across the estate. It is only after it has gone, that I realise I left all but one of my fraying, milk-stained maternity bras in the top drawer. I call the buyer, who is nonplussed having received an empty dresser, and I am then forced to chase down the removal team, one of whom admits to rummaging through the drawers and deciding that some raggedy old bras are just what his wife needed as a gift. I don't know if I am more embarrassed at the state of my now well-travelled underwear or the fact that I so desperately need it back. I feel mortified as I wait for it to be biked back from the village whence it has already been dispatched.

We give away a lot of things to our helpers, to the golf caddies and to my colleagues. What starts as a well-managed sale soon becomes a free-for-all. Everything must go. I give bin sacks full of clothes to Lin who, in turn, has a whale of a time selling them on Facebook - spending hours modelling and photographing them all with her friends. My colleagues come to collect their items at weekends, and I arrange their visits for a time when I will be able to hide my awkwardness behind Jasper. They are also keen to meet or see him and are unaware that his presence masks some of the guilt I feel for leaving when so many people are unable. And when I have said my goodbyes, I bury my face in Jasper's little neck and squash the rising sadness back inside. Today is not the day to fall apart.

We pack boxes. And we pack more boxes. And when the shipping company comes, they pack more boxes. As I sort through cupboards and shelves, I come across the pen that Dylan and I used to sign our marriage certificate - a gift from his grandmother. While I don't necessarily believe in destiny or fate, I can't help but take a breath when I am reminded by the box that it is Rudyard Kipling themed; soft green in colour, adorned with the tiny head of a wolf, inspired by the wolf pack in *The Jungle Book*. Around the top of the cap, the first and last lines of his poem *If* are engraved. Suddenly, I see a faint romanticism to our move from Myanmar, or Burma as Kipling would have known it when he wrote the poem *Mandalay*, to India.

It is sobering to see the sum of our life packed into a series of short cardboard monuments, comprising mostly impractical items like Jasper's toys and an ostentatious excess of golf outfits. But we are so much luckier than many expats who left with nothing but a backpack. I allow myself a couple of items of furniture which are particularly meaningful or beautiful, and I bring lots of sentimental paintings, fabrics and artefacts to fill our new place with happy memories from Myanmar.

Besides the things that go into boxes, I have the luggage we are carrying with us to consider. My faith in any sort of system has been shattered irreparably by COVID, the coup and our passport issues, so I take a glass-half-empty approach and try to pack for any and every eventuality. I think about all the what-ifs of getting stuck in one place or the next, of losing a suitcase and even of the horror of being separated from Jasper for some reason. I think, by the time I am finished, our hand luggage is about forty percent documentation, forty percent nappies, twenty percent spare clothes and a breast pump. All my jewellery is tucked in between the nappies. We hear rumours of military checkpoints between the city and the airport, at which departing passengers are subjected to invasive luggage checks and are forced to hand over gems and jewellery. As with so many things, it is not the monetary value of my jewellery that concerns me, but the sentimental.

I book us a night in Dubai airport and then the obligatory thirteen nights in the Dublin quarantine hotel. I search for nearby supermarkets in Ireland that can deliver Jasper's nappies and check for any evidence that we might get early release for good behaviour or a negative test. Sadly, there doesn't seem to be any flexibility. If hotel quarantine is what it takes for us to enter the Common Travel Area, then hotel quarantine it has to be.

Unless ... Ten days before we set off, my younger sister makes a game-changing discovery that alters our trip and our mental states entirely. She happens to be perusing the Irish immigration website one day when she spots a new section under entry requirements, entitled 'Exemptions for Fully Vaccinated Persons'.

'You and Dylan are vaccinated, right?' says her message, which comes out of the blue one afternoon.

'We are,' I respond, in between work calls.

'I don't think you have to do hotel quarantine.' With this bold statement, she sends a screenshot of the website.

I stare at her message. My heart sinks. We have a plan and it seems to be one that will work. I don't think I have the energy to explore other options at such a late stage and after so much effort. The India pivot already took a lot out of me and I don't think I want to consider a deviation from our current plan.

'We leave in a little over a week. I don't think I want to make any changes.' I send back.

'I called them. And it's true. If you're vaccinated, you don't have to do the hotel quarantine. You could get an Airbnb or something,' comes the reply. I am surprised at her persistence, but then I remember that she's seeing things with fresher eyes than I am and this irritates me.

I sit at my desk with my head on one hand, staring into space for a while. Dylan pops his head round the door. 'What's up? You look stressed again,' he says.

I exhale. 'Alice thinks we don't have to do Hotel Q in Ireland.'

'What? How? We do, don't we? Why did she say that?' Dylan sounds surprised but looks cynical. I show him her messages and the screenshot. And then open the same website on my laptop.

'I mean ... it looks like maybe they've changed the rules. And Alice is a lawyer, and if she says we don't have to do Hotel Q, maybe we don't have to do Hotel Q,' I say studying Dylan's face for signs that he is on the same page as me as far as not making changes to our plan this late in the day. There are none.

'This is awesome news! So, we can rent a house somewhere? Ooh - do you think we can get a tennis court? I'll look for something. We can hire a car. I've always wanted to visit Ireland. I'll ask my friend where his family's from. Maybe we can go there?'

Dylan is as excited as I am reluctant, as energised as I am deflated by the news.

'Fine,' I say. 'If you can find a place and a car, then I'll cancel the Hotel Q. I don't want to cancel it until we really know that we don't need it. I don't think I can handle the disappointment if anything goes wrong with the idea of a house, so I'm going to work on the basis we are doing the quarantine.'

Dylan finds us the perfect hideaway for our time in Ireland. So perfect that I agree to cancel our hotel and recommit to the concept of waltzing through the airport in Dublin and setting off for a staycation, rather than offering myself up to be bundled into a quarantine transit. The Irish holiday house does indeed have a tennis court, and it is well placed for walks to the beach and shopping at a nearby Tesco. It is far too big for us, but at such short notice, and after the month we've had, we don't care that we have four bedrooms more than we need.

I run through my checklist of preparations, double and triple checking that our route meets all necessary criteria. First transit hub accepting passengers from Myanmar? Yes, Dubai is open to all; vaccine or no vaccine. Second transit hub on UK's amber or green list? More than yes for Ireland – a sneaky back door. Australians and Brits allowed to stay visa free? Yes; more points to Ireland.

For our last few nights in Myanmar, we are staying at the hotel in the estate where Jasper was born. I decide it is easier to pack up and completely empty the apartment a few days before flying, rather than having a mad scramble on the day we leave, or having to sleep a night without any furniture. Those days at the hotel are how I imagine the centre of a tornado. We know everything is still swirling outside the hotel, but we have enough peace and quiet to ignore it.

Tony joins us for a day and a night, and then flies out to Thailand on a flight that, much to our relief, leaves a few days ahead of our own. We insisted that he leave before us because we don't entirely trust that he won't change his mind at the last minute and hang around in case fortune is planning to favour the stubborn. Not only would the Australian family never forgive us for abandoning Tony there, we don't like his chances of surviving without us for company. The four of us enjoy one last swim in the pool, one last beer on the terrace, one last dinner in the restaurant and say some very emotional farewells. We don't know when we will next see Tony. His plan, insofar as he has one, is to wait things out in Thailand until Australia reopens its borders, at which point he will return home. We, in turn, are hoping to be reunited in India by the end of the year and we have no idea how much longer COVID will be lurking. We aren't only saying goodbye to one another, we are saying goodbye to a shared experience quite unlike anything we had ever lived through before, and to the country we all consider our home. It is a good thing Jasper is robust, because Tony almost squeezes the life out of him before I dive to the rescue.

The last thing we need to do before leaving Myanmar is pass a COVID test. This is more than a little nerve-wracking considering that we have only recently recovered from COVID. Nothing makes me lose hope more than hearing from our Dutch friend how she continues to test positive for COVID three months after recovering from it. I book us in for tests at the Airport Cargo Terminal, which comes with the added benefit of a lounge pass at the airport while we await our flight. Timing is crucial, of course, for our test to be still valid by the time we arrive in Ireland, after an overnight layover in Dubai. The experience is surprisingly civilised, unless you are Dylan who is convinced the swabber gouges so hard, she dislodges some cartilage in his already twice-hockey-broken nose. There are no lines as only our flight is leaving the next day. But that doesn't mean the labs work any faster. The long wait for the results makes for a highly charged atmosphere over dinner and breakfast.

'What if one of us fails?' I ask Dylan.

'I've thought about this. I think if I fail, you and Jasper leave anyway. If you fail, then we all have to stay because I can't really travel with Jasper but without his food supply!'

'Oh my god, imagine if one of us fails. We have nowhere to stay. We'd have to be in a hotel or something. And the next flight out isn't for almost a month. And your visa might be up before we were able to fly. And then our Ireland bookings, and your India job ...'

'You can't think about it. Because there is nothing we can do at this stage. At least we know we've had COVID and that we've recovered.'

'I know, but I can't help it. I think this is worse than the wait to get Jasper back. And the wait to see if Tony was still alive. This is literally the final hurdle between us and freedom from all this stress!'

To our enormous relief, Dylan and I both pass our COVID tests, and can exhale, pack up and set off for the airport. After a last drive, Dylan and I leave our barely used car with a friend of mine, its glove compartment stuffed with leftover cash. After a considerable test-driving period during which she is supposed to be trying to sell it, my friend decides the easiest thing is just to buy it off us. There's nothing quite like buying a car just before a pandemic, and then having to sell it for half price in the middle of a political and economic crisis, to make you feel a fool.

'Are we sure this is the right decision?' I half-joke to Dylan on the way to the airport.

'What? To leave Myanmar? Or to go to the UK? Or India? Or all of it?' he asks.

'Leaving Myanmar. No, no, it is. It's the right decision. It's easy to forget about the violence and the cash situation and the medical system when you're in a five-star hotel on a private estate. But no, it's the right decision. Not our choice, but the right call.'

We drive in silence the rest of the way to the airport, holding our breath for roadblocks, jewellery thieves and armed patrols. We are also terrified of having our phones taken and searched, as many people have been arrested for content that has either been saved on their phone, or which simply appeared on their Facebook newsfeed when a soldier decided to go snooping. Not that we have anything incriminating on our phones, but the way the rumour mill has been churning lately, we expect they'd find any excuse to give us a traumatic shake down, at the very least.

Luckily, we see nothing.

17

WHEELS UP

OUR FIRST TIME travelling as a three rather than just a two was always going to be different. But this trip isn't only our first as a family, it is our first in almost two years, our first under COVID protocols, our first international relocation together and certainly the first time we have fled a coup. There is so much about the journey that is unpredictable and so much about the circumstances that make me nervous. I find comfort in preparation and rehearsal so, by the time our first plane is ready to take off, I will have mentally walked through every step of the journey many times and roleplayed every potential confrontation.

I am breaking our trip, or mission, as I like to see it, into three stages. For each stage, I have prepared a bulging document wallet and a detailed timeline for all the tasks that we must complete in order to advance to the next level. Stage one is to get out of Myanmar. For this we need originals and copies of negative PCR tests, translated and notarised vaccine certificates, travel declarations and, of course, flight tickets. We also have to find one thousand US dollars, in cash, in case an opportunist immigration officer decides to call in Jasper's visa overstay debt. Technically speaking,

Jasper has been living in Myanmar illegally for almost nine months now because he doesn't have a visa. The reason he doesn't have a visa is because he had no passport for most of those months. The day I collected his passport was the day the VFS office shut down and many of the government administrative offices shut too, including the one which handles visas. I tried to get him a visa to avoid any funny business at the airport but, despite much support from my HR department, there was no way to do it with the office still closed.

Jasper's overstay fine isn't the only hurdle we are expecting to jump at the airport. A couple of weeks ago, a demand was made by the Authorities that financial institutions submit a list of any foreigners working for them and that these Authorities be informed any time one of these foreigners leaves or enters the country. The incident with the salary exposures earlier in the year made me feel as though I was being watched and this move compounds that fear, even before I take into account the fact that I am not only a foreigner working for a financial institution, but I am also attempting to leave the country with an illegal baby. As I arrive at the airport, I realise that I have no idea the degree of success with which this demand was handled by my employer. They confirmed they submitted a letter which detailed the travel plans for my permanent departure from Myanmar, but I have no receipt to show this has been done. This makes me very nervous going through the airport, especially as we have heard stories of foreigners being held up at immigration or, worse still, dragged off their flight for some arbitrary reason.

We approach the immigration desk as a family and hand over our passports. As we expected, the officer picks up that Jasper's passport is short of a visa and sends Dylan off to the cashier counter. While I wait, the officer asks me to pull down my mask, much to Jasper's fascination from where he is sitting, strapped to my front, within arm's reach of the mask. The officer scrutinises my face and goes through my passport. And then he goes through it again. And a third time for luck.

'Entry stamp,' he barks, eyeballing me.

I look back at him over Jasper, who is now determined that he too can play at taking my mask on and off.

'Entry stamp,' he repeats, louder this time.

'It's in …' I trail off. Oh, shit. 'It's, um, it's in another passport.'

'Please show other passport.' He thrusts his hand out over the counter.

'I don't have it,' I say slowly. I know exactly where that passport is: in a box, on its way to storage at the port. The last time I entered Myanmar, at the end of our honeymoon back in early 2020, I did so on an old passport in my maiden name with my then-visa inside. Having changed my name and acquired a new passport, and having renewed my visa during COVID using this new passport, I completely forgot that my last entry stamp would be in the old one.

'What's wrong?' says Dylan, coming back from the cashier counter, stuffing the money he had clearly avoided paying into his wallet.

'I don't have an entry stamp in my passport,' I tell him. 'It's in the old passport.'

'So get that one out,' hurries Dylan. 'You brought it, right? You showed it to me and asked if you needed it. I thought we agreed to bring it?'

'I packed it into a box,' I say with increased panic. 'I don't remember why, I think I just packed it without thinking.'

'What? Why? I thought you were going to bring it?'

'Don't get angry with me, please. It doesn't help. Shit. What do we do?' The last part I say under my breath to

Dylan, avoiding eye contact with the immigration officer, and gently batting one of Jasper's mischievous little hands away from my mask.

Is this it, I think? After all the stress and the planning and the organisation, am I going to be the one who lets the team down and prevents us from boarding the flight? I have visions of myself being bundled off to some holding cell somewhere, boobs exploding, while Dylan and an unfed Jasper are sent on without me.

'Just move back, Milla,' Dylan snaps. 'I'll talk to him.'

Dylan shows the immigration officer his passport and his entry stamp.

'We came in together,' I interrupt from behind Dylan.

'Please, Milla. I'll handle this,' Comes the very abrupt dismissal from Dylan. I feel the tears welling up and bury my face in Jasper's few soft wisps of white blond hair.

The sound of the stamps in the passports snaps me quickly out of my spiralling reverie of self-pity and makes me jump.

'How could you have forgotten your old passport?' Dylan asks as soon as we are through the barrier.

'I don't know, OK. Please just let it go. It doesn't help, you being angry with me.'

I shuffle through security in silence, feeling like a naughty child but making sure to do everything I am told and with smiling eyes above my mask. I am lightheaded and my hands are unsteady as I gather my belongings. Once through security, Dylan takes my hand and apologises.

'I'm sorry. I am just stressed, and that wasn't something we had planned for,' he says. 'But we're a team, right? We just need to get out of here and we can all relax. And from now on, it should be plain sailing.'

I nod, and squeeze his hand back. We join our friends in the airport lounge and slowly my mood lightens.

'You'll never guess what Milla just did,' opens Dylan, by way of a greeting.

'Oh, thanks for that,' I say, giving Dylan a friendly shove.

I confess my stupidity in having packed my old passport into a box, a story which is met with gasps and looks of horror, followed by relieved laughs.

'You're lucky they just want us all out of here,' says Steve.

I nervously sip coffee, spoon some sloppy milk porridge into Jasper's mouth and count down the minutes until they call us to board. As well as our masks, the airline wants us to wear some flimsy, blue, rear-tied smocks, latex gloves and shoe covers as supposed protection gear. Given that I need front access to Jasper's food supply and that the gloves make no sense to me at all, I rebel. I toss the gloves and style my smock into more of a cape.

I don't relax until the wheels are off the tarmac and, even then, I can feel a little ball of fear lodged deep in my oesophagus. Jasper sleeps for some of the flight, feeds for some of it and plays on the floor by our feet for the rest. He isn't happy but his ears don't pop and he doesn't turn into a gremlin either, which I consider a win. I don't stand up once for the entire six hours of the flight. I don't quite have the energy and I don't want to leave our little seat-row bubble. I don't even have the energy to play one last game of 'Guess what colour cake?' for old time's sake. I am nervous and want to be invisible, so I am lucky that Jasper's digestive system is equally still for the duration.

I am grateful for the dead weight of a sleeping Jasper. He is pinning my arms so that I am unable to reach my phone and scroll through old photos. Usually when I leave a country, be it after a holiday or a longer stay, I spend the flight reminiscing about all the wonderful experiences I have had and reliving all the beautiful memories. This time, I try to focus more on what lies ahead to save myself from the sadness I know I will feel if I think too much about what I am leaving behind.

Getting off the plane and walking through Dubai airport is surreal. I feel as though I am sleepwalking or like I have been hypnotised, in step and in line with my fellow passengers. I float through the terminal, marvelling at the bright lights, the functioning air conditioning, the presence of other people buzzing to their destinations. I smell fat frying and hear cutlery clashing - the hubbub of operational F&B outlets. It has been twenty months since I was last in an airport, let alone a different country. Friends who left Myanmar sooner than us told me that, once they stepped off the plane, they felt as though a weight had been lifted off their shoulders. I know what they mean. It isn't just a weight off my shoulders, especially as Jasper's ten kilo mass is once again strapped to me. It is as though my skin weighs less, and my bones and hair. I feel as though my lungs are opening, allowing me to breathe down into their depths for the first time in months, and even my eyeballs feel refreshed. The muscles in my neck and jaw relax, and the lightest of smiles creeps on to my face, raising my cheeks just a fraction underneath my mask.

'We're out,' I say to Dylan. 'We're actually out.'

'Can you believe it? How do you feel?'

'I feel weird. I don't think I realised how much weight I was carrying. Nothing seems quite real.'

Of course, neither the physical nor the emotional journey is over yet, but I already feel revitalised. With our exit from Myanmar complete, we advance to stage two of the journey, which is to get to our holiday house Ireland.

But first, a toast.

Dubai is one of those brightly lit, temperature-controlled transit hubs where it's hard to ascertain what time of day it is and which meal is most appropriate, but we know we want a beer. After checking into our hotel room, we reconvene with our friends to choose a restaurant to enjoy our first taste of freedom. The clink of glasses followed by a crisp sip of a Brewdog IPA and a toast to Myanmar brings with it such a release of emotions. It might be because I haven't tasted a craft beer in so long, or because I have almost forgotten what it is like to have a meal out at a restaurant, but whatever the reason, that beer seems to unlock a world in colour. I sit back and let the tension dissolve as exhaustion and joy wash over me. For the first time in months, I don't really mind what happens next; I have my husband and son with me, I have a functioning credit card and I am no longer being watched. We are just regular people on their holidays.

The second leg of our journey couldn't be more different from the first. We swap water for wine, indistinct baked goods for fresh salads, and dodgy PPE for plush blankets and sleep socks at the hands of Emirates Business Class. Our vaccination certificates cause a slight stir at the check in because, unsurprisingly, nobody has seen a Burmese one before, but the rest of our documentation is accepted without question, as is our confident announcement that no, we do not need to go into hotel quarantine on arrival in Dublin.

I am quite sure we aren't the staff's favourite passengers on that flight. We are repeatedly told off for forgetting to put our masks back on, seconds after eating or drinking, and for letting Jasper play on the floor in front of our seats. I apologise for all our many offences, but the reality is that it all feels so very trivial after what we have been through over the past few months. Adrenalin is leading my, usually very obedient, self astray. We don't cause any real ruckus, however, and are allowed to disembark like normal people. As we collect our bags, we scan the baggage hall for any evidence of lurking Garda or hazmatted minions ready to pounce on anyone silly enough to cough or sweat. But there is nothing. Absolutely no sign whatsoever that a quarantine hotel is even a thing, let alone a thing to which unvaccinated passengers from designated countries are duty bound to submit.

'Thank god we didn't go ahead with our hotel quarantine booking!' I mutter in hushed tones to Dylan. 'I don't see any signs anywhere saying that anyone has to do it. I was expecting a separate line and a shuttle bus for the quarantine passengers. Thank god for Alice, noodling around on that website.'

We smirk at each other in gleeful collusion, hold our heads high and waltz through into the arrivals hall. I am still half expecting someone to ask to see our documentation, but nobody does. All we have to do is collect our hire car and, by the looks of it, we are away.

I say 'all' we have to do is collect the car. If Dylan and I ever get divorced it will be over navigational differences. At its core, the issue is: Dylan likes to set off and then bark orders at me on how to use the GPS and how to guide him to his destination. I would prefer to look at where we are going, load the coordinates into the GPS and then set off. See? Differences. A secondary issue is that I don't like driving. This automatically designates me as navigator and, apparently, I am not allowed to say I dislike both driving and navigating. Although, for the record, I do. We have hired a car for our two weeks in Ireland. We aren't exactly travelling light, with three large suitcases, Jasper's buggy, several small bags, Dylan's golf clubs and a baby, so it is a large car. More like a small van. No sooner have we loaded our things, including an uncharacteristically anxious baby, into the back of it than Dylan takes off out of the car park. I think it is about 15 minutes later that we pull into a semi-urban McDonald's so a bawling Jasper and I can comfort one another, and so I can take myself as far away from the car, and from Dylan, as possible.

Navigation is hard in a city you don't know or understand and in a country with actual traffic laws. Give me a countryside lane and I'll help you identify your turnings from your field entrances all day, but put me on an inner-city ring road and ask me how to find the nearest service station and I am no use to you at all. I think I am shouting. I am almost certainly swearing and I am definitely crying. And then I accept that perhaps all this pent-up anger and emotion isn't entirely the fault of our being lost on the outskirts of Dublin. Perhaps one airport beer and one fancy flight isn't enough to unwind the months of tense uncertainty from which we have just emerged. We don't get divorced and neither do we spend two weeks in that McDonald's forecourt. We do travel most of the rest of that drive in silence, save for the intermittent radio signal which brings us some soothing Irish voices reading inconsequential news and reminding us that it rains a lot in Ireland.

My body feels numb while my mind processes the fact that Myanmar is no longer our home. My eyes see only a blur of green as the Irish countryside rushes past, seeming both familiar and completely new. Now that we are here, I am daunted by the coming days, weeks and months. Suddenly I don't want to look forwards or backwards, I only want to exist in this moment right now, where I am together with Dylan and Jasper.

PART III

18

THE SUPERMARKET

Hot on the heels of our almost divorce in the McDonald's parking lot on the outskirts of Dublin, Dylan and I get into a custody battle in the ham aisle of Tesco Extra. Firstly, I must address the fact that there is a ham aisle. Not just an empty few inches of shelf space in a generic refrigerator section. An entire aisle dedicated to the hams of Ireland. There are smoked hams, baked hams, honeyed hams, crumbed hams, thick sliced, thin sliced and wafer-thin sliced hams. There are multipack hams and hams on special offer. There are fine artisanal hams and basic run-of-the-mill put-me-in-your-sandwich hams. There are hams almost past their sell-by date that look better than anything we have seen in years in Myanmar. And every kind of ham is fighting in at least three different weight classes. As we stand there, bamboozled by the world of hams we have just unlocked by setting foot in the largest supermarket I have seen in years, it becomes clear that we need to divide and conquer. And neither of us wants custody of Jasper in his tired, hungry, impatient state. It is 6pm on the day we arrived in Ireland from our long-haul flight. Dylan and I are riding high on emotion and a lack of substantial food, and Jasper has turned into the Demon Baby of Ballygarrett. We stop just short of a physical fight over who is going to push the trolley and who has to manhandle the kamikaze baby who appears hell bent on throwing himself head first onto the epoxy flooring, but there is a war of words like those hams have never seen before. I end up with the trolley, while Dylan has to restrain the baby, and we learn the hard way that shopping angry is even worse than shopping hungry. Instead of too much of everything, we end up with not enough of anything and are forced to return to the scene of the crime the following morning.

We do so in much better spirits. Showered, rested and fed on the odd assortment of Cadbury's Fingers, black pudding and crumpets that we bought the night before, we hope we are unrecognisable as we stroll into the supermarket with the awe and reverence a normal person might reserve for their first visit to a theme park. Dylan and I are back on speaking terms so it feels like a proper family day out.

There is a Costa Coffee at the entrance to this supermarket. Serving customers hot drinks while they shop is an excellent strategy, in my opinion, if the objective is to turn what could be a quick shop into a slow meander. Personally, clutching a too-hot coffee ensures that I go category by category, aisle by aisle, shelf by shelf in order to finish the drink before I return to the car. Having totally forgotten to buy any store cupboard staples like tea or coffee on our disastrous first visit the night before, both Dylan and I are in need of a caffeine fix before we embark on, what we expect will be an epic and hopefully more fruitful, mission.

Before arriving in Ireland, I had a plan to wean Jasper off the boob and onto formula gradually. But as soon as we set foot in our holiday house, I decide I simply can't face one more minute of the painful 'will he or won't he feed before my boobs turn to stone' dance. I shutter the factory without a second thought. Granted, that decision subsequently leads to several contemplative sessions in front of the bathroom mirror, squirting excess milk out of increasingly lumpy, over-productive milk glands, but I couldn't be happier knowing that I never have to feed him again. I know to some people it sounds terrible, but I can honestly pinpoint the moment I genuinely start to enjoy being a mother as the exact same moment I stop breastfeeding.

My snap decision that Jasper will thenceforth be formula fed leads us somewhat urgently to the infant nutrition section of the supermarket on this second visit. Wow, what a cave of wonders. Since Jasper started on solids, he has been treated to home-steamed, home-blitzed, home-frozen cubes of seasonal vegetables with a side of handheld flavour wands to broaden his palette and refine his motor skills; a hybrid of traditional and baby-led weaning. Proud though I was of my Instagrammable rainbow freezer in Yangon, and easy though I found the 'one cube or two' portion control strategy, Jasper's homemade diet was purely down to necessity. Not only was the milk formula supply chain patchy in Myanmar, but baby ready meals were simply not available. Our options were homemade seasonal fruit and veg blends, or fried rice. 'Seasonal' makes it sound lush, organic and low mileage. All I mean is that I bought and batch cooked whatever was on the supermarket shelf that day, in case there was nothing there the next.

Standing in that aisle at Tesco, I can't believe the choice in front of me. In the same way that hams come in all shapes and sizes, so too, it seems, do the chunks in the helpfully age-labelled baby food pouches. I take one of everything suitable for a nine-month-old. After all, we are in Ireland for two weeks, and I don't have the energy or equipment to cook and freeze a bunch of seasonal veg. And why would I when I am looking at a wall of flavours and textures that will take Jasper months to work through?

Besides the edibles, there are decisions to make about which brand of nappies to choose, what kind of wet wipes and baby shampoo and bibs and water cups and cutlery and crockery and bath toys. Almost everything Jasper owned up until this point was inherited, which was wonderful, not only because we couldn't have bought half of it stuck where we were, but also because standing in front of that vibrant cornucopia of baby items, each more ergonomic or eco-friendly or likely to make your child a genius than the next, I feel incredibly overwhelmed. I see just how much money I might have wasted had I had access to this choice sooner. Before my eyes melt out of their sockets, I grab the tub of milk powder which brought me to the aisle in the first place, and set off to where Dylan and Jasper are already nose deep in the bakery section.

Is there a better smell in the world than freshly baked bread? I would argue no. Back in Yangon, our residential estate had a small bakery from where, if we timed our visit correctly, we would be able to buy a baguette, two or three times a week. Other than the baguette, which was passable, all the other items in the bakery were monstrous amalgamations of sweetened dough, meat floss, chicken sausage and some kind of sugary gunk that didn't know if it was cream or cheese. Before the coup, we had been able to buy a proper farmhouse loaf from a trendy, local deli called Sharky's, named after the owner and Myanmar Master Chef judge Sharky himself. Sadly, the road closures and erratic patrols dampened our enthusiasm for making a ninety-minute round trip just for a loaf of bread, and we settled for some poor-quality sliced loaf instead. At Easter, I made my own hot cross buns, which turned out more like hot cross pebbles, to be honest, and one day when I was feeling particularly homesick, I treated myself to a high tea of homemade scones (no clotted cream sadly). There were a few shelves of bread-like items in our local City Mart supermarket, but they were mostly things I might buy to survive on rather than to enjoy. Anything labelled as 'toast bread' was undoubtedly sweet, had an expiry date five years in the future and didn't fit in the toaster. The one thing we did quite like were the burger buns, complete with sesame seeds, for the rare occasions we could buy burger patties. Don't even get me started on what passed as cake in Yangon, because the thought of those insubstantial, sugary tufts of sponge slathered in the metallic-tasting, violently-coloured byproduct of a school science experiment dissolving on my tongue, makes me genuinely sad for the people of Myanmar. And that's saying something considering what else they are dealing with currently.

Against this background, I probably don't need to explain just how wild we go in this Tesco Extra bakery. Like carb-starved raiders, we load up our trolley with enough warm, doughy comestibles to make up for the two-year deficit. Hot cross buns for breakfast, lunch and dinner. Springy sourdough to accompany the platter of hams we are inevitably going to come away with. Baguettes for snacks. Flapjacks for snacks. Cookies for snacks. More crumpets for tea. And hot dog buns for the many, many sausages we plan to BBQ this evening. We are relatively efficient in the ham section on this second run and barely pay any attention to the sausages as we fling them into the trolley on the basis that they will all be good.

Good bread, good sausages and good ham deserve good condiments too. We ooh and ah at the selection of chutneys, pickles and sauces. In Yangon the pickle selection was gherkins or no gherkins, depending on whether the shipment had come in and chutneys didn't exist. There was one time I had made my own pineapple chutney to use up a massive over order of fresh pineapples but our apartment smelled of vinegar for weeks after and that somewhat dulled our hunger for homemade chutney. For years we carried suitcase loads of Branston Original over from the UK, until I discovered the lifeline worldwide delivery service that is the British Corner Shop. I admit I may have gone a little too hard at the chutneys and pickles section of their website during COVID and before leaving Yangon, I donated hundreds of pounds worth of unopened jars to the one British friend who decided to stay.

As we admire our tower of meats and breads, we realise we have skipped the entire fresh section. Dylan is a self-confessed, cheap and nasty supermarket coleslaw addict, and I am someone who loves salad but can't really be bothered to make my own dressings. For both of us, the fresh food and, in particular, the 'fresh and already prepared food' section in the supermarket is a veritable mecca. And it is also something that didn't exist in most supermarkets in Myanmar. Fried food was easy to come by. Fresh food not so much. Without restraint, I throw one of every flavour of small, unsustainably packed salad into the trolley. It doesn't matter what the base is, if it is in a pot with a dressing on it, I want it. And from salads I move to hassle free, no cook reheatables like sweet potato wedges, buttered corn, potato gratin and pre-chopped veg. And from the lazy cook's corner, I cruise on over to the dips. In Yangon I would make my own hummus, which is admittedly very easy. Easier, it turns out, than navigating the hummus area in a modern supermarket. Either my memory fails me or in the two years we have been away the humble chickpea has been courted and fat-shamed by just about every vegetable and spice on the planet. Flavours here, collaborations there. I come away with a low fat, regular flavour hummus only because I can't find the regular fat, regular flavour variant. From hummus, then, to ready-to-eat crudités and then on to crisps. And with crisps, biscuits. And with biscuits, sweet treats. Gummies, chocolates, fudges, toffees and mints in tubs, bags, boxes, tubes and rolls. Some tea to wash down the biscuits, some juices to perk us up in the mornings. And oh, the dairy section. For Dylan, full fat, fresh cows' milk. For me, pots upon pots of greek yoghurt. Of course, we have to fight our way past all the alternatives to find ye olde cows' products. In Myanmar we had access to a couple of high-sugar soy milk brands, but never before have I seen so many nut and cereal milks and their reformatted offspring.

Having learned the lingo in the dairy fridges, we apply our newfound knowledge to the ice cream freezers, climbing over 'free from' items to dig out the full cream, full calorie Magnums. Even within the Magnum family things have changed. There are new sizes, new flavours and new formats. From ice creams the only logical step is towards the booze. Liberated from my sobriety by the recent factory closure, I am looking forward to the odd craft beer, a couple of glasses of wine and a free pour G&T. The craft beer wall alone takes us a good ten minutes to take in and select from. Realising that our trolley can't accommodate the food, the beer and the baby, we agree that we will just have to come back to complete our craft beer bingo card.

Speaking of babies, ours decides that he's had enough of this adventure. He clearly doesn't share our excitement, and why would he? He has never been to a supermarket like this before and therefore has no idea what he's been missing. I sweep my way round the baby clothing section; a smorgasbord of natural, breathable fabrics on which I will spend far more time and consideration on my next trip, zeroing in on only the essentials this time. One double-bobble hat and matching mittens for Jasper later and we are away. Even clinging onto its summer, Ireland is never going to match the tropical heat of Myanmar. But perhaps it has more to do with the length of time we spent near the refrigerators that Jasper shimmies with his first ever shiver as we emerge into the lethargic sunlight of our first full day in Ireland.

19

IRELAND

WE HAVEN'T EXACTLY CHOSEN to be in Ireland. But we have chosen how we want to spend this period of transition. And that is in a quiet, rejuvenating halfway-house between the life we have left in Myanmar and the new life that will eventually take us to India. After all the intensity and noise of the previous few months, Ireland is most definitely quiet. And it is spacious. The house in which we are staying is large with a large garden, but beyond that, I feel as though everything has more space. The roads are emptier than in Myanmar, the air is crisper, the night skies are clearer and darker, the food tastes fresher and my lungs feel as though they have a far greater capacity. It feels as though we have more time for everything and no reason to rush. The distances we travel each day are greater and the pace at which we do everything is slower. Sadly, there also seems to be more space between Dylan and me.

There I am, preparing as best I can to go to Jersey as a stay-at-home solo parent, living in a place I haven't spent any considerable time for twenty years and where I know almost nobody but my own family. And meanwhile, Dylan is getting ready to move to a country he has never visited and where he knows nobody, with the expectation of setting up a life for us there. While I am winding down, he is ramping up. While I am submitting exit forms and finalising handovers, he is drowning in immigration paperwork and induction packs. A part of me resents being left with the baby, while a part of Dylan resents being sent off as the advance party. Conversely, a part of me feels guilty that I get to keep Jasper with me, while a part of Dylan feels guilty that he is leaving me to parent alone. I worry for him and he worries for me.

We made the decision on India together, knowing that it means a few months of separation, but that doesn't stop us each secretly resenting the other for their role in a plan which is now coming to fruition. We are, of course, united in our desire to spend as much time together as a family as possible while we can. It is just so foreign to us to be in such different places mentally while being in the same place physically.

It is silly for me to begrudge Dylan his exciting new adventure, because deep down I crave some sort of normalness for a while. The trouble is, I am not sure if I will recognise normal when I see it. My perspective on normality has undoubtedly been affected by the coup and the pandemic, as well as by having lived in South East Asia for years. And I have no experience in parenting under any normal circumstances whatsoever.

I have a lot of adjustments to make, as I try to chart a course through the complete upending of my life and the reconstruction of it without any of the support system I built around myself in Myanmar. I am acutely aware of the extraordinary privilege I enjoyed in terms of the support I had in Yangon. Had Jasper not been born in Myanmar, I wouldn't have been lucky enough to engage a nanny, a helper or a driver, and Dylan wouldn't have had the luxury of such a long period of elective unemployment. Suddenly finding myself without them all, however, I feel completely disoriented. I feel as though I am becoming a mother for the first time all over again, except that instead of a new baby, it is a new me that I am dealing with. It is more than a little daunting.

As the dust begins to settle, I realise that despite everything I have lost, I have been left with an incredible gift: a deferred maternity leave. I was fully employed during the first few months while Jasper was little more than an inanimate blob, and have now been released from my professional duties to take full advantage of motherhood just as he becomes more curious, more assertive and more mobile. Of course, more mobile also means more of a danger to himself, which in turn makes my new role considerably more physically demanding than I am prepared for after months of sitting at a desk for eight hours a day.

Amazing as our holiday house is, with its walkable proximity to the beach, 10-bed capacity, its tennis court and huge, manicured lawn, it is also as cold inside as the weather outside, despite it being late summer. The hardwood floors seem specially designed to inflict maximum pain on anyone foolish enough to grovel around on them. Cold weather and hard floors do not make for a gentle induction to my pre-toddler fitness bootcamp. I follow a program of nine thousand squats per day picking up and putting down Jasper, picking up and putting down dropped food items, picking up and putting down toys, balls, clothing items, TV remotes, books, more dropped food items and, as far as I can tell, more Jaspers. I complement the squats with some laundry-weighted bicep curls, grocery deadlifts, bath-time glute holds, and core crunching carrier walks. My knees creak with every level change, my frigid wrists can't hold the weight of Jasper's twists, my back aches from top to bottom and even the joints in my fingers complain every time I open a tightly sealed jar or chop a particularly solid carrot. I assess each activity on a risk versus reward basis. Yes, it would be enjoyable to sit on the sofa for a few seconds, but is it worth the effort of an extra squat then having to stand up again? Yes, it would be fun for Jasper to play with the tennis balls, but is it worth the strain of retrieving them from under the TV cabinet?

Together with having given up breastfeeding, which contrary to popular opinion did nothing to encourage weight or water to leave my body, it's no wonder that this sudden uptick in physical exertion sees me shrink right back down to my pre-baby size. It is a shame that all my pre-baby-sized clothes are in packing boxes on the other side of the world at the time. Not that I need them. One of the big things I am learning from my time in Ireland is that people in the west no longer wear clothes. At least, not structured, tailored clothes made from anything other than Lycra or jersey. Bar a handful of anomalies, who may well be out-of-towners like us, everyone I see is dressed in uniform oversized, grey tracksuits. Initially, I wonder if there is some sort of day release program from a local prison. But then I notice that many of the tracksuits are young women pushing premium strollers. Tracky bums and Bugaboos make for an oddly jarring visual. I mention it to my mother on the phone one day.

'I don't think people wear normal clothes in Ireland any more. I have only seen three people wearing something other than grey tracky bums and a sweatshirt.'

'Ah yes. I think they call it loungewear and it's all you can buy in the shops here now too. Apparently, it's all about comfort these days. It makes me wonder, just how uncomfortable the clothes were which these people were wearing before the pandemic, to make them switch to fully elasticated after it?'

'Wow. This didn't happen in Myanmar. People were still wearing the same things as before. At least I kind of blend in ... my wardrobe hasn't had a refresh in over two years and most of what I brought with me is maternity wear, one wash away from its new life as a cleaning rag.'

I am in a very different headspace from the Irish public as far as fashion is concerned. After two years of pregnancy dictating my clothing choices, I have no beef with my own wardrobe. I am genuinely looking forward to wearing an underwired bra again, and skinny jeans with the top button done up and even, dare I say it, an impractical heel. I just want to dress normally again and this normal is not a grey tracksuit.

Just a few days into our stay, a bout of the world's worst man-flu arrives. It coincides exactly with the arrival of Jasper's first tooth. My two happy-go-lucky exile companions transform simultaneously into sad, sniffling sacks of snot and saliva. It is at this point that I realise that I skipped an entire chapter in the *How to Be a Mother* handbook; I can't remember the words to a single nursery rhyme. I want to sing to Jasper to comfort him in his very tearful suffering, but the only song I can think of is 'On top of spaghetti, all covered in cheese, I lost my poor meatball, when somebody sneezed.' I bemoan the convenience of Spotify's lullaby playlists, which I lazily deploy as a key element in Jasper's bedtime routine but which just won't cut through his wailing, and of having not spent more time studying ways to soothe an unhappy baby. And then, with all the emotion and charisma I can muster, I sing the socks off that meatball.

'It rolled off the table, and onto the floor, and then my

poor meatball rolled out of the door.' I check Jasper's face, to gauge his horror or enchantment, and then sweep through the door and into the garden to complete the rather tragic story of my poor meatball.

'It rolled down the garden, and under a bush, and now my poor meatball is nothing but mush.' I sing it loudly, I sing it softly; I sing it inside and I sing it outside; I sing it as we walk to the beach, as we sit in an armchair and as he tosses and turns in his cot. I sing it as opera, as lilting Irish folk, as jolly as a clown and as sombre as an undertaker. I try humming it but that only seems to cause Jasper further pain. I sing it until that tooth bursts through and until Dylan finally gets up from the sofa he has commandeered for two days. And then I vow to learn some nursery rhymes during my time in Jersey.

Besides a shift in sartorial style, there are other aspects of western society and culture to which I have to readjust. This process of assimilating back into a once-familiar culture is known as 'reverse culture shock' and I have been through it before when moving back to the UK after a year abroad. But this time around, there is so much to adjust to.

Firstly, I am returning to a western culture for the first time in two years, a period long enough for technology to have advanced and for rules and regulations to have changed. On top of that, the pandemic has given rise to dramatic behavioural changes the likes of which I have never known in my home culture. And then on top of that again is the fact that I am now a mother which brings with it a whole new perspective and a whole new set of social rules to adhere to. It's a shame motherhood doesn't come with a handbook. It is a relief that I can process the initial stages of my reverse culture shock in Ireland where I am anonymous and where I at least don't sound like a local. As soon as I return to Jersey, the risk of embarrassing myself or my family in front of someone I once knew is very real.

We are still under some restrictions and are advised to stay home for our first eight days in Ireland. We release ourselves from this partial isolation with a drive-thru negative COVID test, and celebrate by going out for lunch at a local cafe. By the time we sit down at the table, I have stumbled my way through several awkward interactions just trying to establish how things work. I feel as though I have completely forgotten how restaurants operate, having not had much opportunity to visit any in recent months. And even before the coup and COVID, I had grown very used to certain characteristics of Myanmar restaurants which I am not sure apply here. If they don't have my preferred wine on their menu, I don't think they'll let me pop to the local off-licence to bring my own. If I need to pop to the toilet, I am not sure the staff will be happy to drop what they are doing to play with Jasper while I am gone. If I don't have the right cash on me, I am not sure they'll accept an IOU and the promise that I'll return later to settle up. On the plus side, if I order a starter and a main, I am hoping they won't arrive at the same time.

In this establishment, I am not sure if babies are allowed, because I don't initially see any high chairs, until the staff welcome Jasper with open arms and bring a high chair from the back. I am not sure how we pay, until the staff assure me that I have a range of payment options available, including cash and card. I do have to pay today, though, as expected. They inform me that the tap to pay limit for a card is now 100 Euros, which is far higher than I remember. I am not sure if it is OK to bring out packaged baby food, or if that counts as outside food. They tell me it is fine and, what's more, they can heat it for me. I don't know if we can take unfinished food away with us, or if they will think that's strange. They happily box up some leftover chips and wraps for us to enjoy later. On our way out, we pass through a beautifully curated gift shop.

'Wow, imagine if we'd had a shop like this in Myanmar,' comments Dylan. 'It has literally everything we wanted for our apartment - the vases, the candle holders, the frames, the cushion covers, the fake plants. How many years did it take us to build up our collection? Five? Six? And we could have just walked in and bought it all here!'

'Do you remember?' I reminisce. 'We were carrying bed linens in from Bangkok every time we went! Sometimes it feels like a lifetime ago, our Myanmar life, doesn't it? When actually it was just last week.'

At the house, I am struggling with the way things work too. I don't know if Irish tap water is safe for babies. In Myanmar we only drank filtered water, so filtered that it was completely devoid of any minerals and did nothing in the face of the summer heat. We used to rely on oral rehydration salts to replenish body salts lost to hockey, cycling, walking or even a long taxi ride in an unairconditioned cab. I find myself searching on the local government website for the salt content of the tap water, in case I need to worry. I am also not quite sure what temperature it is in the house and if it is too cold for Jasper. In Myanmar our air conditioning units all told us the room temperature, which gave me easy control. In Ireland I am guessing and poking at the thermostat. At least I know what a thermostat is, I suppose, which is more than Dylan.

Ordinary tasks are confusing. I repeatedly try to get into the wrong side of the car, and I often look the wrong way when crossing a road. When it comes to planning our departure from Ireland at the end of our stay, I don't know how many hours before our flight to arrive at the airport, as I don't really know what was originally normal and I certainly don't know what is normal since COVID. Our departure from Myanmar was so stressful that I don't even remember how many hours before that flight we arrived at the airport, but I know it was many. I have forgotten how to top up the credit on my UK mobile phone, and I am not even sure if I can buy the right credit from Ireland. I miss knowing how everything worked in Myanmar.

Then there is the difficulty I have when someone asks the question 'where are you from?'. Ostensibly, I am from Jersey. But that doesn't really explain my look of confusion in the face of basic day-to-day activities. It also doesn't explain why my vaccine certificate is in Burmese, or why I am struggling so much with the exchange rate. It certainly doesn't explain why I sound so odd when I order food. An unfortunate habit I picked up in Myanmar is that of reordering my English words to match the Burmese flow when speaking to a waiter in a restaurant. I made this change to maximise the chances of a Burmese waiter catching the order for the first time, but clearly, this isn't necessary any more.

'What'll you be having today?' the unsuspecting waiter asks after we have sat down at our table.

'Caesar salad, one. Sparkling water, one bottle. Bread basket, one' I respond as his eyebrows twitch in bemusement. The fact that I have already needed to translate the waiter's heavily accented opening question to a nonplussed Dylan results in us being given some subtle side-eye and, I am sure, a wide berth, when other diners arrive to be seated.

As a result of this strange interaction, the waiter asks where I am from. I inevitably freeze and stare at him while I run through all the possible responses to this question in my head. Dylan jumps in and says, 'She's British, and I'm Australian, but we have been living in Myanmar.'

'Oh, right,' says the waiter, clearly unsure of what the

appropriate response might be. From experience, I know that many people haven't heard of Myanmar. Or if they have, it's so far down the list of countries or cities they are expecting to hear that day that it takes them a minute or two to process what we have just said.

It helps enormously having Jasper around during exchanges like this, especially if Dylan is elsewhere or otherwise engaged. On more than one occasion I find myself talking to Jasper, knowing full well that he can't respond, but hoping that someone overhearing will use my chatter to fill in some context around my strange behaviour. I ask Jasper how he thinks we can pay, or if he thinks they have WI-FI, or if he thinks they have a high chair. I consult Jasper on what I should order, on where he thinks the bathrooms might be, or whether we are allowed to sit outside. To an outsider it probably looks like I am carrying Jasper, but really he is carrying me - through the stress of my re-entry into western society.

On walks we take together as two, I revel in the colours, the smells and the sounds of the countryside and the coastline. I do it as though for his benefit, but really it is for me. Showing the world to Jasper helps me to see the beauty in our surroundings and to appreciate the good in however strange a situation we seem to be.

When I am not engaged in working desperately to fit in with the society around me, I am rapidly trying to improve my baby-wrangling skills, particularly where nappy changes are concerned. It isn't that I haven't been changing nappies up to this point. I have tackled my fair share of danger diapers. It is that Jasper appears to be going through some kind of standing rebellion and is resolutely refusing to lie down to be changed. After his third or fourth attempt to twist himself off the chest-height dresser I am using as his changing table, spraying both me and the carpet with a catherine wheel of urine during his freefall, I decide that maybe this isn't just a 'me being out of practice' problem. Maybe this is a 'my baby is a problem' problem. And so, according to the internet, it turns out to be. Despite not yet being remotely steady on his feet, it appears Jasper has decided he is one of *those* babies who demand a standing change. Naturally, as well as advice on how to switch to a standing change, the internet also offers 101 ways to remodel my home to ensure Jasper is a certified genius and fine-motor medallist by the time he is out of nappies. I ignore all that and go in search of a furniture knob at about the right height for him to hold onto instead.

Despite our fortnight in Ireland being something of a forced holiday, it does turn out to be everything a holiday should be. It is a change of scenery and a change of pace. It is two weeks of uninterrupted family togetherness. It is an opportunity to take a collective exhale and start to process the madness of the preceding months. It is a break from reality and a chance to recharge our batteries ready for whatever is coming down the line next. It is a retreat and a bootcamp in one, and I come away from it feeling stronger mentally and physically. As we pack our suitcases again and prepare to leave, I brace myself. I feel as though I am just settling into a rhythm and now it's time to move on again. And this time, the move takes us one step closer to Dylan leaving.

We are unable to fly directly from Dublin to Jersey, which gives us a few hours at Heathrow en route. Jasper assigns Dylan the role of human futon for most of those hours. This leaves me with the role of travel agent, booking Dylan's flights to India for just two weeks later and, I won't lie, I seriously consider messing up the booking. But that wouldn't be fair. Dylan is only doing what we agreed was right for the family. Without flights, there is no job in India. And without a job in India we really have no plan. I book the tickets and look across at Jasper still asleep on Dylan. Knowing that it is the right decision doesn't make it feel any less wrong that we should be separated from one another, but at least I get to keep Jasper with me.

20

JERSEY

JASPER IS HEAVILY OVERSUBSCRIBED in the grandparent department. Both Dylan and I have divorced parents who are now happily together with new partners, giving Jasper a total of eight grandparents to whom he (or we) will, at some point, need to assign suitably grand monikers. I give up trying to label them all because at the end of the day, with two pairs in Jersey and two in Australia, there is unlikely to be much occasion for confusion, and that's saying something considering three out of the four women are called Jo.

Nine months into his life, Jasper has only met one of the eight, but as we land in Jersey, two more are waiting in convoy to ferry our baggage and bodies to my father and stepmother's home where we will be setting up our base. As bad luck would have it, after nine months of waiting to meet her first grandson, seven of which have been spent worrying about *his* health and safety halfway across the world, my mother has caught COVID just a few days before we arrive. So, while my father and his wife load up on cuddles with the little man, it is more than a week before my mother is allowed anything more than a wave from the end of the garden.

My parents have taken polar opposite approaches to their retirements. My father is the busiest retired person in the world, filling every minute of every day with activities and appointments and holidays and social engagements, as though he's making up for the time he lost to his very successful career as a lawyer. My mother, on the other hand, is relaxed and content pottering about in her own space and time, probably due to having done more than her fair share of buzzing around while raising three children without anything like the help I have had.

The temporary home in Jersey for Jasper and me is in a three-bedroomed cottage attached to my father's beautiful, pink granite farmhouse. It is a little much for one and a half people, I'll admit, but having our own space allows me to toddler-proof all the cupboards and edges, and to establish my own parenting routines and practices, without worrying about disturbing anyone. We aren't completely isolated. The patio doors open directly from the living room onto a section of the main garden known as the rockery, where two years earlier Dylan and I had our wedding photos taken. We were married in the garden at my father's house in 2019 and, because of the pandemic and everything that followed, that was the last time either of us visited. The cottage is where we stayed for the few days we were in Jersey for the wedding, and where Dylan kicked off the big day with some tennis, bacon butties and bubbles. I started my own preparations with some yoga and toasties less than a kilometre away, down the road at my mother's house. The cottage holds such warm, happy memories for Dylan and I and, when we arrive there in September 2021, it is still dotted with leftover wedding decorations. But as I unpack the few belongings I have with me, for what is essentially an open-ended stay, I feel sad comparing how settled I felt at the time of our wedding and how rattled I feel now. Back in 2019, if someone had told me that two years later I would be squatting alone in the cottage with a nine-month-old baby, I would have wondered what on earth was about to go wrong in my life.

Dylan and I know that the separation will be tough, and even more so because we don't yet have a fixed date for when we will be reunited. We talk about it as though it is going to be three months. October to December feels like a manageable chunk of time even if, for me, that means staring down my first winter in nearly four years and a lonely, cold one at that.

Our first two weeks in Jersey are such a whirlwind that I don't have much time to think about anything but enjoying showing Jasper off to the family and helping Dylan finalise his plans for India. We even manage to squeeze in a christening for Jasper. I will be honest, neither Dylan nor I is particularly religious, despite having been raised and educated in Christian environments, but we agree on one thing; the awkwardness of an adult baptism is not something we want to inflict on Jasper should he choose a more godly path than us, later in his life. My father is a very active member of the parish community, which is useful when the date of Jasper's christening jumps forwards from December to September, in order that Dylan can attend. Before the coup derailed our outlook on 2021, we had originally hoped to spend Christmas in Jersey, and had arranged a winter Christening accordingly. But our plan now (as much as we dare to make one), is that we will spend Christmas in India this year. Sadly, the customised leather christening booties I ordered for Jasper weren't as easy to change as the date, so not only do they have the wrong date embroidered on the soles, but they also slop off his three-months-too-small feet every few minutes. My younger sister, Alice, also pops over to Jersey for Jasper's christening. By the end of the year, she will be the only one in the family with a job, which means she is considerably more time poor than the rest of us, but that doesn't stop her from doting on her nephew when she has the time. My mother isn't allowed to join the celebrations due to COVID and Jasper's godparents aren't able to join due to living in locked-down New Zealand, but they and several other absent friends and relatives all dial into the church service on Zoom, and we lob a piece of christening cake over my mother's garden fence on our way back from lunch.

I do a lot of shopping over the first two weeks that I am in Jersey in order to equip Jasper for being a baby in a cold climate. My own plan is simply to raid my mother's wardrobe. It is amazing to walk into a shop such as Next or Marks and Spencer, search for the size I need and then walk out with the items in my hand, ready to wear. No three-month lead times and no doubts over whether the courier service will be running when the order finally arrives at the border. Plus, I have Dylan as a packhorse to help with the lifting and shifting. Jasper doesn't have a buggy when we first arrive, as we sold his Yangon one in the move. He isn't anywhere near using his legs to get from A to B either, so everywhere he goes he does so while strapped to me. I buy Jasper some developmental toys, which I imagine will keep him busy while I do other motherly things besides playing with him. The workbench walker is a huge hit, until he decides to use it as a climbing frame and consequently give himself a multicoloured egg on his forehead. The jungle bouncer is less of a hit when, on only its second outing, he bounces so hard that he makes both his feet bleed.

I borrow a lot of things too. Toys from a friend of my sister, whose three children have a cave of wonders so vast and overfilled that I don't think they even notice when the odd wailing emergency vehicle is generously lent to us by their long-suffering mother, who decides she can't bear to hear its siren one more time. I borrow car seats and a camp cot from them too, which saves me a lot of unnecessary expenditure. I borrow clothes and various cooking utensils from my mother. And, of course, I am borrowing an entire house and a car from my father and stepmother. This is the first time I have experienced the camaraderie of motherhood, having gone it alone for all those months in Myanmar. I now realise that I am a member of a very wide-reaching club whose motto seems to be 'be kind to anyone who seems to be having a rough time of it'. It is humbling and encouraging and I only hope that I can pay it forward by offering someone else the same support one day.

A few days before Dylan leaves, my mother is finally released from her isolation and at last meets Jasper in person and at close quarters. Dylan thrusts Jasper into her arms as he steps over the threshold into her hallway. Even a seasoned child-raiser like my mother is initially hesitant, worrying that Jasper will start to cry. Nobody wants a baby to take one look at their face and decide the world is ending. Luckily, Jasper isn't that kind of baby. Whether because my mother smells like family, in the politest possible sense, or because her voice sounds a lot like mine, or because Jasper has always been an unflappable baby, he settles right into his nana's arms and the house that will become his home from home from home over the next few months.

Jasper and I spend a lot of time at my mother's house during our stay in Jersey, mostly out of choice, except for two rather stressful weeks in November when the heating conks out at the cottage, right in the middle of a cold snap. We are lucky that there is a room going spare at my mother's, with only one of my sisters in temporary residence there. It is only stressful for me; Jasper basks in the extra attention he has from his nana, her partner and my older sister, Liv. She has taken our somewhat spontaneous arrival in Jersey as the sign she was looking for to quit her London life and make the move back herself. In the same way Jasper and I are squatting at my father's house, Liv is taking advantage of board and lodging at mum's, until she finds a place to live and a source of income. In the meantime, she is free, willing and able to spend time with Jasper, just not at six o'clock in the morning. The last thing any of the three night owls in that house wants is to be woken at sparrow's fart by someone shouting or banging for their breakfast.

The first two weeks in Jersey are bittersweet. My family is so excited to meet Jasper and some of them even notice that I am there too. They love his chubby, smiley little face, his infectious giggle, his bright blue eyes and his striking resemblance to a mischievous character in a book my sisters and I enjoyed as children, entitled *The Wild Baby*. With his calm, gentle good nature and his attentive expression, that continues to suggest that he is quietly taking in everything and everyone around him, he is a persistent little ray of sunshine breaking through the dark clouds trying to gather over my head.

I force myself to see the silver lining that is the windfall of Jasper time that our little life interruption brings to my family. In ordinary circumstances, they would have seen him once or twice a year at most, and only on flying visits. My mother and Liv barely even try to disguise just how much they enjoy having Jasper on tap for such an unexpected length of time. And why should they? It is impossible not to feel happy when Jasper is around. He starts to make wobbly moves towards assisted standing and when he is finally upright, he rewards whoever is holding his hands with a howl of laughter; eyes sparkling with wonder and pride. He is fascinated by the dogs at my father and stepmother's house and his face lights up whenever one of them appears at the window of the cottage. He explores the power he has to play with his food and the reaction he triggers by putting sticky fingers through his hair. He is the king of funny faces and loves nothing more than making people laugh. He is starting to take control of peekaboo games which means I am always on the lookout for his little face peeking out from behind furniture, toys and his own hands. The joy he sees in my face reflects right back at me from his. He wakes up laughing and he goes to sleep without a fuss. I couldn't ask for a better baby to distract me from the inevitable, impending departure of his father.

The day Dylan leaves starts twice for me. The first time I wake up is before dawn, in time to say a bleary-eyed, light-headed goodbye to Dylan before he bundles himself and his suitcase into my father's car to head to the airport. Dylan decides not to disturb Jasper, instead choosing to slip quietly out of the house without a fuss. Dylan and my farewell is whispered and brief, so as not to wake the sleeping baby.

'I don't know how I am going to do this on my own,' I worry out loud to Dylan, my voice muffled by his shoulder as I hug him close and fight back the tears. 'I'm not sure I'm ready. I still feel frazzled from everything in Myanmar.'

'You're not on your own. You have Jasper. He'll keep you company. And you have your family too.'

'I know. But they aren't you. I'm going to miss you so much.'

'I know you will, but think about me. I'll miss you guys more! I'll be in India, all alone, without my family, starting a whole new job and life over there. Do you want to trade places?'

I laugh. 'You are leaving us,' I say with mock accusation.

'You are sending me away,' Dylan counters.

We both laugh. We both know that going from living in one another's pockets for two years to not seeing one another for months is going to take some getting used to.

I hover by the front door as Dylan walks away from the house and then, once he has disappeared, I listen to the car doors closing. With a last crunch of gravel I know they have turned out of the driveway and onto the main road; my signal to tiptoe back up the stairs and into the empty bed. With Jasper still audibly deep in sleep, my weary body knows better than to waste precious time to rest, and overrides my stirring brain.

The second time I wake up, I feel sluggish and heavy. It is as if I am weighed down by the sadness which didn't fully hit me earlier in the morning. I feel sad for Jasper who is babbling away in his cot, oblivious to the fact that his father isn't here anymore. I feel anxious for Dylan who by now is rushing to make his flight connection; a jarring gear change from the leisurely two weeks we have just enjoyed together in Jersey, and the two weeks in Ireland before that. I feel shell-shocked by the realisation that this is how I will wake up every morning now; surrounded by the quiet, countryside stillness. I pull myself up out of bed, and walk slowly to the door of Jasper's room. As soon as I open his door and see his sunny, happy little face, the tears come rolling down my cheeks. I scoop him up and squeeze him tightly, allowing myself a few seconds of self-pity before, with a sing-song voice and an upbeat bounce, I embark on the morning routine.

Jasper is aware something has changed. It breaks my heart that for the first few days after Dylan leaves, he watches the door as though hoping someone familiar is going to come through it. Even though I know that Jasper won't remember anything of this period, I still feel cheated on his behalf; as though somehow the pandemic and the coup have conspired to swindle him out of a few months of family time. I resolve to channel these feelings into parenting, determined that by the time we are reunited, I will have at least made some headway into usurping Dylan's self-appointed position as 'the fun parent'.

21

BUSY BABY

JUST TWO DAYS into a life of parenting by myself, I have an epiphany. I am going to need a system. Systems and logistics usually fall under Dylan's remit in our relationship, while I bring more of the softer skills like maintaining friendships and choosing cushion covers. Dylan has always been irritatingly organised and I used to goad him for being obsessed with routine and efficiency. On my second attempt at that first morning without him, however, breakfast is an ordeal. With Jasper crawling around unsupervised under my feet, I stumble back and forth across the kitchen, tripping over the moving baby to reach the fridge, the toaster, the fridge again, the cereal cupboard, the condiments, the cutlery, the fridge again, the fruit bowl and the toaster again. The more I rush, the more I make mistakes and the longer it seems to take. I am muttering 'more haste, less speed' under my breath, but the message doesn't reach my body. I continue clattering around the kitchen, swallowing expletives as I go. While Jasper doesn't cry if he is hungry, he does pester. He grabs at my legs and feet, and bangs stolen kitchen implements or toys noisily on the floor. He is surprisingly nimble considering his belly-based army-crawl and appears, disappears and reappears somewhere dangerous at incredible speed whenever my attention is elsewhere. Food in hand, with Jasper shouting at me impatiently, I spin around to face the table where food and baby are to convene, only to realise I don't have his bib, his splat mat or his water ready. I puff out my cheeks in frustration. By the time the baby is in the chair and the food is on the table, my stress levels are through the roof. I feel so foolish. I have vastly underestimated how much harder it is to start the day without Dylan. I am embarrassed by how ill equipped I am to perform a simple task like making breakfast for a ten-month-old baby. As I help Jasper with his rather stodgy porridge, it dawns on me; Dylan's obsession with routine and efficiency isn't something to tease him about, it is something to emulate. I take a deep breath, scan the kitchen and mentally devise my very own breakfast production line; one that I can set up every evening before going to bed and sleep easier because of it.

It is a symphony of efficiency: the squelch and clunk of the fridge door as I pull out the carton of full fat Jersey milk and the spreadable butter. The rustle of the bread bag as I extract a slice, and the squeak of the spring as I push it down into the toaster. The slosh of the milk as I douse Jasper's pre-measured porridge and my pre-poured cereal. The single beep of the microwave as I warm the porridge and the double beep of the coffee machine which kicks off the whirr and trickle of my morning fuel. The thud of the ready-to-grab knife on the waiting chopping board as I slice into Jasper's pre-selected daily fruit and place it on the waiting plate. In the few seconds while everything toasts and heats and espresses, I plonk Jasper in his chair under which his splat mat is already positioned to catch flying food items, attach his bib and hand him his spoon. The toaster pops, the microwave sings, the coffee machine coughs, the spoon bangs and all I have left to do is plate and serve. My very own system. One requiring minimal time and even less brain power, and one that ensures a unidirectional, steady glide across the kitchen that even a commando stealth baby under foot can't disrupt. The cleaning up takes a little longer, but by then Jasper's tummy is full and he is content with his toys for just long enough for me to reset the kitchen for lunch.

End to end, our new and improved breakfast routine takes us about thirty minutes and brings us early birds to around 7am. At this point in the first few days, I deflate and wonder what on earth we should do to pass the hours until Jasper's bed time. The day seems to stretch out in front of me like an endurance run I haven't trained for. I realise that in all the madness of leaving Myanmar, recuperating in Ireland and arriving in Jersey, I have never faced a day without at least one scheduled activity. Furthermore, as I contemplate the weeks ahead, it hits me that I have absolutely nothing to do. I have no life in Jersey which means I have no socialising, no appointments, no meetings, no calls, no errands and no admin to see to. Besides the odd trip to the supermarket, I really have no structure to my days or weeks. I feel more than a little lost.

Not for long. Jasper never gives me much time to wallow. He plucks me out of my puddle of self-pity with a frustrated grunt that I take as a request for help, an excited whoop which tells me he is about to do something dangerous, or a waft of poop as he crawls past with his nappy at full capacity. And with that, we embark on an activity. Often, in those quiet, early hours, we take advantage of the garden. Jasper loves to wobble around on two feet, supported by me stooped in a backbreaking hunch, inspecting the plants, the grass, the tennis balls left, half-hidden, in the flowerbeds by the dogs. We only have to fill two hours before the yawns and eye rubs start, and I tuck Jasper away for his morning nap.

Jasper's naps and mealtimes are the first building blocks of our new life; three meals, two naps and a bath-time routine gives my days a six-part structure. During his first nap I shower, dress, tidy and launder, making myself and the house presentable for the day. During his second nap I talk to Dylan, now five and half hours ahead in Mumbai, and then cook. Between each fixture I only have around one and a half to two hours to fill. This, I feel sure, is manageable.

Inspired by how much time was saved by Jasper's frozen portions in Yangon, I continue this habit, batch cooking and freezing a whole menu of meals for Jasper. A week of cooking affords me three weeks of not, and that suits me perfectly. At any moment in time, Jasper's frozen treasure chest comprises between five and ten portions each of bolognese, roast dinner, fish pie, shepherd's pie, vegetable stew, chicken curry and pumpkin mash. An unexpected benefit of having no husband around is that I only have Jasper to cater for. I am more than happy to exist on Jasper's leftovers, supermarket ready meals and afternoon teas with Jasper and my mum. Dinner for me on many occasions is a slosh of wine and a fistful of chocolates which is arguably more acceptable come Christmas time, with its seasonal diet of 'anything goes', than it is in September when I first arrive. The thought of generating more washing up for myself by using anything beyond a single spoon or fork puts me off most meals entirely. A small part of me dreads being reunited with Dylan and his adult-sized appetite, in yet another country with no ready-to-eat supermarket section. And a large part of me wonders daily how on earth people with present partners and multiple children have the motivation to get out of bed in the morning. I like to imagine they do their washing up in the bath once a day, together with themselves and their children.

It is the gaps between the naps and the meals that I look at next. In the absence of any kind of social calendar for myself, I throw myself wholeheartedly into finding ways to entertain Jasper. While I don't have many friends in Jersey, I do still know a few people whose brains I am able to pick, when I manage to pin them down. I am disheartened by how hard it is to coordinate with them to begin with, because it reminds me how busy everyone else's lives are, especially those people with multiple children. It highlights to me just how empty my own life is of anything other than Jasper. That is until I start to book Jasper into some of the very same classes that keep these mothers and their children so very, very busy. On Mondays we go to the baby gym, on Tuesdays we learn sign language and go swimming. Wednesdays and Thursdays I keep free for ladies and babies that brunch, together with my mother and my sister, and on Fridays we go to a bouncy-castle-based agility class. Outside of classes, we join my father on cliff-path dog walks on Monday afternoons, walk to the local farm shop for coffee most mornings, wander down to my mother's for tea most afternoons and run the gauntlet of cheek-pinchers at the supermarket once or twice a week. It never ceases to amaze me how many people believe that the appropriate action to take on seeing a baby is to grab its cheeks. I would be surprised by it under normal circumstances but, during COVID, it is downright baffling. Every time it happens, I am simply too stunned and too slow to bat the hands away. It's not only when I abandon Jasper near the oranges and traverse the aisle to the apples, either. It happens even when I am pushing the trolley that he is sitting in.

On Saturday mornings I break from the usual breakfast routine for freshly baked croissants and on Sundays it is scrambled eggs. When my sister, Liv, moves back to Jersey full time, Saturday evenings become Seafood Saturdays and we see Jasper gorge himself on the day's catch of prawns and crabmeat like the bougie baby that he is. Even getting Jasper temporarily signed up to the Jersey medical system provides us with something to do, as we catch him up on some of the missing vaccinations that he hasn't had in Myanmar.

Once I have Jasper's schedule and medical needs in hand, I decide I should do something about my increasingly worrying neck tremor and the fact that, when it's not shaking, my neck appears to be locked into a position which makes reversing a car almost impossible. I have a sharp pain all down the right side of my back, I have to turn my entire body when I need to look at something beside me and I am constantly saying no when I mean yes. I take this problem to a chiropractor and, hundreds of pounds and several months later, I am finally able to touch my chin to my shoulder again. Many of my appointments fall just after Jasper's morning nap, so I leave early, allow the drive to the other side of the island rock him to sleep and then enjoy a cup of coffee from a beach cafe, staring out over the English Channel while Jasper snores in his car seat behind me. Sometimes the open expanse of sea makes me feel so incredibly alone. Other days its familiarity makes me feel calmly accepting of the circumstances I am in. I wind down my window or, on days when I am sure Jasper is dead to the world, wander a few steps away from the car up onto the sand dunes to gulp down huge, invigorating breaths of fresh, salty sea air.

By autumn 2021 it is as though COVID never even existed in Jersey. Masks are no longer mandatory, restaurants are up to full capacity and busy, public events like festive markets, charity auctions and amateur dramatic performances are back on the social calendar. I take a while to remember how to interact with other people at close quarters, and to get used to no longer wearing a mask. Once I have a buggy for Jasper, I am able to go out without him strapped to me and I feel uncomfortably naked in public places without my usual protection of a mask and baby. I grow accustomed to expecting things to be open, instead of expecting them to be shut. I find myself shaking hands with people by way of introduction, and I even attend a birthday party where someone blows out the candles with their mouth! I relax into letting Jasper play with other children's toys, knowing full well they are all sharing saliva germs with one another, but safe in the knowledge that there is medicine available, should anything dramatic take a grip on his immune system. Although I am trying to fall in step with the people around me, I find it hard to listen to them complaining about any hardship they think they suffered under the previous year's restrictions. Even at peak lockdown, Jersey still allowed its citizens to take outdoor walks in, what is arguably, some of the most beautiful countryside and coastal scenery in the British Isles. There were no shortages of medical care, beds, or food, let alone any risk of being shot at while lining up to buy oxygen. There are many times when I am part of a conversation about how awful the COVID restrictions were and what a relief it is that this year things are back to normal, and I simply stand there thinking to myself 'if you only knew how good you had it'. It is in those moments that I worry the coup and the subsequent chain of events have hardened me.

Even as the days start to pass more quickly and as I start to feel as though I have a rhythm to my weeks, I miss Dylan horribly. I miss his encouragement and, I like to imagine, admiration for how well I am managing Jasper's enviable calendar. I am proud of the life I am creating for Jasper; of the systems and routines which simultaneously preserve my sanity and support his development. But I miss having someone other than my glass of wine and my chocolates to spend my evenings with. I miss sharing Jasper's care with someone. I miss having someone to decide on the day's activities with. But even more than missing him, I am sad for how much of Jasper's first year Dylan is missing. He is missing the emergence of Jasper's cheeky little personality. He is missing Jasper's increased stability on his feet. He is missing Jasper's ability to reciprocate cuddles and to play games and to make me laugh. He is missing out on helping Jasper with his spoon work, teaching him to catch, and reading books with him.

In his own world in India, Dylan is getting busier and busier with work, which leaves him with less and less time to speak. When we do manage to connect, I feel as though I am talking at him rather than with him. He is distracted by work deadlines and seemingly endless late night calls on his end. I want to keep Dylan abreast of everything Jasper is up to, because it feels important to me. But to Dylan, who is swamped under the pressures of a new job and trying to find his feet in an unfamiliar city, my stories are simply a reminder of how far apart we all are.

Keeping busy helps me to avoid thinking too much about what the coup has taken from me and from Jasper. In the short term, it has taken Dylan, and the fledgling family life we had only just begun to enjoy back in January 2021. It turned the first nine months of Jasper's life from an oasis of calm wonder as we watched him explore the new world around him, into a hurricane of stress, fear and constant worry as to what might happen next. In the longer term, it has taken the future we saw in Myanmar for at least a decade, the job I loved in a market I knew and the stability we foresaw for Jasper's childhood years.

Although we have a new plan of moving to India, the

immediate future is still disconcertingly vague. We hope that Jasper and I will be able to join Dylan in Mumbai at the end of the year, but with COVID still ever-present and visa issuance disrupted in many countries including India, nothing is set in stone. Devoid of a departure date, I hover in a strange kind of limbo, focusing intently on that which I can control; namely, making sure Jasper is the busiest of babies.

22

OCTOBER

At the beginning of October, my employment contract comes to an end and with that, the last piece of my Myanmar life falls away. My team organises a farewell call during which they present me with a tribute video, and as it plays, the realisation that my time in Myanmar is officially over hits me like a bus.

Until that point I still felt connected to my old life by my work email account. I checked it every morning to read the daily reports and status updates, and to see how projects I was involved in were moving along. I was emotionally invested in the things I was working on, even if I no longer had an active role. I knew that eventually this last thread of connection would be detached and that I would have to let my role in Myanmar go. I have left plenty of jobs, had plenty of leaving do's and said plenty of farewells, but none so heartbreaking as this one.

It would have been better to have held the call while Jasper napped, but the team isn't available then, so Jasper joins me, first from my lap, and then from the floor behind me surrounded by his toys. With him there, I can focus the camera on his face instead of mine, and smile and laugh about him and his antics, instead of thinking too much about what I am feeling. Members of my team are in tears, and I am in tears. I am crying to the point of not really being able to see, or hear the video as it plays. And then I am expected to say something.

Never have I been so completely devoid of words. Any words. All words. Under ordinary circumstances I would have said something about knowing that they would all go on to do wonderful things, but it feels inappropriate given the state of the country. I can't bring myself to talk about hopes for the future when it feels like there are none. I hired almost every single one of them, and I feel personally responsible for their professional growth and development, and yet here I am, having upped and left the country when they most need guidance. They are grateful to me for having done everything in my power to make their professional lives as rewarding as possible, something I am proud of, but something that for now seems futile given the uncertainties they face. They look up to me but I feel as though I no longer deserve their loyalty when, by leaving, I have done what so many of them can't. I feel like a hypocrite. I don't know what to say and so, after a few seconds of silence, I say, 'I don't know what to say, except thank you to all of you for making my experience in Myanmar so, so wonderful.'

After the call is over, I sit for a long time wondering how on earth I can continue my day now that I have an enormous hole through my chest. I feel terrible for having failed to say anything motivating or positive to my team, who I love dearly and for whom I have so much respect. I think about the weight that was lifted when I landed in Dubai, and that I am now living in a safe, quiet cottage surrounded by family. And then I think about all of them still in Myanmar under the same heavy pressure and uncertainty. I feel guilty for leaving them, but in my heart of hearts, I know that my priority is Jasper and that I have done what is best for him. I also feel oddly empty. Since graduating university, I have never not worked, and I didn't appreciate how much of my sense of purpose and identity I owe to my career. Knowing that my career is now on hold for an indefinite period, I suddenly feel as though I am adrift at sea.

I am still sitting with Jasper crawling around at my feet when Liv walks into the cottage to pick us up and take us to lunch by the beach. She takes one look at my face, throws her bag on the floor and rushes over to engulf me in an enormous, long hug. I collapse onto her as ten months' worth of stress, anxiety, panic, fear and sadness pour out of me. I haven't processed our departure from Myanmar fully. I haven't even really come to terms with Dylan leaving. But as the book closes on this final chapter of my Myanmar story, the floodgates open and all the pent-up emotion from that series of traumas comes pouring out.

'Oh Milla,' says my sister gently. 'What happened? Did you have your call with your team?'

I take a breath and try to pull myself together. I smear the tears across my face and reach for a tissue as I pull away from the hug.

'Yes. They made ... they made me a video,' I sob. 'And I ... I couldn't say anything. I didn't know what to say. What could I say? What do you say to a team who have lost their entire future?' I sniff and cry, trying to speak clearly.

'I don't know. But they know how you feel. They will know how hard this is for you and how much you care,' My sister comforts, her own eyes watering with empathy.

'I just wish I could do something. Or at least say something that would make them feel better. But I couldn't find any words. All I said was thank you,' I say.

'It's OK to cry. It's OK to feel sad. You have been through

a lot, and maybe this was the final piece that was stopping you from grieving for all of it,' she says, pulling me back into a hug. 'Mum is waiting in the car. We thought we'd go to the Nude Food cafe at St Aubin. Get some fresh sea air and see some seagulls for Jasper?'

I sniff again and nod.

'I have already packed Jasper's bag; he just needs a change before we set off. Maybe I just need to get out of the house. I can't believe how hard it hit me to say goodbye to everyone. That's really it. That's really my Myanmar life over.'

I say the last part as much to myself as to Liv.

'I'll change Jasper while you get yourself ready,' offers Liv and bundles Jasper off up the stairs to the bathroom while I reassemble my face and dry my eyes.

Over lunch I repeatedly well up and have to fight back tears as the memory of the call, the feelings of guilt and then the sense of loss keep rising back up to the surface of my consciousness. Despite it being October, the sky is cloudless and blue, the sun bright enough for sunglasses and the temperature warm enough for shirt sleeves. After lunch we walk along the seafront to the harbour to look at the boats and the gulls and the old fort. Jersey is beautiful to me in all weathers, but it's particularly special during an Indian summer. I smile to myself thinking of what a different meaning the term Indian summer will hold for Jasper when he grows old enough to understand it.

'Why don't you come to London?' suggests Liv as we walk. 'I'm going over next week to pack up the flat to ship things back here. You and Jasper could come over for a few days. It might be a nice distraction?'

'I hadn't thought about going anywhere at all, to be honest. I was just thinking we'd be here until we leave. But maybe you're right. It might be a good distraction and I could see some friends at least. I don't really know anyone here anymore - they are all in London.'

'I'm sure they'd love to see you. And I won't be working so I'll be free to look after Jasper if you want.'

'OK. I'll look at flights. I know it's silly, but I don't want to miss too many of Jasper's classes now that we are signed up to them,' I reply.

'You could even come for your birthday,' says Liv.

'Eurgh. I am just going to ignore that. It doesn't even seem worth observing this year,' I grumble. 'But yeah, I think coming to London is a good idea.'

A trip to London is indeed a good distraction, but mainly because the thought of travelling on my own to a big city with a small baby is absolutely, all-consumingly terrifying to me. As I plan the trip, meticulously mapping out every movement and transit, I demonise London into a writhing pit of thieves and muggers and baby-snatchers. Despite my mum and sister trying to persuade me of the helpfulness of strangers, I am convinced that I need to be entirely self-reliant for the journey, able to carry Jasper, his nappy bag, our suitcase and his buggy without help. I imagine scenarios where opportunists take off with the buggy while I am not watching, or with the suitcase while I am putting Jasper in the buggy, or most extreme, with Jasper while I collapse the buggy and grapple the suitcase. I am conscious of just how vulnerable I am to petty thieves as a mother with a small baby because my attention is so often focused on Jasper, especially in cafes or restaurants.

Once I arrive in London, I have new elements of my reverse culture shock to contend with. Since I was last in London, the payment options for the London Underground have changed. While previously I would have used my bank card, I can now use my phone and, knowing that I want to reduce the pick-pocketable valuables I need to have stashed about my person for my own convenient use, I decide that is the preferable option. I make Liv walk me through the process of tapping my phone repeatedly. I decide that for any excursions I make on my own, I will wear Jasper in his carrier. This leaves both my hands free to use as needed but, more than that, wearing him makes me feel protected from the bustling, frantic world around me. Jasper is my armour. I also wear the forced smile which I believe makes me appear reasonable and open to being educated in child-wrangling etiquette should I do something against the mother-baby code. I think it probably makes me look unhinged, but whether I do nothing wrong or people fear me, the result is that I am left in peace behind my strange face.

I am not used to moving around without either a car or Jasper's buggy to help with heavy bags. But in London, a city of poor accessibility and expensive cabs, in order to avoid the stress of having to do the one-handed buggy collapse every time I meet a staircase, I must carry or wear everything I need every time we go out. On one occasion Jasper and I venture out together with his buggy. We take the bus, to avoid the stairs at the entrance to my local tube station. It is all very civilised on the way into town, because we board at an early station and we are the only buggy in there. It is harder on the way back, however, because by the time our bus arrives at Oxford St, it is already at capacity, with two buggies, one of which is turfed off in front of us in favour of a wheelchair-user, as per policy. On this occasion, I decide that the walk home will do us good and luckily Jasper falls asleep before he can complain.

Every day in London I catch up with friends, none of whom I have seen since having Jasper. Most have their own children and their own parenting horror stories, and they all want to hear the story not only of our escape from Myanmar, but of Jasper's birth adventure too. I am grateful to Jasper for his ability to work the room and lighten the mood. Liv sits through the retelling on numerous occasions and I can tell from her face that it doesn't get any easier to hear. I can see her reliving the worry she must have felt throughout the months which followed the coup. My friends, in turn, do a lot of head shaking, a lot of eyebrow raising, a lot of open-mouthed staring and they say 'oh my god' a lot. The first time I tell the story, I find it draining, thinking back through all the stress and all the worry. There is a lot of information to impart in a short period of time and I find myself darting back and forth between what we were trying to do and all the many ways it felt as though the universe was working against us. But by the end of the week, I have distilled it into a relatively short, spirited tale of survival.

'I can't imagine what you've been through,' says my friend Emma, after she has taken in all I have just said.

'I mean, COVID was hard enough, without a coup and then with a newborn baby! I just don't know how you did it. A hell of a first year as a mum!' she says in amazement.

'Well, I didn't really have a choice. We all just kind of muddled through. I must admit, the mothering part took something of a back seat to dealing with the coup. I am lucky Jasper is such a good baby. I try not to think about what would have happened if he'd had serious health complications or if he'd been a nightmare. I might not have come through it with my sense of humour still intact!'

'It must be such a relief to be out of there,' Emma says.

'Yeah. It's nice to deal with normal issues for a change. So, tell me about you. What's been happening with you?' I change the subject.

'Oh, our life is so boring,' she replies.

'Don't knock boring. Boring is good. Boring is exactly what I'm looking for right now!' I say joking.

'You say that ...' observes Emma. 'But you are about to move to India. I don't think you know how to do boring.'

A phrase I have heard a lot when I have told friends and family about our move to India is 'out of the frying pan and into the fire'. Each time I hear it, I laugh and make a face to say 'I know, right?' It also makes me question whether we are doing the right thing. Even without having lived there, I can tell from news stories, films, Dylan's account of how he is getting on and my own brief experience as a tourist there fifteen years ago, that India burns with a ferocity which Myanmar does not have.

At the end of my week in London I wonder what I was ever worried about. I have come to love travelling around with Jasper. I have thoroughly enjoyed showing him the sights, playing with him in the park, putting him down to sleep in his makeshift den of a bed on the floor, spending the afternoon with him and Liv at a Westfield Shopping Centre and taking him out for lunch at the local pubs. On the flight home, I look back on the trip as a huge success. I can see now that I don't need to worry so much. I realise that it's time to shake off the doomsday mentality that I am clearly still carrying around. If my plans go awry, it isn't as though I am going to be arrested and thrown in a Burmese jail. I can simply sit in a nearby cafe, grab a coffee for me and a pastry for Jasper and think of a Plan B.

Jasper and I arrive back in Jersey two days before my birthday, which is just enough time to make myself a birthday cake. I won't say I celebrate the occasion, but I acknowledge another trip around the sun and blame the coup for the appearance of my first sprinkling of grey hairs. For the first time ever, I do feel another year older and another year wiser. I am still fragile, but I can feel the stirrings of some confidence as a mother. Spending my birthday outside of Myanmar for the first time in six years, I also feel some semblance of closure from my time in Yangon.

23

HIGHS AND LOWS

I ORIGINALLY DECIDE that I can't face organising anything for Jasper's birthday because the thought of throwing a first birthday party from which Dylan will be absent makes me cry. But as 2 December gets nearer, I realise that failing to mark the occasion will be far worse. I owe it to Dylan and the Australian family, and to my family, and to Jasper himself, to celebrate his rather extraordinary first year of life. The remote family are all living vicariously through a private photo sharing app onto which I upload as many moments of Jasper's days, weeks and months as I can capture. I am a one-woman paparazzo and his birthday is as good an excuse as any to take some special photos.

With Jasper as my muse, I throw myself into planning a small but beautifully decorated, highly photogenic party. I line up a balloon artist and cake designer to assist me but, a few days before the party, they both inexplicably vanish. After the year I've had, I don't waste any time before formulating a Plan B and roping my mother into some arts and crafts.

We accept that blowing up balloons while a baby sleeps directly overhead is a high-risk strategy, so balloons become a day time activity, with Jasper's help. Jasper is in charge of quality control. If a balloon can't withstand a bit of rough and tumble with an almost-one-year-old, it has to be replaced. Jasper doesn't mind at all when a balloon bursts, but he does not trust a balloon that has yet to be tied. The unpredictable, high-speed escape of an untied balloon turns Jasper into a trembling koala, scrambling up my torso and trying to disappear into my jumper. Eventually we have enough baby-proof balloons to attempt an arch, which soon becomes a pillar, and then ultimately a short, uneven stack of unruly, mismatched balloons held together with a lot of sticky tape and draped with fake ivy in a futile attempt to cover up the tape. Fortunately, the balloons are not the focal point. Strung up in front of the patio doors, outside which the tousled green of the wintry, windswept garden complements the artificial foliage inside, is a row of smiling faces: absent friends and family unashamedly Photoshopped onto the bodies of parrots, elephants, tigers and monkeys and displayed as bunting. Front and centre is Dylan - arguably the most important of the absentees, surrounded by Jasper's Australian family, his godparents in New Zealand and his aunt and uncle in the north of England who can't get time off work.

I go with a tropical jungle theme in honour of where Jasper was born, as well as out of respect for his obsession with animals and plants and all things Sir David Attenborough. This means that our balloon sculpture is justified in its jumbly, tangled form, and our cake needs some animal figurines. The evening before Jasper's birthday, my mother and I sit down to ice the cake that I made during one of his naps earlier in the day. Strewn across the table are the entire contents of the Waitrose 'Home Baking' aisle, together with a sketch of how I hope the cake might look and two large glasses of wine. I assign my mother the task of making a monkey, while I get started on the river, some palm leaves and the base layer on which it will sit. I admit, I have grand visions. I turn away from the table to make use of the larger counter space for my rolling and smoothing and am engrossed in my work until I realise my mother is weeping quietly behind me. I spin around to find her doubled over in hysterical laughter, tears streaming down her face and what I can only describe as a crime against monkeykind slumping drunkenly in front of her on the table. My mother, it turns out, is no fondant sculptor. Her so-called-monkey has a sausage for a body, a tiny pea head and long, spaghetti arms which she has squashed into the table to hold him upright. He has no tail, no legs, no discernible facial features and absolutely no chance of survival in the wild.

'What have you done?' I snort.

'I made a monkey,' she cries back at me, wiping away the tears. 'Except I forgot what a monkey looks like, and then I ran out of the orange mix I made.'

'You ran out because it's all in his body! What is that? He's 90% body! And where's his face?' I move closer to try and make out something which might constitute an ear, a nose or an eye, but find nothing. I dissolve into laughter and the more I laugh, the more my mother laughs until we are both completely overcome with muffled hysteria, as we try to avoid waking Jasper. I am first to regain my composure.

'OK. Having failed so spectacularly with the monkey, I am reassigning you to make a grey colour for an elephant. I think maybe if you mix some blue, green and red, it'll be about right?'

My mother rearranges her face and nods in acceptance of her new challenge. I return to the counter behind me to put the finishing touches to my river. It isn't long before I hear the familiar snort of my mother's laughter once again, and when I turn around she is again crying, but this time into an enormous lump of blueish-green fondant.

'Now what are you doing?' I enquire as straight faced as possible. I can see very clearly what has gone wrong.

'I keep trying to make it greyer, but it's not changing colour. The more red I add the more fondant I seem to have. But it's not turning grey or brown,' she says when she catches her breath.

'Your elephant could eat the entire cake at the rate it's going! It's supposed to sit delicately on the top, not squash the whole thing! I could make a herd of elephants with that much fondant, if only there was space on the cake.'

We collapse again into fits of suppressed giggles, glancing with trepidation at the monitor which will show us if our nonsense has reached Jasper's room. We are both covered in fondant icing and in no fit state to calm a disgruntled baby. I reassign my disgraced mother to clean-up duty, while I take over as sculptor, fashioning a suitably sized, but still green, elephant and an appropriately appendaged monkey to perch elegantly on Jasper's cake.

I realise I haven't laughed like this in months. For days afterwards I crease up with the memory of just how uniquely awful my mother proved to be at her tasks. When the rest of the family arrives for the party the next day, they are oblivious to the literal tears that went into the cake, which is given pride of place below the bunting and beside the balloons, most of which, luckily, haven't burst or come unstuck overnight.

The party goes exactly as planned, which isn't unexpected seeing as there are only five people invited besides Jasper and me, and all of them live within a two-mile radius. I raise a glass of bubbly in a slightly tearful toast to absent friends and family and help Jasper open his humble collection of small and portable presents. At my insistence, he is only given things which we can carry with us on our onward journey. As I am inflating a ride-on giraffe, I hear the clink of a spoon on glass. I look up to see my mother ready to speak.

'Another toast – to Milla. To your first year of motherhood. Goodness only knows it hasn't been easy, but you are doing an amazing job.' She begins to tear up as she continues, 'It's wonderful what you are doing with Jasper. He's a very lucky baby. To Milla.'

As the others join the toast and slurp their bubbles, I smile through my own tears and let out a puff of acknowledgement.

'It's been quite the ride, hasn't it?' I say after a few sniffles. 'Thank you. But honestly, I am only doing whatever it is I am doing because of Jasper.'

Later, when Jasper is in bed and I am happily curled up on the sofa, I think about the year that has passed since Jasper's birth, and I realise that despite having brushed it off, I do feel worthy of my mother's toast. I realise that I didn't just survive Jasper's first birthday, I genuinely enjoyed celebrating it. Celebrating him. And if I am being completely honest with myself, celebrating me.

Buoyed by the new sense of achievement this major milestone gives me, I start to look more seriously into visas for India. I feel as though I have absorbed enough normality and stability to embark on the next leg of the journey.

Dylan went to India on an electronic visa which was issued quickly and with minimal fuss. In my blissful ignorance, I am working on the assumption that Jasper and I will enjoy the same experience. I couldn't be more wrong. Through many hours of Googling, several calls to VFS in London and a few to the Indian High Commission in Australia, I establish two things. The first is that British citizens are not eligible for electronic visas. And the second is that Dylan is on the wrong visa to bring in dependents. What we have lazily tagged as 'and then Milla and Jasper join Dylan in India' is suddenly a lot more complicated than we have anticipated. The more I learn about the process by which Jasper and I can join Dylan, the angrier and more frustrated it makes me. I find myself yet again in a situation that I couldn't have avoided, other than by Dylan not taking the Indian job. On calls to Dylan, I question the sanity of the India plan in its entirety and vocalise a scenario where Jasper and I never make it to India at all. I put pressure on him to try and resolve the visa issue from his end, despite knowing that he has no bandwidth to do so on top of his work.

'I am sorry it's not going to be as easy as we hoped,' says Dylan once I finish my latest rant about the Indian visa process. 'But we will find a way. I have these consultants here who are looking into whether I can convert my visa in-country.'

'You can't,' I snap.

'They are looking into it, like I said,' Dylan repeats.

'Yes, but I already know that you can't,' I retort. 'I don't understand why you put so much faith in the consultants. They clearly don't know any more than I do, or they would have presented you a solution by now. How long will it take them to come back to you? Are we going to be able to join you before the end of the year? Or in January even?'

'It's not going to be this year, Milla, and you know that,' Dylan says trying to reason with me. 'It's already December.'

'Well maybe we just give up. Maybe you have to quit the job and we come up with a new plan.'

Dylan sighs. 'I think you and Jasper need to come here first, and see what it's like. I think you'll like it,' he says.

'Why would we like it? You keep saying we will like it but you haven't told me anything about it! What is there to like?

You never send photos, you never tell me what you've been up to and you haven't given me any good reasons to be interested in coming there.'

I am being unfair to Dylan and I know it. He is not an avid photo-taker and he is not someone who can paint a vivid picture with words. Those are my jobs whenever we travel anywhere. He is also working too hard to have any time to distil his first impressions into anything other than a few snippets of useful information. He has found an apartment, after a few weeks of looking, and has moved out of his hotel to live in an unfurnished box awaiting delivery of belongings from Yangon. He tries on a couple of occasions to show me the facilities within the apartment complex; the tennis court, the squash court and the pool, but my vision is too clouded with frustration to take anything in.

'I thought you said you'd been here?' Dylan reminds me.

'I have. But I have pretty much no memory of it. I don't know why, but Mumbai clearly never made an impression on me, other than one restaurant that I went to with my dad.'

'Oh. Well, I still think you are going to like it. It's what we enjoy - a bit chaotic, but very livable. Let's wait until the end of the year, when the consultants come back with a solution, and then we can talk about whether India is going to work for us. Right now, we can't make any decisions because we don't have all the information,' Dylan says persisting.

'Fine. But I don't think they will find anything I haven't already told you,' I say as I hang up.

I feel so completely and utterly powerless to do anything about the situation I am in; a situation not unlike the one I was in during those last few months in Yangon, in so far as I am stuck somewhere I do not want to be. But if I could trade the feeling of hopelessness I have during that December in Jersey for fear of bombs and violence in Yangon, I would.

Yangon was stressful at the end, there is no doubt about it, but there was an end in sight; a strategy, a plan. I was busy with work and packing and travel arrangements. And I had Dylan there with me, going through what I was going through. It was a stress that on some occasions I mistook for exhilaration. Now faced with Christmas apart, and Dylan's birthday and New Year, and however many more days or weeks or months after that, I have nothing to do but wait.

The smallest hiccup in my day's plans, the slightest change to Jasper's routine, the tiniest misunderstanding between me and a family member feels like an insurmountable obstacle. Issues that I would ordinarily resolve swiftly weigh on me and drag me deeper and deeper underwater. I cling to Jasper as though he is the only thing keeping me afloat. He is my reason for getting out of bed in the morning but also my excuse for going to bed early at night.

At the last sign language class before the Christmas break, one of the mums turns to me as we are packing up.

'Will we be seeing you next term? Do you have a departure date yet?'

My mouth forms a smile, but I am quite sure my eyes are saying something different. 'Do you know what? I have no idea. I don't have a leaving date yet because we still haven't worked out how to get a visa for India. So, it's looking like my husband will have a lonely Christmas in Mumbai - just one day off to spend alone in an empty apartment, and we'll be here. He can't even get the time off to come back here for a few days. He'll be there for New Year too, which is his birthday. We can't go there, and he can't come here. We are waiting for some consultants to confirm what visa we can get and they aren't working over the holidays. I've actually started looking for jobs for me, in case I can get my own visa and take Jasper in on that, but I doubt that's going to work out.'

I pause for breath.

'Oh I'm so sorry,' says the mum, taken aback by an answer I imagine she wasn't expecting. 'But you are staying with your family here, right?'

'Kind of. Next door to my dad. The heating is half-broken in the house we are in, so it's freezing downstairs. We'll have Christmas at my mum's but we can't stay there overnight because my other two sisters are there and there's no space for Jasper and me. So, we'll just walk down on the day. I know I shouldn't complain. At least I have people. Dylan has no one. And that just makes me feel so guilty for complaining. I think if it weren't for Jasper, I would just stay in bed and hibernate until the festive season is over. Gosh, you didn't really need to hear all this, did you?'

As I climb into the car and drive home with an almost-sleeping Jasper I can't quite believe what I have just unloaded onto that poor unsuspecting mum. I am all over the place. I am speaking to Dylan less frequently and the conversations we are having feel less meaningful. I am angry and he is stressed. And then I am angry because he is stressed. And then I am stressed because I am angry that he is stressed. I know that I am not supporting him as I should be. Quite the opposite. I am loading all my troubles and grievances onto him, and blaming him for our extended separation. I am in completely the wrong place, but there is nothing I can do about it. I convince myself that I am becoming an unwanted presence in the cottage; those awful guests who never leave. I turn down invitations for lunches and dinners with my family, using Jasper's nap and sleeping schedule as an excuse, but really, I just can't face having fun when I know Dylan is all alone.

Christmas is the worst part; my so-called festival of togetherness and I feel anything but together. I dress Jasper as an elf and we open his stocking with Dylan on a video call. It is as fun as it can be, but I feel heavy with sadness once the call ends. Jasper and I ring the Australian family to wish them well and to show off his elf outfit and then, after his morning nap, we walk down the road to join the festivities at my mum's. Jasper is the greatest gift. He is the centre of attention and is spurred on by the laughter, the silliness and the fact that he can pull baubles off the bottom of the tree when we aren't looking. Any lull in conversation is easily filled with a game of peekaboo as Jasper's mischievous, entertaining little personality shines through and chips away at my self-pity.

Dylan's New Year's Eve birthday passes with him playing squash on his own with some newly purchased squash shoes and a new racket; gifts to himself. The image of such an isolated birthday breaks my heart into even more pieces than it is in already. Jasper and I spend New Year's at my mother's sipping on whiskey sours (me) and milk (Jasper). I am in bed long before midnight and awake to a feeling of disappointment on 1 January. I am also in pain. I went for my COVID booster on 31 December and twenty-four hours later, aches and pains kick in. I have long been hoping for 2022 to be better than 2021, but it doesn't feel like an auspicious start – still feeling unwanted at the cottage, still no closer to India and battling through a day of solo parenting in a body that feels as though it has been run over.

A few days into the new year, Dylan tests positive for COVID again and begins two weeks of solitary confinement in the apartment in Mumbai. I find the thought of him being even more alone than he already is very hard to deal with. It brings back shuddering recollections of Tony's solo COVID ordeal and I insist Dylan let me know daily that he is still alive. I can't do anything to help him or to support him, and instead I absorb the injustice of his situation into the frustration I am already feeling about mine. During those two weeks we have almost nothing to talk about when we connect. There are a lot of long silences punctuated only by the clang of a spoon on the side of a pan as I stir Jasper's latest batch of bolognese and the tap of the keys on Dylan's laptop as he keeps ploughing through his deliverables. I am too caught up in myself and he is too isolated from anything outside his work emails to contribute to a conversation. Talking to him makes me feel worse about everything, but not talking to him makes me feel uncaring.

True to form, Jasper breaks me out of my funk. On 11 January, at thirteen months and nine days old, Jasper launches himself onto two feet, at pace. And with that, I accept that I have to take a run at 2022, whether I like it or not.

24

COUNTDOWN

WHEN DEALING WITH A SMALL BABY, taking life in chunks of three months is a good thing for one very important reason: this is how clothing is sized. Until they reach one year old, that is, when the temporal wedges expand to half years. I was secretly chuffed at the timing of our supposedly short stay in Jersey because it coincided with Jasper's ninth to twelfth month. I took full advantage of the end-of-summer sales, which were in full swing when we arrived in September, to buy up all the twelve-to-eighteen-month summer gear that Jasper would need on our arrival in India sometime in early January. And I purchased a capsule collection of nine-to-twelve-month-sized winter essentials to see him through until his first birthday and our departure soon after. That was the plan, anyway. The reality doesn't quite align.

As January melts towards February, Jasper's baggy jumpers and slouchy tracksuits are starting to cling like muscle tops and leggings, and no amount of post-wash stretching can make the bottoms of his trousers meet his shoes. With every week that goes by, without a concrete plan for our travel to India, the risk of Jasper bursting out of his clothes increases, until I have to concede defeat. Sometime in January, it becomes clear that for Jasper and I to join Dylan, he first has to go to Australia to get himself onto the correct visa; a visa which allows for dependents. The state of Dylan's project, and his dedication to its success, mean that his absence for any prolonged period is going to be a problem. Another problem is that nobody at the VFS office (at whose mercy we find ourselves once more) can confirm whether, as Brits, Jasper and I can apply for our dependent visas in Australia too. While Dylan searches for an appropriate break point in his project, and the consultants dig around online to verify information that I have already found, Jasper keeps on growing.

Jasper isn't only growing in size. He is taking leaps in skills too. In just a few weeks, he becomes a master of walking; finally bringing his forward momentum under control and learning to stop on his own, without a sofa or a pair of arms to collapse into. Dylan and I have never given the revered list of baby firsts much consideration, partly because the early days of Jasper's life were so fraught with other concerns that we forgot to keep track of his life skills, but partly because while there is undoubtedly a first, there is also a second and third and then suddenly it is as though he has always been able to smile, or roll, or sit, or clap. I think we both find more joy in Jasper as a whole, than as a sum of his first-time parts. With walking, however, something feels a little different. That Jasper will be walking the next time he sees Dylan really brings home the length of time we have been apart. It doesn't matter to us that Dylan has missed Jasper's first steps, but it seems so unfair that he has missed almost half a year of his life. This new two-legged self-propulsion also presents a whole new parenting challenge on the next long-haul flight we will be taking, and adds an urgency to my impatience to leave.

Deciding that the guilt I feel over Jasper's cold ankles outweighs the guilt I will feel for buying clothes that might only be in use for a few weeks, I grudgingly go shopping for Jasper's second minimalist winter wardrobe. On the same expedition into town, I join the library. As well as clothes, Jasper is beginning to outgrow the tiny selection of books we have with us from Myanmar. We have read all six of them cover to cover so many times that between my mother, my sister and I, we have exhausted all possible vocabulary and excitement that can be squeezed from their pages. Just when I am considering starting Jasper on the local newspaper, a fellow sign-language mum mentions that she goes to weekly nursery rhyme sing-along sessions at the public library. Jasper and I join her and her son one day and discover the cave of wonders that is the children's book section. Not only does Jasper now have clothes that fit, but he also has an endless selection of books. And some freshly enthused readers.

I am exceptionally lucky that the same family who lent me the infant car seat that Jasper now barely fits into, also has a spare booster seat of the next size up. So, in the space of a few days, Jasper upgrades his wardrobe, his bookshelf *and* his transport. That I can solve the various trivial issues as they arise doesn't mean that it is an easy period for me. I am in limbo again. Again, I know what needs to be done but I have no control over making it happen. I have no idea if I am planning a week ahead, a month ahead or longer. Buying clothes which can be later donated and borrowing books and car seats which will be returned are manageable, but they aren't the only things I have to consider. I don't know whether to sign Jasper up to another term of his classes and they are all non-refundable. I don't know how much food I need to have in the freezer. Too much and all my carefully portioned but unsalted, blended food will go to waste. Too little and poor Jasper will be back on pouches and packets. I don't know if we will still be taking up space in the cottage at Easter, which is more of an issue for various step-siblings than it is for me. I have one eye on flight availability out of Jersey as those seats seem to be selling out fast. I don't want to get the green light on Australia only to find that the twenty-five-minute short hop to London is my downfall. I want to avoid a mad scramble if we have to leave suddenly but, at the same time, I don't want to waste the time we have left in Jersey. I remind myself that I have dealt with weightier worries back in Yangon, but that doesn't quell the familiar sense of rising stress.

I take the executive decision to behave as though we are staying, as far as Jasper is concerned. It isn't fair for him to miss out on anything, including clothes that fit, because his parents are pushing the limits of emigration during a global pandemic. Conversely, as far as I am concerned, I act as though I am leaving. I ignore my sister's encouragement to take advantage of the winter sales and buy a few things that can live in Jersey. Instead, I simply rotate the selection of jumpers and jackets that I borrowed from my mum back in September and refresh my wardrobe that way. I make little or no effort to deepen friendships I have begun with some of the mums at Jasper's various classes, something I later regret. I spend hours plotting imminent travel routes, only to watch the proposed dates and connections come and go, and find myself still very much grounded.

One morning at the beginning of February, while Jasper and I are out on our usual walk to the farm shop, I spot an early spring daffodil poking above the long grass on the verge. In the same way Jasper's graduation to two legs alerted me to the time we have been away from Dylan, the daffodil makes me realise that we have survived a whole winter! I was expecting far worse from my first winter in years. Although the air is still crisp and the sun more aesthetic than ambient, spring is here. I feel vaguely optimistic. It is 2022, the season is starting to change, and surely this means that we are one step closer to being reunited with Dylan.

February also means one full year since the coup. Myanmar-based friends mark the anniversary with silent strikes and darkened Facebook profile pictures. Thinking about the same day a year before gives me pause to reflect on my current situation in the context of what I have been through. I am hit by conflicted feelings of relief and frustration. I also feel heavy-hearted. It makes me sad that Myanmar has all but dropped out of the international news, save for a spattering of articles on the day of the anniversary itself, most of which highlight that nothing much has changed in a year; the volatile stalemate between the military and the people continues with no compromise or resolution in sight. The attacks, the fighting, the danger, the fear, the cash shortage, the hopeless waiting for the world to do something to help; and the loss of jobs and income as international organisations pull out of the market continue. Some journalist friends release and promote documentaries on the Myanmar situation, and social media groups fight to retain some global attention on the plight of the people, but I am sad that the world has lost interest in Myanmar.

Just a few weeks after the one-year anniversary of Myanmar's coup, Russia invades Ukraine. The frenzied outpouring of global outrage and aid is unprecedented. For me, it's also heart-wrenching. Everyone is talking about the situation in Ukraine, and I find it hard to listen without wanting to shout 'But what about Myanmar?' I feel almost offended that Myanmar should have been forgotten so quickly. But then I remember how rarely anyone I mention my life in Myanmar to asks a follow up question, and how little most people know about the country. I also remember how Dylan and I reacted to the image of the crowded military aircraft evacuating people from Kabul back in August, when the Taliban seized control of the country as the U.S troops withdrew. It was an iconic image and one that appeared to incapsulate the urgency and the scale of the operation. I was in no place to take on the emotional weight of the suffering in Afghanistan. We commented on how much more there must be going on behind that one headline image, and how lucky we were that we were catching a commercial flight out of Myanmar two weeks later, not a having a military evacuation. And then we promptly pushed all thoughts of Kabul to the backs of our minds. I assume that, for most people, this is what has happened with Myanmar: something newer, nearer and potentially deadlier has come along and pushed the already-distant Myanmar out of their field of vision. I realise what a rare privilege it is to have lived in and loved Myanmar the way I have.

I talk to a friend in Yangon about how she feels about the anniversary of the coup.

'I watch the sunset from my window every evening, and every time the sun goes down, it drags me a little further down with it,' she says, rather poetically. 'Everything is hopeless. My husband thinks I am being dramatic, but I don't know how else to be.'

'If ever there is a time for justified theatrics, this is it,' I say, joking.

'Maybe. Have you seen Henry, yet?' she says, changing the subject back to her favourite Jerseyman, Henry Cavill, as she always does.

'Ha. No, not yet!' I laugh. 'I do love how your future is falling apart but all that you are thinking about is whether or not I have carried out your stalking requests on your favourite superhero, though!'

I think about how relatable my friend's unwavering celebrity fandom is, despite the context for it. News stories that are published about Myanmar show the violence and the impact of international investment being withdrawn, but on a day-to-day basis, the people there are going about their lives in as normal a way as possible. It would be easy for someone who hasn't lived through something like this to assume that from dawn until dusk, people think about nothing but the coup, but the reality is more complex and less one-dimensional. I appreciate how hard my own family found it to reconcile the news stories they saw in the early days of the coup with the photos I was sharing from our life in Star City.

I take advantage of donation drives for Ukraine to offload most of Jasper's winter gear when the time comes. Someone in Europe will need his snowsuit far more than he will in India. I feel tearful as I look around for anything else that might be of use to the Ukrainian evacuees, and reel with a wave of sadness for how much the people of Myanmar need the same support but how little they are receiving. As Jasper and I walk our donations down to my mother's house, to combine with her offerings, I take the long route down the empty, winding country lanes and explain everything to him. I know he doesn't understand, but it helps me to express my thoughts out loud.

I find the limbo we are now in far harder to tolerate than any of the intensity of trying to leave Myanmar, or the struggles with the reverse culture shock of settling into my new life in Jersey. At least in both of those situations I had a plan of action and was able to set myself a series of tasks to keep my mind off the bigger picture. This time I have nothing to do but wait; wait until someone tells me I can stop waiting. I am powerless to speed up the wait and this frustrates me as much as it annoys me that I can't plan anything. I try to find someone to blame: Dylan, Dylan's job, Dylan's HR department, India, Myanmar - as though personifying the reason for the long wait will make it easier to endure. It doesn't.

It is mid-March when Dylan finally finds an upcoming lull in project milestones and the consultants finally confirm that Jasper and I should be able to apply for our visas in Australia.

'We have a departure date!' I whoop to my mother on the phone as soon as I have booked our tickets. 'We will fly Jersey to London, London to Doha on 17 March. We'll meet Dylan in Doha, and then do the mega, fifteen-hour flight to Brisbane as a threesome!'

'Oh, that's such good news.' My mum sounds relieved.

At her suggestion, I am already working my way through a bucket list of all the things I want to do before leaving Jersey. My list is filled with delicious food, outdoor activities and nostalgia; a way for me to show Jasper all my favourite places, even if he won't remember them in the long term. It is a showcase of the best Jersey has to offer. But my mum knows that on the quieter days within our hectic what's what Jersey tour, I have been riding the waves of hope and disappointment every time I think we have a date which is then postponed for one reason or another. She knows that I am putting on a brave face, even on the days when I am really beginning to wonder if we will ever make it to India.

'Let me grab the calendar. Seventeenth ... ooh gosh. That's in two weeks. What's left on your list? We'd better start scheduling day by day,' she says and laughs.

'I know. It will go very fast from here, I think. There is still a lot of admin to do like the PCR test, Australian visas, and tons of printing for all our documents, but I can't believe it is finally happening! As far as activities, we are doing weekly cliff walks with Dad and the dogs, and we've walked to the pub for lunch and had tea at the garden centre. So, still to go are breakfast at the Hungry Man, sunset at St Ouen, lunch at the museum and another trip to the zoo. I think Dad is keen to do the zoo again next Monday. So, one of the others?

'Actually, let me check with Liv,' I say before my mother has a chance to choose. 'It's partly her list too! Except for her it's not a bucket list, of course. More of a re-entry 'get to know the island again' list. I must admit, it's making me wonder why we are so desperate to leave!'

My remaining days in Jersey become a blur of coastal walks, beach cafe pit stops and packing attempts. The cottage begins to empty of Jasper's and my paraphernalia and the suitcases begin to fill with all the same things I brought with me, and Jasper's new summer wardrobe. I hate packing, despite having done a lot of it. It brings out all my worst character traits; impatience, poor spatial awareness, frustration and then ultimately, a ruthlessness that leads many a regrettable dismissal of something I later decide is essential. On this occasion, however, I pack like a woman possessed. Possessed not only by an extraordinary determination to be prepared for all imaginable eventualities, but also possessed of a fortune large enough to ignore the fact that our excess baggage is going to cost almost as much as our flight tickets.

Some people call their honeymoon the trip of their lifetime but, for me, this journey wears that crown. Flying to the opposite side of the world with a mischievous toddler now in tow, staging an in-transit reunion with my husband who I haven't seen for six months, and arriving upside down at my in-laws' house feels like the most undeniable justification for throwing all sense of frugality to the wind. This truly is it. A trip of a lifetime, so emotionally charged and fraught with things which might go wrong: COVID tests that we might fail; connections we might miss; Australian ESTAs which might not be accepted; a baby who might choose not to sleep and a life's worth of belongings which might be lost in transit. In the days running up to the journey, I worry that Dylan is so busy that he might miss his flight, leaving me to fly all the way to Brisbane on my own.

When the day comes, I am sizzling with excitement and nerves, as I check into the first of our three flights. These flights will take Jasper and me almost twelve thousand miles in just shy of thirty hours, bringing us simultaneously both further from and closer to India.

PART IV

25

FAMILY REUNION

In much the same way as our farewell all those months earlier was one of hushed whispers, my reunion with Dylan is similar. Jasper is enjoying the last few minutes of his afternoon nap, tucked up in his transit hotel cot while I lie on the bed next to him, in the dark, distractedly skim-reading the day's news, and updating my family on our journey's progress. I know that Dylan's flight has landed from Mumbai and he is somewhere in the airport, but I don't know how imminent his arrival at the hotel is. It feels silly to be nervous about a reunion with my husband, but this is the first time we have spent such a long period apart, and I am a little worried that our individual experiences might have somehow changed us. I am also concerned that, despite my daily slideshows and our many video calls, Jasper might not recognise his father. I don't think my fragile heart can take the sadness that would cause Dylan. I hop around in the doorway for a while, once I know Dylan is off his plane, but then return to the bed realising the door is too much the proverbial watched pot.

The knock is quiet but, with my ears out on stalks, I hear it clearly. My heart leaps, I spring up, rush to the door and yank it open, catching it just before it bangs loudly into the wall. There he is: my favourite fully-grown person in the whole world. Dylan registers the fact that it is dark and quiet and places his bags carefully on the floor, before pulling me in for a long-awaited hello.

'We made it!' I say quietly once our arms grow tired from a long, tight hug. 'What a mission.'

'I've missed you,' says Dylan sincerely.

'I've missed you more. How was your flight?' I ask.

'Yeah, you know. It was short. I just realise I've gone in the wrong direction. We are behind India here. What a roundabout route,' says Dylan.

'Ha. What about us? We have to fly all the way to Australia to then go back on ourselves to reach India which is only an eight-hour direct flight from London! Nothing about this has been straightforward, has it?' I remind him. 'But at least now we are together.'

'How much longer does he need to sleep?' asks Dylan, peering past me down the hallway, and over to the cot.

'Oh - not long. Come in, come in. I thought we'd go and grab some lunch when he wakes up. We had breakfast when we first arrived, and we have another seven or so hours until our next flight. For Jasper, it's already the afternoon, so I hope he'll be exhausted by the time we board the next flight.'

'How were your flights so far?' asks Dylan, as we step into the hallway and close the door, plunging ourselves back into darkness.

'The first flight was OK except he kept kicking the guy in front,' I say in a low voice. 'His legs are so much longer now; they can get us into far more trouble. And then the second flight was amazing. We had a pod! I didn't realise Qatar Airways had them. Jasper was already out cold by the time we boarded, so all I had to do was slowly recline my seat and detach him from his carrier and we both slept the entire way in our little room. I was almost sad that I didn't have a chance to take advantage of the menu, but we left at 9pm and I knew I should sleep too.'

'Oh wow - I didn't realise they had the pods. And what about our next flight, is it the same?' Dylan asks as eagerly as a low volume allows.

'I have no idea, to be honest. But I guess it will be pods again. I hope so anyway. It's such a shame that we have to pay for him once he turns two. I could get used to this style of travel!' I say grinning.

Dylan and I tiptoe further into the room and resume my earlier silent vigil, awaiting some movement from Jasper. To my enormous relief, there is no space between us, no awkwardness, no difference. It is as though we have never been apart, and the previous six months seem suddenly inconsequential.

A rustle and a toot announce Jasper's return to consciousness. He rolls and writhes for a few seconds before coming to and taking in his unfamiliar surroundings. He pulls himself up to standing and is about to cry out when he sees me. And then he sees Dylan. Jasper rubs his eyes and stares at Dylan. Before he has a chance to do or say more, Dylan is up off the bed and scooping Jasper up into his arms.

'Hello little man,' Dylan says. 'Oh, I've missed you.'

I wait with bated breath to see if Jasper is going to cry or fight the tight grip his father has on him, but he doesn't. There isn't so much as a hint of hesitation or wariness. Jasper melts into Dylan's arms, resting his head on his father's shoulder. I feel left out. I jump up and muscle in on this first of many family hugs. After a few seconds, Jasper signs for some water, so I leave Dylan and Jasper for a few minutes to refill his cup. I want to give them some time to get to know one another, so I dawdle in the bathroom, and by the time I re-emerge a minute or two later, Dylan is lying on the bed while Jasper menaces over him with a pillow.

'I see Jasper's shown you who's boss now then?' I say laughing.

'He's so strong! I can't believe he can lift this pillow. He's so much bigger now. He's just the best,' Dylan says, and then to Jasper, 'I have missed you so, so much, buddy. You are the best baby.'

'He really is. I honestly don't know how I would have got through the last few months without this little guy,' I say with agreement. 'Shall we get ready to go out for a wander round the airport, and then go and grab some lunch? I read somewhere that there are buggies we can borrow for Jasper. His had to go in the hold at Heathrow.'

'I'll carry him,' says Dylan before I finish speaking.

'He's heavy,' I warn. 'And wiggly.'

'We don't need a buggy. I'll carry him,' repeats Dylan with conviction.

I look at them, thick as thieves, romping around on the bed. I remind myself that Dylan hasn't seen his son for six months. He deserves whatever he wants by way of time and physical contact with Jasper. And I, in turn, have to learn to share the responsibility and accept that I have help again. There are two of us again now, and only one of Jasper. Everything is so much easier this way.

If there's one thing a family reunion calls for, it's champagne. So that's what we head for, via a quick leg-stretch around the concourse. Jasper soon wiggles free of Dylan's arms and takes off towards the neatly stacked toy shelves in Harrods.

'He's quick,' I warn Dylan. 'And he's a pickle. He'll have things on the floor in no time.'

'Wow, he really does have some pace on him now that's

upright,' exclaims Dylan as he sets off after the sound of Jasper's wild laughter. 'It's an escape baby!'

'He's testing you,' I shout after Dylan. 'You can see it in his face. He wants to know if you'll stop him. He doesn't know that you have much faster reflexes than I do!'

I wonder if we look like a family who hasn't seen one another for a long time, but I can't see how we do. Jasper and Dylan have blended into one big ball of mischief. And with the communication we've had over the months apart, it isn't as though Dylan and I have much catching up to do; we can simply look forwards to resuming the life which was so rudely interrupted by the Myanmar military coup, a little over a year ago. It is almost anticlimactic how normal everything feels within minutes of being reunited, but I take it as a sign of the strength of our relationship.

As we sit down in the restaurant, I raise my glass of bubbles and make a toast.

'To us. Cheers!' I say.

As Dylan raises his glass to meet mine, a little blue beaker makes its way up between the flutes, and Jasper's little face lights up from where he sits on Dylan's lap.

'Did he just cheers us?' says Dylan incredulously.

'Yes. Yes, he did,' I say with a smug smile. 'Do it again.'

'Cheers!' says Dylan again, shifting Jasper to one side of his lap so he can make eye contact and extend his glass towards him. Again, the little beaker bobs up to meet Dylan's flute, this time with more force and an audible clink, and then Jasper proceeds to take a huge gulp of water. He releases the cup from his mouth with a loud 'aaah' and a proud, toothy grin.

'That's amazing,' says Dylan laughing. 'Did you teach him?'

'Yep. Liv and I did. At Seafood Saturdays. We've been

eating prawns and drinking champagne every Saturday,' I confess.

'Little man, you are just the best baby,' he says, squeezing Jasper tightly. 'Can you believe it's been so long since we were together as a family?' Dylan says to me.

'I was just thinking about it. It feels like no time has passed. It's like those months have just vanished,' I reply. 'I mean, we still don't know for sure if we are going to be able to get our visas for India, I suppose, but I really hope this is us now. For the rest of the year, we do everything together as a family. Deal?'

'Yeah. Deal. Once we get to India, we aren't going anywhere. I think we just need to settle in as a family before we plan for any visitors or any travel,' says Dylan with a hint of the travel fatigue I feel too.

We enjoy our champagne lunch. Or is it brunch? Or afternoon tea? For Jasper it is more like dinner. For Dylan, perhaps it is breakfast. Whatever time it is, we eat, we drink, we shower (not in the restaurant, you understand) and we check out of our hotel to drift slowly towards the departure gate. I am dreading this flight. It is fifteen hours long, and while some of it is overnight, I am not sure I have enough of the right things to entertain Jasper with. At this stage in his toddling, all he really wants to do is explore, and that's just about the one thing passengers are not allowed to do on planes during COVID. I walk Dylan through the contents of my hand luggage, with all its nappies, spare clothes, books, flashcards, new toys, old toys, balloons and snacks. The balloons are a last resort, but if I am allowed to inflate one inside a plane, I know it would keep him entertained for at least 20 minutes. Twenty minutes may seem like a small dent in fifteen hours, but I will take what I can get.

As we board the plane and wander down towards our seats, Jasper surveys his surroundings with interest and, as we move further into the plane, he begins to beat his chest. One of the stewards comes towards us, with a concerned look on his face.

'Is he OK? Is he scared of flying?' he asks.

'The baby?' I say. 'Oh no. It's sign language for gorilla,' I explain.

Seeing the man's face shift from concern to confusion, I realise I have to go further.

'It's sign language for gorilla and he's doing it because he's seen the TV screens. He wants me to put Sir David Attenborough on for him,' I say.

'Oh, I see,' he says.

'I can see you speak fluent Jasper,' says Dylan, from the aisle on the other side of the plane. 'He learned that in sign-language class?'

'That's what's so weird! During the classes he was always super distracted, playing with toys instead of paying attention to the teacher. I thought nothing was going in. But apparently not. He beats his chest for gorilla. And he can do elephant and crab. You've seen him signal for water with his hand on his mouth, right? It's been a surprisingly useful way for him to communicate before he can speak. I'm so glad I did the classes.'

Hearing the word 'water', Jasper dutifully indicates that he is thirsty.

'There you go!' I say. 'I'll get your water, Jasper.'

'Would *you* like something to drink?' the steward offers, recovering his composure but still staring at Jasper with intrigue.

'Ooh yes, champagne please,' I say enthusiastically.

By the time the steward, my champagne and a toy pack for Jasper arrives at our pod, we are engrossed in episode three of *Our Planet: Jungles*. The one with the elephants and the gorillas. We have also discovered that better than two adjacent pods, Dylan and I have a giant adjoining pod, which becomes a double bed. Or, for Jasper, a giant, soft playpen. Lulled by the hum of the engine, the familiarity of the gorillas and the cushioning of the quickly converted bed, Jasper is soon in the land of nod. Dylan and I enjoy our dinner sitting either side of our little snoring monster, and then join him to get some rest.

Overnight I wake to see the two of them snuggled up together. Everything is heightened at altitude – emotions more than anything. As the joy of being reunited as a family finally extinguishes the last few smouldering embers of my frustration at being apart, I cry huge, Hollywood tears of happiness. Whatever happens next, at least we are going to face it together.

26

JET LAG

What happens next is baby jet lag and it really knocks us around. Travelling from the UK to Australia is about as upside down as it's possible to turn yourself, and while it's one thing to handle jet lag as an adult, it's quite another to coach a fifteen-month-old baby through it. Especially if this coaching has to take place between the hours of 11pm and 5am within the confines of a single room.

We stay at Dylan's mother's house in Queensland, having decided that, while renting our own space would be lovely for whatever indefinite period we might be in Australia, the expense is less appealing. On previous visits, it would never have occurred to Dylan and I to stay somewhere other than at his mother's house, but with the first time the Australian family can meet Jasper coinciding with the first time Dylan, Jasper and I have seen one another in six months, something tells me that we might want a safe space to retreat to when the situation overwhelms us. Of course, once Dylan's family catches wind of our hesitation, they tip the scales heavily in favour of accepting their hospitality by unearthing the old cot, high chair and toys which

Jasper's cousin, Austin, outgrew a decade ago. And they offer us the use of a spare car.

For Dylan, this house is home. His mother, Joanne, and her husband, Dee, are as grounded as Tony and Jen are nomadic and a younger Dylan saw this house as his base when he wasn't spending school holidays abroad with Tony. Younger than his siblings by seven years, he is the only one to have had his own room here, a fact signified by questionable nineties fashion choices still lurking in the dusty corner of a wardrobe adorned with stickers telling me, 'Get out or I snot'ya' and other similarly mature teenage warnings.

Our room for our stay is this room, with Jasper's cot set up next door. Both rooms have been temporarily taken over by Dylan's mother during the intervening years, and have been used as trophy storage for her ever-growing collection of dog agility and dog dancing awards. But with her newest grandson on his way across the globe, Joanne has reduced the ribbons and stashed them in the room Austin is about to occupy for his school holidays. With the four award-winning dogs, we three and Austin, it is going to be a full house.

Joanne and Dee, or Jasper's new Nana and Poppy as they will come to be known, collect us from Brisbane Airport. They have long been envious of the British side of the family, enjoying month after month of seemingly never-ending Jasper time, and their delight at it finally being their turn is written all over their faces. As is customary for anyone meeting Jasper for the first time, their eyes barely leave his earnest, intrigued little face as they introduce themselves to him with a wave and a coo and a cuddle. As an afterthought they greet us. It is around 5pm on a

Saturday evening in the middle of March which, on the outskirts of Brisbane, means a late summer's warm twenty-five degrees and another couple of hours of daylight. Jasper is in shorts and T-shirt for the first time in months and his winter socks and trainers look out of place at the ends of his pasty little legs.

'Have yous had dinner?' Joanne asks from the front seat, as we pull out of the airport carpark and onto the highway.

'Er, we had some things on the plane,' I reply, wracking my brain to work out which meal we ate last and what might be most appropriate as the next. 'Jasper and I have been in transit since Friday morning UK time, so I honestly don't know what his body clock might be up to. He's been subsisting on a weird diet of fruit pouches and Cheerios for the last however many hours.'

'We stopped at KFC on our way here. There is some chicken left, if you'd like it?' Joanne says as she passes a small box of chicken pieces to us.

Before I have a chance to suggest that perhaps we might aim for something a little more nutritious as Jasper's first meal in Aus, Jasper has already reached out to accept the gift. Seeing my grimace, Dylan laughs.

'Relax, Milla. It's only a few pieces of chicken. It's not going to spark a lifelong fast-food addiction,' he says mocking gently.

'I know, I know,' I say conceding. 'He's never had anything deep fried before, except the odd portion of chips,' I say.

I watch Jasper examine a couple of pieces of chicken before putting one to his lips. It makes me irrationally uncomfortable watching him exploring his first taste of fast food. I don't eat any of it and have never understood the place it has in peoples' lives. It's not that my diet is perfect. It's simply that I have a sweet tooth and would far sooner choose a cake or a dessert over anything battered. Jasper's diet is as near perfect as I can make it, with all his home-cooked, varied and appropriately portioned food. Something about the way he devours those greasy little balls of mystery meat and flavour feels like a smack in the face after all the effort I have put into balancing his nutrition for the past six months.

'He loves it!' roars Dylan, high fiving Jasper. 'Yeah! There you go, Jasper, your first taste of the dirty bird. Welcome to Australia. Can I have one?'

Seeing how happy Dylan is, and how adorable the two of them look sharing their tiny box of leftover chicken, I realise that this is just the first of many things I am going to have to let slide. I have to relinquish some of the control I have over Jasper's life now that I am, once again, sharing responsibility for him. I also need to make space for Dylan and his family to share their lives and habits with Jasper, as mine did while we were in Jersey.

By the time we pull into the driveway of the house, it is dusk and Jasper is starting to fade. The house is a bungalow at the end of a quiet, rural, cul de sac. There is a large flat lawn at the front, which used to be a paddock for horses and is now a training arena for Joanne's dogs. There are gum trees along the borders of the property and the garden runs back a long way behind the house, boasting foliage dense enough to hide a few resident kangaroos, Dylan's mother confides to Jasper. I have never seen a kangaroo at the house and can never quite tell if Joanne is joking when she says they see them all the time. But that doesn't stop me demanding to kick off every morning with a 'nature walk' with Jasper in the hope that we will spot one. And to my absolute disbelief, one morning spot one we do!

We rush Jasper through an introduction to the dogs and then offer him a quick dinner of Vegemite toast and banana before launching into his bedtime routine. While Dylan cools his room with a fan and an open window, I bathe, brush and bag Jasper. As soon as he is in his sleeping bag, I realise that he is going to be too hot with his long, winter PJs, so I quickly undress and redress him in a more climate-appropriate outfit.

Jasper, for reasons unbeknownst to me or any of my family, has always insisted on bouncing and shouting himself to sleep. Ever since he was about four or five months old, he has been a noisy settler and, as soon as he was able to stand, he added the bouncing action to his loud objections. I have always thought of it as him releasing every ounce of residual energy before he calls it a night and to me it's totally normal. But tonight, I am self-conscious about it and, if I am honest, a little ashamed. I read him his usual story and say my usual goodnight, before closing the door on him as he pulls himself up to standing to begin his usual loud jumping routine. I know it will only last a few minutes before he will give up and go to sleep as usual but, as I rejoin Dylan, his mum and Dee in the kitchen their faces tell me that Jasper's racket is not something they were expecting.

Joanne has a look of horror on her face. 'Is he OK?'

'Yeah, he always does this. He jumps around for a bit and then settles himself down,' I say. 'I don't really know why, but he always goes to sleep in the end.'

'Don't you want to go back in there?' Joanne asks.

'No, it only prolongs the process,' I say with a shrug of apology.

'Well, if you're sure,' she says, clearly unconvinced, and sits down at the table to join Dee watching a TV show.

I go to fetch a glass of water from the kitchen and beckon to Dylan. 'Do you think we can ask them to turn the TV down a bit?' I ask quietly. 'I don't know if Jasper will go to sleep with all the noise. He's used to it being quiet.'

'Not really,' says Dylan. 'They always have it this loud. And it *is* their house. I'll put a towel along the bottom of Jasper's door.'

'I really hope he goes to sleep soon. Your mum clearly thinks it's weird that he cries so much at bedtime. But it's just what he's always done.'

'Don't worry about it. As you said, it's just the way he goes to sleep. It doesn't matter what my mum thinks anyway.'

I make a face. 'It does matter, Dylan. She's my mother-in-law. I don't want her to judge me!' I say, with an expression of mock exasperation. 'Well, I am going to go and find some of our things in our suitca ... oh, hang on. Our cases are in Jasper's room, aren't they?'

We look at each other and exhale with amusement.

'OK, I won't go and do any unpacking. I'll have to sneak in once Jasper is asleep,' I say. 'Are you sure we can't ask them to lower the TV volume? He's going to wake up if I open the door and go rummaging,' I say grumbling.

Jasper does eventually stop jumping and goes to sleep, at which point I brace myself to sneak into his room and find my own pyjamas and toiletries. Once in his room, I hover for a while listening to his peaceful snoring, to the rustle of the leaves in the trees outside the open window, to the geckos blowing their nocturnal kisses and to the explosive action sequence on the TV next door. I feel tired and disoriented, and am attacked by a wave of homesickness for the familiarity and routine of Jersey. As much as I was desperate to leave Jersey, I have to admit that my life there was starting to feel like home. I take a deep breath. We are in Australia, which is bewilderingly one step closer to India. Tomorrow Dylan's brother and sister are driving down to meet their nephew. I just have to relax.

Dylan and I don't stay up much longer once Jasper is out

and not long after we retire, we hear the TV go quiet too. Besides the occasional patter of canine footsteps outside our bedroom door, the odd cackle of a cicada and the hoot of an owl, the house is silent overnight. That is, until a little before midnight, when Jasper starts to cry out. We know that the dogs have free run of the house at night with the daytime baby gates being retracted after Jasper goes to bed. We also know that if they hear noise or sense movement in the house, they will bark the entire neighbourhood awake. I throw myself out of bed, tripping and stumbling, far less quietly than I intend, into Jasper's room to scoop him up or settle him back down. But he is not interested in sleeping. He is interested in shouting and crying, and clambering and crying some more, and reading his book, but definitely not sleeping. I wonder if he is hungry, or thirsty, or hot, or cold. I offer him whatever snacks I find in our suitcases, take his sleeping bag off, and put it back on again. I read the only book I have to hand ten times over and then, finally, after a fruitless hour, I take him into Dylan's and my room where I hope he might fall asleep between us. He does not. Photo evidence suggests he rampages until 5am, refusing to sleep, or to allow us to extinguish the light, or to be soothed by his lullaby music, or to eat any of his snacks, but fights for the freedom to bang on the bedroom door, his way of demanding to be let out into the rest of the house.

The room we are in is large enough for a double bed but, with only about a metre perimeter between the bed and the walls, a toddler playground it is not. Were we in the UK, I would suggest going out into the garden to calm him down and walk him back to sleep. But this is Queensland, home to some of the world's biggest, ugliest and deadliest nocturnal creatures and, as a self-diagnosed arachnophobe, I am not setting foot outside if I don't have my full field of vision. We watch *Our Planet* on my phone, but not even the gorillas can keep his attention. We read books. We empty my wallet. We dig around in our hand luggage in the corner of the room for more snacks and toys. We listen to music. We look at photographs. I try repeatedly to switch off the light and ask him to lie down. I am frazzled. Dylan and I are both drained; me from the long-haul trip, Dylan from months of working fourteen-hour days on top of the travel. Unlike Dylan I am at least familiar with Jasper's antics, but this refusal to sleep is surprising even to me, and I have soon exhausted all the tricks I have up my sleeve. I try to stay upbeat and to work on the basis that surely at some point he will run out of steam and go to sleep.

'What's wrong with him?' I ask Dylan a hundred times. 'What are we supposed to do? We can't take him out of the room, but he doesn't want to be in here. Neither of us can get any sleep either. Is it jet lag? Is he sick? Is he just a monster?' I wail.

At some point, Jasper does finally run out of juice. What feels like moments later, I am woken by the sound of something scratching its way into my subconscious. I pry one eye open and wait for it to focus. I take in the room and the sunlight peeking through the curtains. I pat around on the floor by the bed to find my watch or my phone to check the time and groan as I see it is 7.30am.

'Dylan,' I say, shuffling carefully so that I can give him a whack without disturbing a deeply asleep Jasper, whose head is nestled under my chin and whose feet appear to have commandeered Dylan's pillow.

'Mmmm. It's Peaches. At the door,' he mumbles, not moving. Peaches is the smallest of Joanne's dogs; a gentle, white miniature poodle, who, on regular visits from Dylan and me, would be welcomed into our bed with open arms each morning.

'I know it's Peaches. Do I have to let her in? She'll wake Jasper.'

Some grunting and snuffling tells me Dylan is as discombobulated as I am. 'Um. What time is it?'

'Seven thirty.'

'Mgh. I don't feel as though I slept. Aren't we going to wake Jasper anyway? Don't we need to get him onto an Australian schedule?'

'I don't know anymore. I am not sure I can bear to wake him up after his all-night rave. I only dropped his morning nap a few weeks ago, but maybe he's going to need more sleep now we are here.'

I put my head back down on the pillow and lie there, staring at the ceiling. I listen to the kookaburra chuckling to herself in the gumtree in the garden. Further in the distance, I can hear the hum of the highway starting to ramp up to its usual weekend level, as beachgoers and shoppers ferry themselves up and down the Gold Coast. Closer by, I hear the slide of the screen door from the kitchen to the patio and I hear Dylan's mum call out, 'Joy! Story!'

'It sounds like your mum is heading outside with the other dogs,' I say. 'Let's wake Jasper then, and go and say hello.'

Dylan, Jasper and I must look like an absolute fright, emerging slowly, all blinky-eyed and ruffled from our terrible few hours' sleep.

'You're up late!' exclaims Joanne from the patio outside, knowing Dylan and I to be habitual early risers.

'We only just went to sleep,' I tell her. 'Jasper would not sleep.'

'Oh dear,' Joanne says, watching Dylan slump down at the kitchen table with his head resting on his hands. 'Well, tea's in the pot and there's some bread for toast. What'll Jasper have for his breakfast?'

'Toast is good and some fruit. He eats most things really,' I reply, dropping an eye-rubbing Jasper onto Dylan before heading into the kitchen to start preparing Jasper's food.

'That was brutal,' says Dylan after some time. 'What's your strategy today, Milla? Let him sleep when he wants or try to stick to the routine?'

'I think I'll try for a routine,' I say, without much conviction.

Our first few days in Australia are not enjoyable. After two more sleepless nights we have to admit that my strategy isn't working. I go ten rounds with Jasper every night as he tries to battle his way out of our room, or destroy what is in it, waking like clockwork at 11pm, and finally falling asleep again at 5am. He is napping during the day, but I have to wake him up every time, an action that attracts commentary from Dylan's mother who claims never to have woken any of her children from their naps. Her inputs make me second guess myself, and I am about to change tack and let Jasper take over his own schedule when, as if by magic, he sleeps through the night. I stop just short of panic when I wake in the morning to find the sun already up, but no baby in our bed. My heart leaps and I startle myself trying to make sense of where I am and what is going on. I feel that Dylan is already awake and on his phone, responding to emails in bed next to me, and ask, 'Where's Jasper? Is he OK?'

'He's fine. I think he's still sleeping,' says Dylan reassuringly.

'Oh thank god. I don't know how much more of this nightly confinement I can take. I was thinking that perhaps we would have to get our own place after all. I just feel like I am going to snap. It's such an adjustment being in someone else's house with Jasper. What with him not sleeping and him trying to take everything off the shelves everywhere. This house is not really toddler friendly and I'm not used to being in such a busy environment with him.'

'I know, but fingers crossed, he is going to start sleeping normally now. And there are other people around to watch him. You have to remember you are not the only one who has to look after him. Just give him to my mum. She'll love it.'

To my enormous relief, Jasper's body clock appears to have caught up with the right time zone, which in turn allows Dylan and I to begin to enjoy ourselves and our time with one another. Jasper basks in the fresh attention and warm sunshine. It makes me so happy to watch family member after family member fall head over heels in love with him. I wish that I had been a little more practised in parenting at other peoples' homes before arriving at my in-laws' on the opposite side of the globe with a toddling tornado, crippling jet lag, and a husband who is six months behind on his own parenting journey. But, besides the one occasion when Jasper's grabby little hands almost upturn the urn containing the ashes of Joanne's favourite dog, he can do no wrong in the family's eyes. And after two years of COVID restrictions, it feels as though Dylan's family are grateful for the excuse to spend some time with one another as much as with us.

27

AUSTRALIA

In March 2022, COVID is down but not out. As our seemingly typical bad luck would have it, the virus graces Dylan's Australia-based family for the first time two days into our visit, when Dylan's sister, Kara, realises she has caught it from a nurse in her veterinary clinic. Under normal circumstances, her needing to quarantine for a week (or until a negative test result) would only have inconvenienced Kara, but our arrival in Australia has stirred up a flurry of activity among the Australian contingent and so a lot of plans suddenly need postponing.

Jasper belongs to an elite community of people fortunate enough to have a great grandmother. Still sharp as a whistle, she may not look or act her ninety-five years, but her immune system suggests otherwise and so the top priority becomes minimising any risk to GG (as she requests to be known). We have allowed for a few days' incubation period before meeting GG but, having spent our first day in Australia with a now-infected Kara, we have to restart the clock.

A pivotal activity in the calendar is a family photo shoot,

which has been painstakingly scheduled to accommodate not only the local family's work commitments, but also any need for Dylan and I to hotfoot it up to Brisbane, in case we are required to attend a face-to-face visa appointment. It doesn't help that Dylan and I can't define the timeframe within which we will be available in Australia.

'How long are you here for?' Kara asks on the phone, as she looks at new dates for the photo shoot, safely in isolation back at home.

'We don't know,' says Dylan, wearily.

'But, I mean, roughly?' asks Kara.

'I honestly don't know,' says Dylan.

In Kara's loud sigh, I hear years of long-suffering sibling frustration and so I try to offer a little more context.

'They said it could be seven to ten working days from the day we submit the application. But we still don't know if we have to submit the application in person or by post. And, if it's by post, we don't know how long that will take to arrive. And then we don't know for sure that we will get the visas, so, I would guess we're here for at least two weeks. But as soon as we have the visas, we will need to book flights and get Dylan back to his project.'

'OK. That's helpful,' Kara says, glaring at Dylan through the video. 'It would be great if you're here for longer, though!'

'I mean, we could be here forever. What we thought was a three-month stint in the UK ended up being six, so be careful what you wish for!' I say joking, but more bitterly than I intend.

'You aren't going to stop posting photos on the app, are you now that you are here? I will still want to see what you guys are up to, even if I am just down the road,' Kara says.

'Of course not! Now *my* family is relying on photos and

videos to get their Jasper fix. And to be completely honest, that app is often the only reason I do anything. I had so many days in Jersey when I didn't feel like leaving the house, or doing anything at all, but then I would remember my responsibility to post photos, and it made me think of something to do,' I say. 'If I hadn't set myself the task of posting daily, Jasper and I would have had a much less active lifestyle.'

'We love it here. I admit I don't check it every day, but I know Grandma and Dad do. So did you really manage to post every day?' asks Kara.

I take a deep breath. 'Every day except 21 February. That little empty square on the calendar taunts me, showing that I failed. We went to the doctor that day, which I usually classed as an activity, but it tells you something about my mood that I couldn't muster the enthusiasm to take a single photo. Of course, I'll regret it for the rest of my life now,' I say with a laugh. 'I mean, it's easy enough to take a few photos or videos every day when you have such good subject matter,' I add, taking a couple of pictures of Jasper cooling off in a bucket of water on the patio.

The family photo shoot is duly rescheduled and Kara soon frees herself from her isolation. Nobody else catches it, which is good news, especially for those of us who are looking forward to showing Jasper the Gold Coast, reuniting him with Tony and introducing him to his great grandmother.

Once we are over the jet lag, we fully embrace what is Dylan's first holiday in over six months. And his first series of consecutive days off in that time. His phone still buzzes non-stop with work-related communications. I can see how tiring he finds it to split himself between being a parent, a son, a husband and a professional. I, in turn, am adjusting to adding daughter-in-law, wife and house guest to my usual far narrower remit, as mother. We bicker more than we used to back in Myanmar, but I hope it is only because we are out of practice parenting together. I am used to making decisions on Jasper's behalf, but when things also involve a member of Dylan's family I feel as though he must be consulted. And so, it takes us twice as long to decide anything.

As expected, Tony is impatient to see Jasper again. They are reunited at a pub and, either Jasper is very easy to kidnap or there is enough residual familiarity to make Jasper instantly comfortable enough in Tony's presence for them to wander off hand in hand to explore the kids' play area. Knowing how much Jasper loves nature, Tony organises a visit to the Currumbin Wildlife Sanctuary, where Jasper is mesmerised by the rainbow lorikeet feeding and where I completely lose my cool when a very large lizard invades my personal space at the cafe. Tony almost falls off his chair laughing at me, while Dylan accuses me of using Jasper as a shield to protect myself from the lizard. This incident, and the mind-blowing kangaroo sightings we make in Dylan's mother's garden, remind me that despite many cultural similarities between us, I am not an Aussie. In the UK our wildlife doesn't try to kill us. I make a mental note to sign Jasper up to dangerous creature training whenever we do finally move to Australia. He's half Aussie so undoubtedly better placed to protect me from all that crawls, slithers, bites and jumps.

Jasper's first encounter with his great grandmother is magical. GG's eyesight is going, but her brain is still firing on all cylinders. Jasper's eyesight is top notch but he doesn't yet have any command of spoken language. Despite the disconnect in their abilities, and the ninety-four-year age gap between them, they huddle together at one end of the lunch table pouring over Jasper's farm book laughing, pointing and making animal noises. GG displays an impressive array of intrigued facial expressions, much to Jasper's delight and Jasper is more than happy to be the centre of her attention while we wait for our food. Despite being a COVID baby, Jasper is surprisingly social and has no issue with being passed around family members like a new toy. He rolls out his Cheers-ing party trick time and time again, and it never seems to grow old.

We take Jasper to the beach - a warm, sandy beach, this time, with no Irish pebbles, no Jersey seaweed, and he has his first swim in the sea. He isn't yet steady enough on his feet to withstand even gentle movement of the waves, but he is fascinated by the sight and sound of the water.

'Are we sure we shouldn't just move to Australia?' I ask Dylan, after a particularly enjoyable afternoon visiting his brother Fred in his new beachfront apartment.

'Ha. Why do you say that?' asks Dylan.

'I mean, the sea, the sunshine, the clear air, the food, the fact that your family would love to have Jasper around ...' I trail off, imagining a life where I take a dip in the sea at the end of a long day at work.

'You don't think following your six months in Jersey that we should go there?' Dylan asks.

'Nah. It's too normal. I think we'd go mad. Don't get me wrong, it was exactly what I needed when we arrived there, but I still think it's not for us,' I say reflectively.

'Australia is normal too, I think. I guess that means we are making the right decision with India, then!' Dylan says.

Besides the challenges of parenting a toddler in someone else's very breakable house, and of having to take many other peoples' opinions into account when deciding on what to do each day, I am adjusting to my own loss of independence. As I don't like driving and because the roads and cars are so much more intimidating in Australia than I am used to in Jersey, I am dependent on Dylan as my chauffeur. This works well for the first couple of weeks because we do everything together, but when his work starts to struggle without him and he sets himself up an office in the caravan in the garden, I start to feel a little stifled. It's not that I have anything particular I need to do. I just want some alone time; alone time with Jasper. He is the axis around which my sanity revolves and I find myself missing the privacy we enjoyed so much in Jersey. It would re-centre me when I start to feel anxious or irritable. I miss my life in Jersey. And then I remember that while I was there, I missed my life in Myanmar. And towards the end of our time in Myanmar, I longed to be anywhere else but there. I accept that perhaps the grass always looks greener wherever I am not.

One day I announce that I am going to walk Jasper to a nearby playground. My idea is met with a questioning look and the offer of a lift from Dylan's mum, but I politely decline on the basis that it's not far. Even Dylan offers to take a break from his work to drop us off and come back to collect us. While it's a short distance, I am forgetting that I am no longer dealing with country lanes and fifteen mile an hour speed limit. By the time Jasper and I reach the playground, we have crossed a busy highway twice and fought our way through long grass on a very uneven verge with his buggy. Once the adrenalin from the terrifying road crossings has receded, I enjoy watching Jasper clamber and slide but, on returning home, I feel foolish and jittery enough never to attempt something like that again.

The initial excitement of our visit to Australia dies down as Dylan begins to spend longer hours cooped up in the caravan, working on Indian time. Instead of enjoying the time in Australia, Dylan is increasingly impatient for it to end. He is keen to get back to India and back into a room with his work team. Each day his temper shortens and I see in him so much of what my family must have seen in me towards the end of my Jersey stint. I don't even try to placate him because I know that there are no words which will make the wait go any faster or seem any less frustrating.

Before we know it we are approaching a month in Australia. A month of living out suitcases, a month of refreshing email inboxes in the hope of news on our visas, a month of not wanting to leave the house unmanned in case a courier arrives when there is no one around to sign. When we do finally get word that our visas have been issued, and the courier does suddenly appear, it is ten-year-old Austin who does the honours and signs for the package, while the rest of us are out in the back garden or down at the supermarket.

'Ok. Flights,' says Dylan as he checks that all three passports are now sporting the correct new visas.

'What a relief,' I say. 'I was so worried that Jasper and I might not get ours at the same time. This is it, then. The final, final, final leg of the epic journey. As wonderful as it's been to spend all this time with your family, I admit I'm looking forward to getting to India and settling in. I want my own space again. I'm looking forward to getting back into a rhythm with Jasper's meals and things. And god, I cannot wait to *not* have to travel anywhere for a very long time.'

'Well, we certainly have space. You remember that there is no furniture yet? I haven't bought anything other than beds and a sofa. And when you say 'Jasper's meals', you know there's no oven,' Dylan says.

'Wait, what? No oven? But you have a microwave, right?' I ask confused.

'Nope. Nothing apart from the hob.'

'No kettle?'

'Nope.'

'How do you make tea?' I ask.

'I don't. I've told you this. No toaster, no kettle, no oven, no microwave, no table and no chairs. Apart from Jasper's high chair,' Dylan says, as though he's told me a hundred times before. In his defence, he probably has but it hasn't registered until now.

I feel myself beginning to get angry. 'How am I meant to cook for Jasper? What am I meant to do when we arrive? I thought you had bought all this before you left? I thought it would be ready for us.' I am winding myself up.

'When? I have barely even had a break while we've been here! Do you think I have had time to go shopping in India? All I do is work!'

'I don't know. But I also don't know how you expect Jasper and I to do it when we arrive. And what's he going to eat?'

'I don't know what you want me to say, Milla. I haven't had the time,' Dylan snaps.

We are alone in the caravan while Jasper plays with Nana and a bucket of water outside. I am conscious that we might be arguing audibly and I feel ashamed of the person I seem to be at the moment.

'I know,' I say. 'I know.' I say it more quietly the second time. 'I'm sorry. I hate how quickly I fly off the handle. I think it's a hangover from the coup and everything, but I know I'm too quick to get angry. I'm sorry.'

We sit quietly and look at our laptops, Dylan searches for flights and I look up COVID travel testing sites.

'We will manage,' I say after a while. 'We always do, right?'

'We do. Your job as soon as we get there is to finish setting up the house. I gave up trying to buy a dining table when you vetoed marble, so you need to find something else,' Dylan says, laying down what is clearly a challenge.

'We don't need a marble table,' I say decisively.

'I agree. But now it's your job to find something that isn't marble.'

'I just can't believe that it's so hard to find non-marble tables,' I mutter under my breath.

'Neither did I,' says Dylan with a knowing smile.

'I accept my challenge of finding a non-marble table', I say in a sunnier voice, feeling far more like myself again.

We book flights to leave less than 48 hours after receiving our visas. The farewells are swift, emotional and open-ended but, I have to say, Jasper and I are getting quite used to saying goodbye to people. As we await our flight, I think what an amazing experience our stay in Australia has been for Jasper; he has connected with a whole new family, he has spent hours outside observing and enjoying the wildlife, he has taken a sudden change of climate in his stride and has even overcome his first bout of monstrous jet lag. I am reminded of the saying 'it takes a village to raise a child'. For Jasper, it is more like a network of villages and a dispersed one at that. I think about how open-mindedly he approaches everything and I tell myself to try to take a leaf out of his book when we arrive in India.

The journey to India is a test. Jasper behaves exactly as a toddler is expected to behave on a long-haul flight: terrorising the other passengers and tormenting his parents. I am forced to inflate and deploy a balloon to try to distract him from unplugging the headphones of the passenger in front of him. On what I hope is my last long-haul journey until COVID is well and truly over, I am acutely aware of how much harder it is to travel with a toddler while wearing a mask. This has nothing to do with the discomfort of the mask but everything to do with the innumerable times I find myself trying to dispose of some stray food item, quickly and into my mouth. As a fruit puree or soggy Cheerio slides down my leg for the umpteenth time and I am unable to take off my mask fast enough to perform my usual role of human dustbin, I long for the days of mask-free travel.

28

INDIA

Our arrival into India is a blur of immigration, baggage collection, thick, fume-filled air in the underlit car park, deafening car horns, a midnight drive through the bright city lights and arrival into a warm, dark, echoing apartment. As I step through the doorway into what is my new home I am shocked by just how empty it is. Besides a sofa and rug the living room is completely devoid of any sign of life. The floor-to-ceiling windows along the far wall make it feel like an observation deck, out-of-hours, offering us a view into the neighbouring tower blocks and, behind them, across the dimly lit racecourse and out over the Arabian Sea.

I turn to Dylan. 'What the hell?' I say with unwarranted venom. 'Where is all our stuff?'

'What stuff?' he says curtly. 'We didn't ship any furniture, remember? Our boxes were pretty much just kitchen utensils.'

'But, what about stuff you've bought?' I say, feeling my face contorting as I speak. 'I didn't think you'd been living with literally *nothing*. It looks like a squat!'

Dylan exhales sharply. 'For the last time, when have I had a chance to buy stuff? I barely have time to scratch myself let alone to go shopping. I told you this over and over but you were just too angry to listen to me. You were always too busy ranting about what a terrible decision it was to move to India to take in what I was saying.'

Of course I knew there was no furniture, I think to myself. But, somehow my imagination has failed to prepare me for what an empty apartment would feel like. Looking at it, I struggle to see how this might ever feel like home. The challenge of protecting Jasper in such alien surroundings looms large in my mind and I begin to feel tiredness clinging to my body like a suit of wet clay.

Dylan and I glare at each other in the semi-darkness and Jasper seizes the moment to wiggle free from my arms. I put down my handbag and move further into the apartment, following a wobbly Jasper and sizing the place up as I go. I see the kitchen with its two empty spaces where an oven and a microwave should be. I let out a theatrical sigh and slump my shoulders.

'Don't do that,' says Dylan behind me. 'I have had such a crap time being here alone. Don't come in here and judge me for not having done more. You were so wrapped up in your own issues that you didn't listen to how hard I told you things were here. Think of me - I have been living in this apartment for four whole months with no furniture and no way to cook anything!'

I hate fighting with Dylan because we are a team: always have been and always will be. But sometimes I get so wrapped up in my head, as he observed, that I try to make him the enemy. The other reason I hate fighting with Dylan is because I never win. He is annoyingly rational and a good debater. He prefers to argue things through to a resolution while I like to stew. On this occasion, I can clearly see that he is in the right and that I am being unfair. I know that I will get no satisfaction from tying myself up in knots over what might or might not have been done differently, but tie myself up I do. I huff and puff around the apartment looking through our suitcases for the essentials Jasper needs for a reasonable night's sleep. He, at least, has a cot set up in an otherwise empty bedroom. Similarly, Dylan's and my room has a bed and a TV but nothing else. The bare, white walls offer no cupboards, no shelving, no mirrors and no artwork. Only a pile of Dylan's clothes and some paperwork shoved in a corner suggest he has spent any time here. A more reasonable version of myself would have broken down in tears at the thought of Dylan coming home to this lifeless box every night after long, stressful days at work. Not to mention how his fourteen-day COVID isolation must have felt.

'Are you going into work tomorrow?' I ask, as I stomp about.

'No. I should, but I'll stay here to show you guys around,' responds Dylan.

'OK. Thank you.' I can't stay mad at him any longer.

'I'm sorry,' I say, swallowing my anger. 'It was just a shock. I don't know what I was picturing for the apartment, but seeing it all empty makes me worry about how I am going to feed and look after Jasper. I find it so hard to adjust to all these big changes. It's like as soon as I get into a rhythm somewhere it all changes again. First Jersey, then Australia, now India ... it's so tiring.'

'I know. And Jasper's lucky that you care so much. But as I've said, it hasn't exactly been easy for me,' Dylan says with some sadness.

'Is it weird to have us here in the apartment finally?' I ask.

'Yeah, it is weird. But it's good to have you here too. I feel as though I might finally start to have a life in Mumbai, rather than simply existing.'

It is well into the early hours of the morning when Jasper falls asleep and we finally collapse into bed. I will my brain to stop whirring because I am sure I will need to be well rested for the adventure of tomorrow.

Jasper wakes early but not *too* early the next day and starts to bounce in his cot, crowing tunelessly like a defunct cockerel. It takes me a few seconds to work out where I am when I open my eyes but, once I do, I immediately feel comforted by the familiarity of Jasper's morning routine. As I go to retrieve him from his room, I see the apartment properly for the first time. Sunlight streams through the windows on two sides of our corner unit and reflects back up off the shining, white marble floor before landing on the empty, white walls. It is almost too bright for my unaccustomed eyes. We are high up; a little too high for my liking but Dylan assures me that Jasper won't be able to open any of the windows. From the living room I look out at the sea and marvel at how close we are to it. I had tried to look at a map of Mumbai while I was still in Jersey but, until I am in a place, I find it hard to get a sense of how everything relates. I now see that our apartment is in one of the tallest buildings in the area and, as a result, the view over the city and sea makes me feel very small. I also see very clearly how Mumbai is a city of extremes: extreme wealth and poverty living side by side; extreme heat and noise already seeping through the windows before most of the city is even awake. I feel very far from the soft blues and greys of the fresh Jersey skies. Even the kookaburra's gentle chuckle which woke us each morning in Australia feels like a distant memory.

Dylan is up too now and comes to join Jasper and me at the window as we take in our new surroundings.

'Well, what do you think?' he asks.

'I think that I can't quite believe we are finally here,' I say. 'It feels as though we were waiting so long that I stopped bothering to imagine what it might be like. I don't know what I was expecting, but I suppose it was probably something like this. It's surreal, being here now.'

'Let's have something to eat and then I'll show you around the compound,' suggests Dylan.

On my quick scan of the kitchen the previous night I didn't see evidence of any food, so I am a little surprised to watch Dylan motion that we should follow him in there. I locate Jasper's cereal in one of our suitcases, all of which lie open and over-flowing along one wall of the living room, and head to the kitchen.

'There's not much here,' explains Dylan. 'I had the house boy pick up a few things yesterday so that we weren't arriving to a completely empty fridge. You have no idea how long it took him to come up with a normal loaf of bread.'

I am a little confused. The term 'house boy' immediately makes me think of 'house elf' from Harry Potter but I assume that Dylan isn't dabbling in some casual domestic slavery here.

'What's a house boy?' I ask.

'Anthony. I've told you about Anthony. He's like a housekeeper, I guess, but they call them house boys here. You'll meet him when he arrives this morning. He comes in every day for a few hours to clean and do some laundry and sometimes he helps buy groceries for me,' says Dylan in a voice which tells me he has tried to explain this to me before, more than once.

I listen this time, wondering how I can avoid *ever* using the term 'house boy' myself.

We review Anthony's purchases: UHT milk, something called 'protein bread' which doesn't look like it will taste or behave anything like normal bread, a box of cereal, an orange juice carton, some bananas and some butter.

'Your first objective should be to find real milk,' says Dylan as he pours UHT on two and a half bowls of cereal.

I laugh. 'I'll add it to my list!' I say, thinking that I am joking.

I put Jasper in his high chair and sit down on the cold, hard floor to eat my own breakfast. Jasper looks down at me, bemused.

'We also need a table and chairs,' says Dylan from where he is standing, leaning against the back of the sofa, bowl in hand.

'Yep. I noticed that,' I say. 'And some wardrobes and maybe a rug for Jasper's room.' I spin around slowly, cross-legged on the floor, scanning the place. 'And some shelves or something, and a kettle and toaster. And an oven, a microwave, some pans. I actually am going to need to make a list.' I grab my phone and start jotting down everything which we are missing.

Every minute that we are in the apartment my list grows longer. Before I am overwhelmed by the enormity of the task I see in front of me, I suggest that we take our walking tour of the compound. It is only a little past seven in the morning, so the grounds are ours alone. It is unbelievable. I genuinely cannot quite believe that this is where we now live. In one of the world's most densely populated cities, it is mind-boggling to learn that we have ten acres of carefully manicured, private land to enjoy. As we circumnavigate the compound following the running track, we pass the indoor tennis court, the football field, the basketball court, the volleyball court, the outdoor tennis court, two cricket nets, a building which houses a badminton and two squash courts, a dog park and the swimming pool with its vast, shaded cafe. I am instantly in love. Everywhere I look are frangipani trees bursting with thousands of my favourite flowers. The garden is lush and beautifully kept by an army of landscapers whose garden hoses Jasper is itching to play with. I feel some of the stress of our empty apartment dissipate as I realise that it is definitely not *all* bad.

'So, what do you think?' asks Dylan for the second time today.

'It's incredible,' I say. 'Really. You've done so well to find this place. The facilities look amazing, and everything feels so grand and well-kept. I can't believe this is where we live!'

Dylan is visibly relieved. 'I'm so glad you like it. When I saw it, I knew immediately that it would be good for us. Jasper can run around like a wild thing and we can play sports together. Like the old days! And you can swim whenever you want.'

He pauses.

'I know that we said we weren't going to invest emotionally or financially in our life in India ...' he starts to say.

'Sod that,' I interrupt. 'This place is worth it. I already feel emotionally invested. I just hope we don't have to leave in a hurry this time! I am not looking forward to filling the apartment, I'll admit. But I also accept that it's my job for now. I am sorry I was so horrible when we arrived yesterday.'

When we return to our apartment, Anthony is there, waiting for something to do. His presence immediately makes me uncomfortable. In his defence, that's the job: to hang around in the house until something needs doing. But perhaps due to my six relatively solitary months in Jersey, I find the perpetual presence of anyone somewhat irritating, with the notable exceptions of Jasper and Dylan. I decide instantly that Anthony has to go, but not before I have established at least the bare bones of a routine for us as a family, or Dylan will be going to work unfed and un-ironed, and the electricity bill won't get paid.

Dylan's tense shoulders, clenched jaw and close attachment to a persistently buzzing phone tell me that he really needs to get to the office. He has been away almost a month, and during that time things have not gone smoothly. We agree that he will go in when Jasper goes down for his afternoon nap and that before then, he'll walk us to the nearby shopping mall to show me something that vaguely resembles a supermarket. That it's inside a luxury mall tells me everything I need to know: you don't see people lugging a month's supply of loo roll and corn flakes past Luis Vuitton.

The instant we step outside the gates of our compound we are in India. It is busy, rushed, colourful, loud and chaotic. It's a sensory overload compared to the quiet oasis from which we have emerged. It's as though a rainbow has exploded into a thousand, tiny, splintered shards of colour which have fallen on the women now threading vivid patterns through the hot, dusty streetscape. I feel very drab in my muted neutrals. There is a stack of caged chickens behind a fruit stall on the street corner, and a man using a circular saw to cut marble in front of the shop next door. The mall is only a ten-minute walk from where we live, but that's ten minutes of Jasper being strapped to me in hot season heat and I feel the sweat start to race down my back, pooling on the waist strap of the carrier. The would-be pavements are a treacherous clutter of people, marble-cutting equipment, motorbike parts, banyan trees and chai drinkers. The road is a fast-moving weave of black and yellow cabs, public buses, scooters, vegetable carts and very daring pedestrians.

I realise Jasper's buggy won't see much action here.

Jasper can walk, but the crowds, the rubbish strewn across the streets, the stray dogs, the uneven surfaces and the bin-diving crows convince me that he won't do a lot of that outside our compound. Even with him safe in his carrier, I am a little jumpy as we duck and dive through the mechanics, chai vendors and rubbish pickers. It has been a while since I have been anywhere so unfamiliar and I can't work out whether Jasper's presence is making me feel more or less vulnerable. His oversized bucket hat might cover his wispy, white hair but it can't disguise the uncooked sausages that are his pale, dangling arms and legs, and I can sense the eyeballs following us. Individually, no one aspect is particularly worrying, but combined, the pace, cacophony and brashness are intimidating. I don't feel threatened, but I do feel noticed and until I know my way around I would prefer to blend in, as I had in Ireland and Jersey.

The supermarket is as heartbreaking as I imagined and our tour of the mall is cut short by Jasper's early morning catching up with him. From what little I see of it, the mall appears to be perfect for high-end luxury shoppers and of very little use to someone looking to decorate an apartment. I feel marginally more confident on our walk back to the apartment compound but I realise that the deafening volume of Mumbai will take some getting used to. It is a relief to step back through the gate to our compound, where the only hazards are low-hanging branches and the odd, bold snail on the path. As soon as we are back at the apartment, Dylan heads to the office and I put Jasper to bed.

I settle onto the sofa - the only available place to sit. I can sense Anthony's presence and so I send him home; I'd rather iron Dylan's shirts myself. I look at the beginnings of my shopping list again, and I add to it essential services such as a local SIM card and a bank account which I now realise I will need urgently. Without a SIM card I can't order an Uber or use google maps - or call Dylan if we get into trouble outside the apartment. And without a bank account I can't pay for anything. Even using Dylan's card is problematic because I have to interrupt his meetings to ask that he forward on a one-time passcode (OTP) any time I try to order something online. (The security is wonderful but the lack of independence is not.) I also add nappies, hand soap, toilet roll, Tupperwares and cleaning products to my list. It hits me that I am starting from scratch all over again, in just the same way as I did in Yangon, except this time round things are so different; I don't have the freedom to wander the streets of Mumbai searching for quirky, bespoke household items. More importantly, I don't have the enthusiasm either. Having taken one walk outside our compound, I have an inkling as to how hard it will be to bring Jasper along on my furniture quest. Dylan has already warned me that I am best to start searching online first, using a variety of apps and websites, and only to take a physical trip to a shop if I really must. This is to avoid spending hours stuck in traffic in a taxi with no air-conditioning and a bored baby on my lap. So, I dutifully begin to trawl the internet. I realise that I have a whole new code to crack and it has nothing to do with the fact that I don't speak any Hindi. I have to learn the language of local brands, products, materials, addresses, city districts and delivery times if I am ever to decipher where to buy what and how.

I look around the empty apartment again and I don't know where to start. And then it hits me: I do know where to start, because I have done this before. I can start with Jasper and his routine as a way to structure my days. And once the framework is there, I will find a way to weave in my errands. While Jasper sleeps I can scour the Internet for possible stores to visit when he's awake. And with him by my side (or strapped to my front), I can pass my own lack of knowledge off as his curiosity.

Dylan works long hours which means my days alone with Jasper are also long and not nearly as productive as I would like. A tedious wait for a local SIM card leaves Jasper and me borderline house-bound for days. I can't even take Jasper outside to the garden, in case a furniture delivery arrives and I am not around to make sure things go smoothly. Anthony is still employed with us, but after watching him oversee the hanging of some paintings (for which I had already given clear instructions), I realise he has no eye for detail and can't be trusted with stage directing a wardrobe installation.

I talk to my family back home during those first few days: partly as a way to pass the time, partly as a way to entertain Jasper and partly so that I don't have to make small talk with Anthony.

'Are you starting to feel settled yet?' asks my sister, Liv, one day.

I sigh. 'Getting there, I suppose. The oven and microwave arrive today which will be a relief. Jasper has pretty much lived on a diet of bananas and breakfast cereal for a week.'

'That doesn't sound like a very Indian diet!' exclaims Liv. 'How are you finding Mumbai in general? Do you have a feel for the place yet?'

'To be honest, I haven't had much chance to form an opinion. In some ways it seems like an easy place to live because it's quite sophisticated (compared to Yangon in my early days there, anyway). There's an app for everything and most things can be delivered. But in other ways it seems so hard; the sheer size and density of the city makes moving around very difficult (which probably explains all the deliveries). I haven't been able to explore much at all yet, but I can already tell that setting up a life here will be an entirely different beast compared to Yangon.'

'How does Jasper seem to be settling in? From the photos you send it hardly looks like he's roughing it!'

I laugh. 'Oh he's taking it in his stride, as always. He's my little rock. I just let him decide what to do and then follow him around like a lost puppy.'

'I was thinking the other day about what a crazy first year he's had. How on earth do you think you'll tell him about it? How will he know what an amazing support baby he's been?' asks Liv.

'I've been thinking about that too. There's so much to tell him. I think I probably need to write it all down - while it's fresh in my mind,' I say. 'He's the only one who has been through it all with me, but he's not exactly going to be a useful source of details.'

I laugh. 'At least if it's documented, he can read about it when he's older.'

ACKNOWLEDGEMENTS

There are many people to whom I owe enormous thanks for their support throughout the 'making' of this book, but none more deserving than my husband, Dylan. You are my best friend, my truest measure of what's good in the world and an irreplaceable part of my heart. As I wrote the chapters about our time apart I repeatedly broke down at the realisation of the sacrifices you made in terms of time with Jasper in order to establish a new life for us in India. As I have often told friends and family, the separation from you was far more difficult than anything that went before. And that's because what went before, we handled together - as a team. And so, in words which are in no way big or wide or deep enough to represent the enormity of my gratitude or my love: Thank you, Dylan. For everything.

Thank you too, to my family in Jersey without whom Jasper and I might have sunk into a small hole in the ground. You kept me busy, you made me laugh, you fed me (Liv), you did a huge amount of washing up (Mum) and you took me for invigorating north-coast dog walks (Dad) - all of which gave me more time and energy to share with Jasper. I will always be grateful for the unexpected amount of time that Jasper was able to spend with you all during those months of uncertainty.

Thank you to everyone who took the time to read early drafts of this book - your inputs were invaluable: Alice, Liv, Mum, Tony, Hannah, Ali, Emma, Sally, Tess, GG and those who I can't name.

Thank you to all my colleagues in Myanmar for your friendship and hard work and for never letting me take my foot off the pedal.

Thank you to the Yangon Pythons Hockey Club for being my social home for so many years. I think I will spend my entire life searching for that level of togetherness and fitness again. Although I won't miss the monsoon grime on that pitch...

Thank you to the community in Yangon for your friendship and solidarity, especially during those early months of the coup. An extra thank you to D for your stealthy doorstep deliveries of much-needed food in the first two weeks after we brought Jasper home from the hospital. Thank you to Tony for your roast lunches, your optimism and for not dying of COVID. Thank you to midwife Jess Rawlins for your invaluable remote assistance through those first few hours, days and weeks of motherhood.

Thank you to Lin and Wai Wai for taking such wonderful care of Jasper. Your love and kindness made you a part of our little family and Jasper was truly the luckiest of babies to have you both in his life.

Thank you to the wonderful community in Mumbai who welcomed us with open arms. Your warmth and generosity made our move to India so much easier than it might otherwise have been.

Thank you to Tom Glazer for the lyrics to the song 'On top of spaghetti'. You carried me through a rough patch there.

And finally, a note on the details in the book. Some names have been changed in order to protect the identities of certain individuals, and some details have been omitted. While I have done my best to research the dates and timings which have fallen to the back of my mind, I accept that there may be areas where my memories do not quite match the exact order in which things happened, especially under the relentless, chaotic pressure of the coup. For this, I apologise and I ask that you allow me to present my story as I best remember the experience of it.

For more information about *Not Quite To Plan* or to contact the author, please visit: www.millachaplinrae.com